30 YEARS ON AND OFF

THE BOX SEAT

HRH The Duke of Edinburgh

30 YEARS ON AND OFF
THE BOX SEAT

HRH The Duke of Edinburgh

J.A. ALLEN · LONDON

© HRH The Duke of Edinburgh KG KT, 2004
First published in Great Britain 2004

ISBN 0 85131 898 3

J. A. Allen
Clerkenwell House
Clerkenwell Green
London EC1R 0HT

J. A. Allen is an imprint of Robert Hale Limited

British Library Cataloguing in Publication Data
A catalogue record for this book is available from the British Library

Edited by Jane Lake
Design and typesetting by Paul Saunders

Frontispiece photograph of HRH The Duke of Edinburgh by Tracey Elliot-Reep

Origination by Tenon & Polert Colour Scanning Limited, Hong Kong
Printed in China by New Era Printing Company Ltd

Contents

Whether we look upon Driving from the point of view of business or of pleasure,
it is certain that no man who has had much of it but feels his pulse quicken, and
a sense of enjoyment pervade him, when sitting behind one, two, or four quick and
well-put-together horses. What is more delightful than a good and picturesque road,
a well-built and a well-running carriage, harness properly fitted, horses bitted and
put-to so that they go with ease to themselves and do their fair share of work?

From the introduction to *Driving* by THE DUKE OF BEAUFORT, KG
taken from the 'Badminton Library' Series, published 1889

INTRODUCTION

I STARTED COMPETITION carriage driving in 1973, which means that, by the end of the 2002 season, I had completed thirty years in a sport derived from a very ancient means of transport. Horse-drawn carriages have been used for thousands of years but, as a result of mechanization, they are no longer needed for any practical purposes, although horses are still remarkably popular for riding sports of all kinds. It so happens that I came to carriage driving after twenty years playing polo, itself an ancient sport. I think the experience of playing polo gave me a certain advantage when transferring to driving. I got to know about the temperament of horses, their management and the almost endless list of diseases and conditions to which they are liable.

When I started driving, the only carriages available were virtually antiques and hardly suited to driving across country and tackling tight and complicated obstacles. It was therefore only a short time before the modern sport of carriage driving began to take advantage of the development of technology and new materials to improve carriage and harness design. In the same way, technology has 'modernized' the bows and arrows used in the sport of archery. I suspect that the bowmen at Agincourt would hardly recognize the implements used in present-day archery competitions.

Sport comes in all kinds; from team sports, like football, to single combat sports like tennis and boxing; from water-sports – yacht racing and rowing – to what might be described as 'single achievement' sports, like most forms of athletics. There is one rather different set of sports that involves a willing co-operation of human and animal. It includes, for example, hawking and field trials for gun dogs and, in particular, those which require co-operation between horse and rider. I think the latter are in a class by themselves. For people who are accustomed to human-only sports, and to the mechanized world, it must be very difficult to appreciate the complexities of the partnership between human and animal. This partnership is a crucial feature in all the equestrian sports.

You cannot force a horse to do anything well that he does not like doing. You may be able to cow him sufficiently to make him do something unwillingly, but that attitude will never produce a happy and successful sporting partnership. Some people have a remarkable talent for understanding horse character and temperament, and some of this talent is required by all equestrian competitors, but what matters as much, if not more, is to establish a rapport, or a compatibility, between an individual human and one or more horses. Horses may look a bit dim sometimes; they do not wag their tails like dogs when they are happy or pleased, and they do not change the expression in their eyes very obviously, although they can express their displeasure by putting their ears back and baring their teeth. The fact is that horses do have their likes and dislikes of people and other horses, in exactly the same way that individual humans can get on with some people and not with others. You can be certain that if a horse does not like you, you will not stand a chance of building the trust, confidence and compatibility, which are so essential for success in any of the equestrian sports. Even jockeys, who ride any number of horses, know that they get on better with some horses than with others. Equally, a good polo pony will go better for some players than for others.

The essential difference between riding and driving is that a rider has direct contact with the horse with the whole body, although particularly through the hands and legs. The only contact that a driver has with a horse is through the reins, the voice and, to a certain extent, the whip. 'Whip' sounds rather fearsome, but drivers do not – as a rule – use the whip for punishment or with the intention of hurting the horse, and they should not need to use it to get the horse to go faster. It should be used as an 'aid', in much the same way that spurs are used by riders. For all other purposes, the horse has to learn to respond to the voice.

It is also worth bearing in mind that competition horses need a natural courage and ability of their own. A horse lacking in these qualities will never be successful in any competition.

Things begin to get more complicated when two or more horses are being driven together. Not only do they need to get on with, and trust, their driver, they also have to get on with each other. There is only so much that drivers can do to control animosity between their horses. Beyond a certain point, nothing is gained by persisting in putting horses together, no matter how talented, if they simply cannot stand each other.

I came to competition carriage driving from the administrative side of the equestrian sports, and the business of writing the rules. In my experience, the art is to write rules in such a way that the sport is fair for all; strict enough to prevent misinterpretation and flexible enough to allow reasonable initiative. There will always be tension between the rule makers and the participants, particularly when the participants are professionals. Rules that might be perfectly acceptable to amateurs, may be seen to limit the ability of professionals to make a living. Good examples exist in the ridden three-day event and the equivalent driving event. The full competition in both disciplines is very demanding and there is an obvious limit to the number of such competitions that horses can be expected to do in any given time. This is not usually a problem for amateurs, but professionals are naturally anxious to participate as often as possible in order to earn more prize money and to satisfy their sponsors. There is currently considerable pressure on the International Equestrian Federation (or FEI, from the French, Federation Equestre Internationale) – the international governing body – to introduce international one-day events and three-section, as opposed to five-section, marathons for the driving sport.

I have been fortunate enough to have been actively involved on both sides of equestrian sport, and it is not easy to keep a proper balance between the two. It is made even more complicated by national differences of perception. In the early years of my Presidency of the FEI, the Iron Curtain still existed, and it was only too apparent that attitudes to international sport were very different on the two sides of the Curtain. This has changed now, but differences in national talents and aptitudes remain, and it is inevitable that each national federation will press for rules and conditions, which serve the best interests of their competitors.

I decided to put this book together because of my experience on both the administrative side with the FEI, and as a competitor. I have the written record of the former, and, as it happens, I have kept a series of scrapbooks of my competitive driving activities as a record of the latter. I appreciate that the market for such a book is rather limited, but I hope that this account of the conception, introduction and development of what is essentially a new sport, may also interest the general reader.

Chapter One

How it Started

1968–1974

Like so many things in my life, I came to driving horse-drawn carriages quite
by chance. I had started riding when I was quite young – in spite of the
warnings of my father, for many years a professional cavalry officer, that all
horses were dangerous and to be avoided at all costs.

My first recollection of riding was on the endless beaches of the Black Sea
while on a visit to my cousin Michael who, owing to the erratic behaviour of his
father, King Carol, and the vagaries of Romanian politics at the time, happened to
be King of that country. This was in 1928 when we were both seven years old. After
that my riding was spasmodic until my uncle Dickie, at that time Lord Louis
Mountbatten, got me onto one of his polo ponies and sent me off to try to hit a
ball about with a polo stick. This might have led to my playing the game, but
unfortunately the war intervened.

Fate, or rather the Lords Commissioners of the Admiralty, decreed that I
should spend 1949 and 1950 in Malta, where my uncle was commanding the 1st
Cruiser Squadron. This time he succeeded in persuading me to take up the game
properly. The fact that the Queen was patently more interested in watching polo
than naval cricket and hockey, also played a part in my decision to accept his offer
of a couple of ponies. I then played regularly in Malta and later at Cowdray and
eventually at Windsor for the next twenty years.

I only mention this because it has some bearing on the reason for the invitation from Prince Bernhard of the Netherlands to let my name go forward for election to succeed him as President of the FEI. Polo was not then, and is not now, one
of the equestrian sports controlled by the FEI, but, as an equestrian sport, it did
at least give me some credibility in the horse world. I was elected in 1964, after the

Fig. 1.1 Riding with my cousin, King Michael of Romania on the beach near Constanza on the Black Sea in 1928. In those days, there were miles of deserted beach. I gather that it has since been heavily developed as a holiday resort. (*Press Association*)

Olympic Games in Tokyo, and I then served a further 5½ four-year terms until I retired in 1986 after twenty-two years in the office.

This has been rather a long-winded introduction to the business of driving carriages but, had I not become President of the FEI, the chances are that I would never have started driving carriages. It came about in this way. In 1968, at a meeting of the FEI Bureau (Executive Committee) I was approached by Eryk Brabec, the Polish member of the Bureau, with the suggestion that the FEI ought to develop international rules for competition carriage driving.

I should explain that most of the international sports federations were formed to compile international rules so that everyone could compete on equal terms at the newly established Olympic Games (following their reintroduction in 1896). Before that, each country had its own rules for each sport. The FEI was formed in

1921 in order to agree common international rules for the three Olympic equestrian competitions: show jumping, three-day eventing and dressage.

I had, of course, heard of the Coaching Club and Coaching Classes at Agricultural Shows, and I knew about the British Driving Society and what has become known as 'pleasure driving', but I had no idea that there were such things as carriage-driving competitions in Europe. So I asked Eryk Brabec where these competitions took place. He assured me that they occurred all over the continent, but that the main events were at Aachen and Hamburg in Germany and in Hungary. He pointed out that the trouble was that each event was run under different rules. I thought the best thing to do would be to have a look for myself, so I arranged to visit Aachen, the site of one of the major German international horse shows. There I was astonished to see some twenty-four four-in-hand turnouts in the ring and to discover that they had been competing in cross-country and obstacle-driving competitions. This was enough to convince me that there might well be a good reason for producing international rules for driving events.

At that time Sir Michael Ansell was Chairman of the British Show Jumping Association and the guiding spirit of the equestrian sports in this country. He was also the British member of the FEI Bureau. When Prince Bernhard invited me to succeed him as President of the FEI, I asked Mike for his opinion. As he had persuaded me to agree to stand for election, I felt I was entitled to get my own back by asking him to chair an FEI committee to propose appropriate international rules for carriage driving competitions. He protested that he knew nothing about carriage driving, but I pointed out that he knew a great deal about rules and equestrian competitions.

The committee duly reported, and its recommendation was that the competitions should be based on the existing FEI three-day event rules (the rules which govern the Badminton International Horse Trials). I inevitably became involved in adapting the rules and then in steering the draft for what became the *International Rules for Driving Events* through the Bureau and the General Assembly.

The general idea was that the competition would consist of three phases, as in the ridden three-day event. However, the 'old hands' felt that there was a need to ensure that the horses and carriages were properly turned out and the driver and grooms appropriately dressed for the dressage and obstacle-driving phases – the latter was later to become known as 'the cones'. It was therefore decided to add an initial 'presentation' phase. Each entry was to be inspected individually by the dressage judges and marked out of ten before driving the dressage test. It was assumed that competitors would use the same dress and turnout for the cones phase. This presentation competition came to be hotly resented by most of the Europeans, largely because it was usually won by the British. It was really a competition for the grooms, but they claimed it gave us an unfair advantage. This was in part because of the British tradition of turnout classes at Agricultural and other shows, and in part because of the standards set by the Crown Equerry, Sir John Miller, and the grooms at the Royal Mews. The separate presentation phase was abolished in 1986, although marks for turnout were included in the dressage score sheet instead.

Nothing was laid down about dress for the marathon phase until much later, when grooms were forbidden to wear shorts. I am not sure quite when, but I know that I was struck by the untidy appearance of the competitors and their grooms during the marathon, and decided that everyone on my carriage – except the referee, of course – should wear the same outfit during the marathon phase: we all wore moleskin trousers, green pullovers and tweed caps. It was not long before most of the other competitors similarly adopted a 'uniform', which, in many cases, was associated with their sponsors.

Presentation was followed by dressage (or compulsory figures) on the first day. A cross-country phase followed on the second day (which, for some curious and historically inaccurate reason, became known as the marathon). Obstacle driving, to correspond with the show-jumping phase of the three-day event was to take place on the third day.

Fig. 1.2 I thought that it would look a bit tidier if the whole party on the carriage (except the referee) adopted the same form of dress for the marathon phase. I settled on moleskin trousers, white shirts and green pullovers. It has remained the same, with a few minor changes, ever since. It was not for some time that hard hats became compulsory. This photograph was taken at the 1984 World Championships at Szilvasvarad in Hungary. (*Author's collection*)

At this stage it was envisaged that the competition would only be for teams of four horses. However, it was not long before classes for singles, pairs and tandems, and for ponies as well as horses, became established. Thus, most driving events involve eight separate classes, although most classes drive the same dressage test and all classes have to drive the same marathon course. At some events, the earlier sections of the marathon are shortened for novice classes.

The dressage phase caused few problems. The dressage test would be judged in the ordinary way, i.e., in those days, in plus points which then had to be subtracted from the minus points earned in the marathon and obstacle phases. It was a fairly simple matter to devise a test consisting of various movements at collected, working and extended trots, a walk and a rein-back. We decided that it should be driven in an arena of 100 m x 40 m and judged by the President and four members of the ground jury.

The problem with describing it as 'dressage' was that it implied that it was simply a driven version of the ridden test. Needless to say, there were very few drivers with any knowledge of dressage. As a result, ridden dressage judges were invited to judge the driven version, but very few of them had any experience of driving a

Fig. 1.3 One of my first efforts in the dressage phase at Lowther in 1974 (there was snow on the ground in 1973!) The carriage is the much-battered Balmoral Dogcart with the Balmoral tartan upholstery. The horses are in the classic English neck-collar harness from the Royal Mews. Notice the prominent wheel hubs: these are what caused such problems in the marathon obstacles. It was to allow for such hubs that the cones for the cones phase were designed with sloping sides. (*Author's collection*)

carriage, and what four horses – or one, for that matter – do when pulling a carriage is not quite the same as that which a single horse does under saddle. A rider has reins, legs, a whip and spurs as aids, while a driver only has reins, a voice (sometimes rather too much and too loud) and a whip. Trying to use a four-in-hand whip on a leader during a dressage test is almost impossible anyway. This is because, while the thong has to be long enough to reach the leaders, this very fact makes it too long to leave dangling down, so it is wound around the shaft of the whip, leaving a loop in the top end. In order to use the whip on the leaders, it is therefore necessary to unwind the loops from the shaft, which would take too long whilst trying to drive a dressage test.

The marathon phase followed the pattern of the three-day event and was to consist of five lettered sections: A, over roads and tracks at a medium trot; B, a 1 km walk followed by a compulsory halt of ten minutes; C, at a fast trot with up to eight obstacles. These were termed 'hazards' in the original rules in English, to distinguish them from the obstacle-driving phase on the last day, but it turned out that the only suitable French translation of 'hazard' was 'obstacle' because 'hazard' in French means 'risk'. Then came section D, a second walk of 1 km, followed again by a ten-minute halt, and finally section E, at a medium trot. The marathon was to be a time trial in that there would be penalties for being late, or early, in each section. It very soon became obvious that there was really no point to section E when the obstacles were in section C. The obstacles were therefore moved to section E while C was reduced in length to 4 km and the speed increased so that it became the fast section. The distances and speeds for sections A, C and E have varied over the years, but the overall length has gradually been reduced to a maximum of 22 km (as of 2002).

The average speeds required for the five sections caused a lot of argument – and still do. In section A, 15 kph was chosen for horses and 13 kph for ponies. Competitors could finish in not more than two minutes less than the time allowed without penalty. Originally, it had all to be done at a trot, but, in order to simplify judging, section A can now be driven at any pace. It was some time before the kilometres were marked along the course, and so, prior to this, competitors had to drive the course by car in order to find reference points at kilometre intervals. Now that the distances are marked in advance, it is just a matter of judging the pace.

Horses are required to walk at 7 kph and ponies at 6 kph over a distance of between 800 m and 1 km. There is no minimum time for the walk sections. Section C is supposed to be the fast section and competitors may finish in up to one minute less than the time allowed, but the speeds (originally 19 kph for horses and 17 kph for ponies) have been reduced over the years to the extent that very few competitors incur any time penalties in this section. Some maintain that this

9

hardly constitutes a competition and that higher speeds would give an advantage to those with faster horses. The speeds set for section E have also been a bone of contention. If the speed is set too high, the competitors who get through the obstacles more quickly gain a double advantage: because they spend less time in the obstacles, they do not have to go quite so fast between the obstacles. As there is always the danger of getting stuck in an obstacle, most competitors try to get a few minutes in hand, otherwise, if anything goes wrong, a mad gallop is required to finish in time, and this can lead to comments that the horses have been driven to exhaustion. It is now forbidden to gallop after the last obstacle.

We thought that the relative value of the three phases on the final result should be in the proportion 3 for dressage, 12 for the marathon and 1 for the cones – the same proportions as in the ridden event. This roughly translates into an average score of 30 penalty points for the dressage, 120 penalty points for the marathon (which allows for an average of 75 seconds or 15 penalty points for each obstacle) and 10 penalty points (equivalent to one cone down at that time) for the cones. Incidentally, in the early days of competition carriage driving each obstacle was given a 'bogey time'. If you could get through within that time, you incurred no penalties. This meant that it was possible to do a clear round in the marathon. While this system penalized the slower drivers, it did not give the faster drivers any significant advantage. The system was later changed so that the time taken to drive an obstacle was converted from seconds to 1 penalty point for every five seconds (or 0.2 penalty points for every second) inside the penalty zone. This was a much fairer system and, as the points were all penalties, or 'negative', they could be added to the dressage and cones scores, which made it more easily understood by competitors, scorers and spectators. It was an informed guess at the time, but the scale has stood the test of time.

Incidentally, penalty zones around the obstacles were inherited from the ridden competition. However, it soon became evident that they created serious problems for the obstacle judges. Each obstacle was surrounded by a penalty zone set at 20 m from the obstacle. Any competitor leaving the zone at any time prior to completing negotiation of the obstacle was subject to elimination. The problem for the obstacle judges was to decide whether one of the horses had put a single foot outside the zone, or whether some part of a carriage had crossed a sometimes indistinct line. They were therefore replaced with pairs of entry and exit flags, and the time is now taken between passing the entry flags and leaving the exit flags of the obstacle. Where you go in the meantime is your problem.

The obstacle-driving phase was to consist of driving between pairs of markers set at between 20 cm and 40 cm wider than the track widths of the carriages and judged exactly as for the show-jumping phase of the three-day event. Each

Fig. 1.4 This photograph is of Sir John Miller, when he was Crown Equerry and in charge of the Royal Mews, driving the Queen's Oldenburgs at the first European Championships in Budapest in 1971. The enlargement shows what the original 'markers' (the predecessors of the plastic 'cones') looked like. They were basically wooden triangles with cross pieces at the bottom to hold them upright. Needless to say, if anyone drove a wheel over them, it broke with a loud noise and had to be replaced. Nearly all the spares had been used by the end of the competition.

The obstacle he is driving required the competitors to drive between the fencing until the back of the carriage had passed beyond the striped poles, and then to reverse out. Such obstacles requiring reversing have since been disallowed. (*Author's collection*)

knock-down would cost 10 penalties and every second over the time allowed would cost half a penalty point. The penalty for hitting a cone was later reduced to 5, in line with the ridden three-day event.

In the early days of competition driving, virtually every carriage had a unique track width, inherited from the days in which it was built for other purposes. This meant that the arena party had to reset the cones for every carriage and this sometimes led to mistakes. I well remember starting a round only to find that I could hardly get between the cones, and on another occasion when I had to appeal to the judges to remeasure the distance between the pairs of cones.

This was the general idea for an entirely new international equestrian competition, and we thought it would be prudent to have the draft rules tried out before they were introduced. The Swiss Federation kindly volunteered to run a competition during the summer of 1969. Sir John Miller was the Crown Equerry at the time and responsible for all the horses, carriages and cars in the Royal Mews, and I knew that he had taken to driving a four-in-hand under the instruction of the Head Coachman, Arthur Showell. I therefore set about persuading him to enter for this trial event and to let me know how it went. It was not an unmitigated success, and we learned a lot from the mistakes. The main thing was that the competitors were enthusiastic, and the Bureau agreed to pursue the project.

However, before the rules could be amended, or even printed, the Hungarian Federation applied to the FEI for permission to organize the first European Championships in Budapest in 1971. This was galloping long before we had learned to trot and I had considerable misgivings. However, the Bureau agreed and I decided that I had better go and see what happened. There were no unusual problems with the dressage on this occasion. In several subsequent championships there were suspicions that some judges were showing favouritism towards their national competitors, but that was nothing very new; favouritism could be found in ridden dressage judging or in the judging of any event subject to personal opinions.

I borrowed a horse to follow the competitors on the marathon, and I found this a very useful way of watching what happened in the obstacles. The marathon went reasonably well, but all sorts of minor difficulties emerged. The problem about the penalty zone became immediately apparent. Until the rules could be properly refined, points of this nature tended to be decided arbitrarily by the ground jury or the Chairman of the organizing committee and this frequently left the competitors in the dark.

The obstacle driving on the third day was almost a shambles. It turned out that there had been similar competitions before the war, and the organizers had simply copied what had happened in those days. The trouble was that the markers were made of wood (illustrated on page 11) and on most occasions, when a driver hit one of these markers, it not only broke, it made a nasty noise behind the horses, with predictable consequences. Long before all the forty competitors had driven the course, there was an embarrassing shortage of markers. The other snag was that, whereas in show jumping it is perfectly obvious when any part of a jump is knocked down, it was sometimes quite difficult to decide whether a marker had been displaced by a horse or carriage.

When I got home, I got in touch with a manufacturer of traffic cones and invited him to make some plastic markers (now commonly known as 'cones') with a hole, or depression, in the top to take a ball about the size of a tennis ball. In this system either the ball comes off or it stays where it is, and thus avoids any uncertainties for both judges and drivers.

In those early days, all the carriage wheels had prominent hubs, therefore the markers needed to be triangular in shape and plane with the slope on the carriage side in order to clear the hubs, and about 60 cm high. The 'outsides' were vertical. My cones were constructed in yellow plastic with red and white circles on each of the flat sides, so that, as they approached the obstacle, competitors would see a red circle on the right and a white circle on the left – as in show jumping. I thought these covered the essentials, but within a short time the Europeans had produced a different pattern. These were certainly smaller and lighter, but the cones were made of red rubber in the shape of a dunce's hat but with the bottom cut at an angle so that they sloped outwards. Since they were red, and circular, it meant that they could not show red and white circles. An additional problem with this shape is that the slope goes all the way to the ground, which means that there are no obvious 'edges' to mark the passage between the cones. Furthermore, because the cones are circular, it makes it more difficult for the drivers to judge their exact position in relation to the cones and for the arena party to set them precisely facing each

Fig. 1.5 This photograph was taken at Lowther in 1987 and it shows the original yellow plastic cones which were produced at my suggestion after seeing the wooden 'markers' used at the first European Championships in Hungary in 1971. The yellow cones were produced by a company making traffic cones. To avoid arguments about dislodging a cone, I proposed putting a ball on top. Penalties are only incurred if the ball is knocked off. (*Alf Baker*)

other and at an exact distance apart. The cones currently in use in this country are made with the European cone on one side and my straight and sloping shape on the other, but they are red.

Immediately after the European Championships in Hungary, the German Federation sought the approval of the FEI to organize a World Championship in Munster in the following year, 1972. I was fortunately able to get to that event as well, and here again there was quite a lot of ad hoc rule making by the ground jury. The most awkward problem arose because we had adopted a system of points for placing in the three phases. As far as I can remember, the winner of each phase was given 1 point, the second 2 points and so on. The points gained by each competitor in each phase were added together at the end of the event with the lowest total deciding the overall winner. Our mistake was not to exclude anyone who failed to complete any of the phases. The winner of the dressage also won the cones phase, but failed to complete the marathon. His combined total for winning two phases, however, put him close to, if not in, the medals. We quickly reverted to the system in use in the ridden three-day event.

One of the most contentious issues was the design of the carriages for this new discipline. There were those who wanted all the carriages to be of 'traditional' design, while the more practical felt that competitors should be allowed a bit more freedom of choice. I drew on my experience of yacht racing and suggested that

Fig. 1.6 These are the cones designed by the FEI to replace the yellow ones shown in Fig. 1.5. They are rather less imposing than the yellow ones and, as they are round, it is more difficult to judge whether you are approaching them square-on. The inside slope goes right down to the ground and it is possible to drive over the lip without displacing the ball.

The driver is Sue Mart, the daughter of Michael Mart the carriage builder, who built the first all-metal dual-purpose carriage for me in 1975. He then built the undercarriage and wheels for the 'Sandringham' marathon carriage built by George Bushell. He later built a very smart phaeton for the horse team for dressage and cones and, finally, the marathon carriage for the ponies. (*Sally Taylor*) there should be a general 'formula', which would just lay down the minimum weight and track width and leave the rest to competitors. In yacht racing, and in air racing for that matter, such a formula allows for innovation and, through the use of current technology and materials, for improved safety. This is exactly what happened. When I started driving, it certainly did not take me long to realize that traditional carriages were not the ideal vehicles for going across country and getting round the marathon obstacles. Breakages were the cause of most problems. On one occasion when I was out in the Home Park at Windsor, the horses took exception to a tractor and spun round in a narrow track breaking the wooden pole. They then spun back again and took off. With the pole broken, there was nothing to steer the front wheels and when the front axle turned sharply to the left, I was pitched off the box and, as I flew through the air, I distinctly remember seeing the hooves of the off wheeler coming up to meet me. As luck would have it, one hoof caught me across the lower ribs and my hip bone. The result was quite painful for a few days, but it might have been much worse if it had caught me in the stomach. When I came back to look at the site a few days later, I saw from the hoof prints that the horse in question had then gone on to jump a six foot hedge with an iron railing in the middle of it.

Modern carriages – particularly the cross-country carriages – are built on a metal frame with open backs, aluminium wheels, disc brakes and what have become known as 'bendy poles'. As a result they are much more robust, more horse-friendly and more stable.

Meanwhile, I had been working on John Miller to persuade the Royal Windsor Horse Show to include an international carriage-driving competition under the new FEI Rules. This was agreed and the first event took place in 1972 and it is now the longest running international event of its kind in the FEI calendar. In those days each competitor was obliged to take a referee with him on his carriage for the marathon phase to ensure that he followed the course and that all the horses maintained the correct paces in the various sections. He could also record the time lost by any hold-ups caused by extraneous events.

I thought this event at Windsor would be a good way to find out a bit more about the competition, so I volunteered to act as referee for one of the foreign drivers, and I was allocated to Sandor Fulop one of the Hungarian entries. I did indeed learn a great deal from him and later on I got to know him, and the other Hungarians, quite well as fellow competitors. The one hazard about visiting the Hungarian stables was that you immediately had a glass of barack (peach brandy) thrust into your hand, whatever the time of day – or night.

The process of introducing this new sport was going on just at the time that I was in the throes of giving up polo. The moment comes for participants in any

Fig. 1.7 Sitting next to the Hungarian, Sandor Fulop, as his referee for the marathon phase at the first Royal Windsor Horse Show International Event in 1972. The carriage was wholly unsuitable for this phase as it was easily damaged in the obstacles. Notice the Hungarian breast-collar harness. I suspect that this was the first occasion on which such harness was seen in Britain. It is instructive to compare it with my harness in Fig. 1.3. (*Author's collection*)

sport when they have to make up their minds when to give it up. I had watched, and played with, several elderly gentlemen, who seemed determined to go on playing until they dropped dead in the saddle. Naturally the younger players made polite allowances, but when the result of a match is in doubt, politeness is sometimes strained to the limit. I was therefore determined not to follow the example of those elderly gentlemen, and to quit before my handicap was put down. In any case I was already beginning to notice that each year it took me longer, and required more effort, to maintain my handicap and injuries took longer to heal. Furthermore, I was plagued with a dodgy wrist. As my fiftieth birthday was in 1971, I thought this would be a good age to give up the game.

I suppose I could have left it at that, but I have never felt comfortable as a spectator and I started thinking seriously about what I might take up as an alternative to polo. Various options crossed my mind: I rejected golf, tennis and squash because of my wrist, and gliding and sailing would require permanent absence from home at the weekends. It then suddenly occurred to me that this carriage driving might be just the sport for someone in middle age. The Mews at Buckingham Palace was full of horses and carriages; the stables at Windsor, where I kept my polo ponies, were available, and I could do all my practising in Windsor Great Park or at Sandringham. As I did not foresee that there would be all that many competitions, the whole thing seemed to provide an ideal replacement for polo

Fig. 1.8 It was obviously about time that I gave up playing polo. Competing with your children is fraught with problems. Jamaica, 1966. (*Jamaica Tourist Board*)

during summer weekends – with the added advantage that I remained within the family of equestrian enthusiasts. The snag with doing any sport with animals is that you cannot treat them like a bag of golf clubs and only use them when you feel like it. Horses need regular exercise, feeding, watering, grooming and the attention of vets and farriers. There is therefore a strong inducement to use them as much as possible.

I started by learning to drive two horses – Cleveland Bays from the Mews – but this was only the first step to driving a four-in-hand in a competition. However, I knew absolutely nothing about driving a four-in-hand, so I thought it might be sensible to try with a team of ponies first. Initially I asked the ponyman at

Balmoral to go to the Mews in London to discover how to harness four stalking ponies together and put them to an elderly pony carriage, which I found in a store. Meanwhile I bought a couple of books on how to drive a team of four horses. One of them had been recommended to me when I was in Hungary, but it was in German. *Die Kunst des Fahrens*, or, *The Art of Driving* by Max Pape. It turned out to be a gold mine of information and instruction and I eventually persuaded Cynthia and Frank Haydon to get their German-speaking secretary, Annie Weber, to translate it into English. Meanwhile, I had to struggle with the original German.

The first outing with the team of stalking ponies at Balmoral was an interesting occasion. This was a completely new experience for the mixed team of Haflingers and Highland ponies and they were quite evidently mystified. The ponyman knew even less about the business than I did but I had at least read a book about it, and so with Herr Pape's book at the ready and the whole turnout surrounded by anxious volunteers, we set off gingerly down the drive.

Fortunately all went well, and I had started a new and somewhat unlikely leisure career. One factor was in my favour; the ponies were more used to walking than trotting, so they had no great ambition to rush off. This became quite a handicap later on when I took them to a proper event for the first time. Whenever I got to an obstacle, there was nothing I could do to persuade them to go any faster than a sedate walk.

The following January, I borrowed five Cleveland Bay horses from the Mews together with a set of neck-collar harness and a big wooden carriage known as the Balmoral Dogcart and took them to Sandringham. Meanwhile John Miller had secured the services of Major Tommy Thompson as my Head Groom. Lately Riding Master to the Household Cavalry, Tommy had grown up with horses and his knowledge of their management was encyclopaedic. He had ridden at Badminton and was also an accomplished four-in-hand whip. He was an invaluable help while I tried to master the art of driving, but he knew less than I did about 'combined driving', as it came to be known. By the time we came back from the winter holidays at Sandringham in 1973 we reckoned that I had made sufficient progress to risk entering a competition.

It just remained to ensure that the horses would go through water. This may sound elementary, but it must be remembered that these were ceremonial horses and their only experience of water was limited to avoiding puddles in London streets. There was nowhere at Sandringham at that time with any convenient water crossings, so I had one made in the Home Park at Windsor and decided to introduce this hazard to the horses in pairs. I had been advised by a brother-in-law that the way to get horses willing to go into water was to get them warmed up first so that they would enjoy the cooling sensation. I am sure this was good advice, but it does not solve the problem of getting them into water in the first place. My worst fears were realized and the first pair flatly refused to get their feet wet. I had made a habit of giving the horses lumps of sugar on return from exercise and it occurred to me that they might respond to a little bribery. I got Tommy to take my jar of sugar lumps across the bridge and rattle it at the horses from the other side of the water. One of them was sufficiently overcome by greed that he dragged the other one through the water to get at the sugar. This also worked with the other pair, but it still took some time before I was confident that they would face most water obstacles.

There was one occasion when I took a friend for a drive at Windsor with a pair and I thought I would show off their willingness to go into water. Just as we got to the edge, one of the horses stopped dead, but the other kept going. The effect was to slew the carriage so that, instead of crossing the stream, we set off down it and towards a tunnel under a bridge that might have barely allowed a single Shetland to get through. My passenger was not deeply impressed and his knuckles were white as he clung to the arms of his seat. By using every inch of the water, I was just able to turn the whole thing round without breaking the pole. Even after much further training, there were occasions when they seemed to be saying 'we know about water, but not about *this* bit of water'.

A couple of years later, I got someone at Sandringham with a bulldozer to dig an approach and exit to what was only a large ditch. I have to say that it was not a success. The only time I used it, the leaders jumped the ditch taking the wheelers with them. Unfortunately the carriage had sunk into the mud on the way in so the traces broke and the horses parted company with the carriage. I was still clutching the reins when this happened so that I was heaved bodily across the ditch and dumped on more or less dry land on the other side. Tommy Thompson was left feeling a bit lonely on the box seat, while the horses set off to explore Norfolk. One of them was stopped by my daughter, who happened to be riding in the vicinity, and, guessing that Father had come unstuck somewhere, rode to the rescue.

Getting the horses, carriages, harness and grooms and learning to drive a team is only the beginning. If you want to enter a competition, you need to get the whole circus on the road. For this you need a horsebox capable of carrying five, preferably six, horses and a trailer for the carriages. You also need accommodation for the grooms and horses when you get to the site of the event. I do not know who first had the idea of attaching portable stabling to the sides of the trailers carrying the carriages, but when I first started, the organizers of the event provided temporary stabling. This worked perfectly well, although it was an added expense. Accommodation for two grooms was available in the living end of the horsebox, but a caravan was needed for the Head Groom. This was no problem since the party needed some form of transport at the event and this could tow the caravan.

I started out with a horsebox from the Royal Mews and a flat-bed trailer for the carriages. I hired a caravan whenever it was needed. It soon became obvious that I needed a horsebox and trailer of my own. I had a good look round to see what other drivers were doing, and eventually in 1985 I ordered a six-horse box with some modifications to the standard layout. Instead of a side-to-side bed in the Luton head, I asked for two beds placed fore and aft, which left a space between them for a cupboard. Since the Luton head is not deep enough to allow a full fore and aft bed space, I had two fold-down flaps attached in such a way that they closed off the Luton head when the beds were not in use. They then folded down towards the rear to make a full length bed space.

When the horses were taken out of the box during an event, the stable part of the box was left virtually empty. I suggested a moving wall between the living end and the stable part of the box. This would move forward to allow the full use of the stable area, and move back, when the horses were out of the box, to make more living space. This had the added advantage that the door in the side of the box, normally used to enter the living part, would open directly into the stable end, when on the move, and then into the living space when the 'wall' was moved back.

The trailer for the two carriages was so arranged that there were two fold-down bunks attached to the front wall with a loo and shower on either side. It only needed one carriage to be taken out and there was room to pull a curtain across to contain this extra living space. As it happens, I do not think these bunks were ever used, as the grooms usually managed to find their own accommodation else-where. Cupboards and racks were fitted on either side of the trailer for the two sets of harness.

Meanwhile, John Miller had successfully persuaded the Earl of Lonsdale that Lowther would be an ideal place for a driving competition and I secured a place in the very first event to be run at Lowther in April 1973. The Lonsdales kindly invited me to stay at their home built round an old peel tower in Askham village.

Things did not start auspiciously. It had been a very wet spring and I had done most of my dressage practice on a cinder arena near the cricket ground at Windsor Castle. It had been built for the King's Troop when they were accommodated in Windsor while their barracks at St John's Wood were being rebuilt. My turn to do the dressage test came fairly early in the morning and it had snowed overnight. The ground became sticky as it thawed out and the horses found it much harder work than on the cinders at Windsor. This was bad enough, but I had also fallen victim to the nightmare of all dressage drivers, by going wrong in the test, with the result that I had the worst score of the ten entries. Things improved somewhat after that and I finished up in fourth place. John Miller won the event.

I had known that the FEI had allocated the second European Championships to Windsor for 1973, but it had never occurred to me that I might participate in them. I can only assume that my fourth place at Lowther must have had something to do with the invitation to take part as one of the individual entries. Since the Windsor Horse Show is always in the middle of May, there was not much time for any serious preparation for what was to be only the second competition I had ever entered. Fortunately the sport was so new that there were few other drivers with a great deal more experience. I was rather pleased when I came sixth out of twenty starters in the dressage, but disaster struck in the last of the eight obstacles, when I hit a pile of logs with the hub of the offside front wheel of the Balmoral Dogcart and bent the front axle. I managed to keep going, but as the front wheels were what might be described as wall-eyed, the carriage veered from side to side. I eventually struck a post on a narrow bridge, which bent the axle even more and broke some of the harness. So I had to retire within a few hundred metres of the finish. John Miller, driving a team of Windsor Greys to a very smart Beaufort phaeton from the Mews, had the misfortune to turn over in the third hazard, but he managed to finish and ended up in eleventh place. My morale was somewhat restored on the following day when I drove one of only four clear rounds in the cones and climbed up two places to end up in seventeenth position. The Great Britain team, consisting of Douglas Nicholson (3rd), John Miller (11th), and Jack Collinson (18th), collected the bronze medal. Switzerland took both the individual (Auguste Dubey) and team gold medals and the individual silver (Robert Doudin). Germany won the team silver medal. I took part in one more event at Cirencester that year, where I came in fourth out of eight and I was firmly hooked on this new sport.

RESULTS FOR 1973

EVENT	Dressage	Marathon	Cones	Pl/No
Lowther	10	8	1	4/10
European Championship – Windsor	6	17=R	2	17/19
Cirencester	4	4	3=	4/8

Horses used: Buttercup, Doric, Castlegar, Cadogan, Rideau.

1974

The 1974 driving season started with the International at the Royal Windsor Horse Show in May. There were five foreign entries and thirteen home drivers. The latter included George Bowman, who won it (the first of many wins), Douglas Nicholson (2nd), Jack Collinson (3rd), John Miller (6th), me (7th), John Richards (8th), John Parker (10th), Cynthia Haydon (11th, driving Hackneys), Alan Bristow (12th), Trevor Morris (15th, Household Cavalry), Joe Moore (16th). John Cowdery and George Mossman did not finish.

Alan Bristow's story is interesting. He had flown helicopters for the Navy and then had a spell with the Foreign Legion before getting a contract to fly a helicopter for an Onassis whaling fleet in the Antarctic. He later expanded his company by merger and takeover and eventually developed a major helicopter base at Aberdeen to service the North Sea oil rigs. He started driving a team at about the same time as I did, but it seemed that his business success had rather gone to his head and he expected everything to be organized for his convenience. He did not make himself very popular in the driving world by arguing with the organizers of events and he made life very difficult for the Chairman of the BHS (British Horse

Fig. 1.9 Driving through the outflow from Virginia Water during the marathon of the Royal Windsor Horse Show Event. The carriage is the famous Balmoral Dogcart fitted as a wagonette – the rear seats facing inwards. Tommy Thompson, my Head Groom, is standing behind me in a bowler hat. The other groom is Ian Garnett. (*Srdja Djukanovic*)

Fig. 1.10 Sir John Miller driving a team of Windsor Greys at the Royal Windsor Horse Show Event. The carriage is the '...very smart Beaufort Phaeton'. This carriage was really too good to use on the Marathon. (*From Show Programme*)

Society) Driving Trials Group by setting up a 'shadow committee' and producing all sorts of proposed changes to the rules. He thought nothing of withdrawing his team and sending it home if the course was not to his liking.

Lowther followed later in May. On this occasion things did not go well for me. I had lost the services of an experienced leader through injury and I had to put in two virtual novices. Disaster struck in the very first obstacle when the leaders pulled the carriage onto a stump where it rolled over and the team broke free and ran off – and the long-suffering Balmoral Dogcart was off for another rebuild. My referee on that occasion was a well-known 'sporting judge'. Fortunately, as a steeplechase rider, this minor accident caused him no qualms or injuries. The next day I started the cones, but I found the horses very difficult to control – in fact they were on the point of running away – so I retired. Cirencester followed in July where I managed to come in fourth out of seven.

I continued to bring the horses to Sandringham in January, largely because I could drive them fairly regularly and it was a good way to get them fit. Sandringham is an ideal place for driving anyway. There are miles of farm tracks, the ground is sandy and free draining and the climate is relatively dry so that it is possible to go out in most conditions. It is cold work in January but the going is

Fig. 1.11 Sandringham House in the snow. (*Sandringham Estate Office*)

always good. Further preparation went on at Windsor until the first club event at the Windsor Park Equestrian Club at the end of March or beginning of April.

One of the critical aspects of driving a four-in-hand is the method of holding the reins. The so-called 'English' system involves the driver holding all four reins in his left hand. The nearside leader rein goes over the index finger, and the off-side leader rein goes under the index finger. Next, the nearside wheeler rein is held directly under the offside leader rein. Finally, the offside wheeler rein goes by itself under the second finger. This system works splendidly for general purposes and is the most convenient way of driving a team for long distances on reasonably straight roads. It is also manageable for the dressage, but it is not – certainly for most people – the most convenient way of driving through the marathon obstacles or the cones.

After trying various alternatives, I came to the conclusion that a better way of driving the obstacles, and the cones, was to couple the two offside reins together and the two nearside reins together. I did this by punching holes in the reins and then inserting an H-shaped buckle, with the two 'uprights' screwed together at the horizontal link. I then held the two offside reins in my right hand and the two nearside reins in my left hand, with the leader reins over my index fingers and the wheeler reins under my little fingers and the buckles roughly in the palms of my hands. I found that this made it much easier and quicker for me to take loops in the leader reins to bring the leaders round while 'holding-off' the wheelers. I suspect that most drivers of teams and tandems have now adopted this method.

While thinking about this problem of handling reins, it occurred to me that there is a lot of evidence to suggest that the reason that traffic keeps to the left in this country can be traced to the way coaches and carriages drawn by four horses were driven in the eighteenth century.

Agricultural vehicles all over Europe were driven by the driver sitting in the middle of the driving bench and holding the reins in both hands – the left rein, or reins, held in his left hand and the right rein, or reins, in his right hand. When I was a boy in France and later in Germany, I well remember seeing farm carts being driven in this way. Hungarian competitors in driving events use this method to this day. In any case, there was so much room on the wide open plains of the Hungarian *pusta* that there was no problem about avoiding other vehicles. Consequently, it did not matter to them whether it was eventually decided that traffic should keep to the right or to the left.

With the improvement of public roads in this country and the development of large passenger vehicles – private drags and stage-coaches – a new technique for handling the reins needed to be introduced.

As I have pointed out, the English method of driving a road vehicle drawn by four horses over long distances, is for the driver to hold all four reins in his left hand. In the very simplest terms, the left hand can be said to control the speed of the horses and is in use all the time. The right hand is only used when required to steer. This is done by pulling on one or the other leader rein and so turning the leaders to the left or right. The driver can do this and still hold his whip in his right hand. He then only has to put the whip into its holder for him to have a hand free to blow his nose or to scratch his ear.

In order to exert a straight pull on the four reins, it is obviously best for the driver's left hand to be roughly in the middle between the two wheeler horses. This means that, in order for the left hand to be in the middle, the coachman needs to sit on the right-hand end of the box seat. As he is carrying his whip in his right hand, it slants over to the left and is out of the way of anything near the vehicle on the right including the whips of oncoming vehicles.

It should be evident that if the driver were to sit on the left-hand end of the box seat, the reins to the horses on his right would slant diagonally from his left hand awkwardly across to the right. If he then held his whip in his right hand, it would stick out to the left of the vehicle and would be liable to catch pedestrians in top hats, lamp posts and branches of trees on his left. While, if the vehicle is driven on the right of the road, the whip would catch the whips of coachmen coming the other way.

Driving on the left of the road with the driver sitting on the right, must have become customary quite a long time ago, since the left side is still known as the nearside – the side nearest the edge of the road – and the right side as the offside. However, the custom of mounting a horse from the left side may also have had an influence on the decision to drive on the left. For practical reasons, swords are kept in scabbards and slung from a belt round the waist. As most people are right-handed, the sword is worn on the left side so that it can be drawn by grasping the handle with the right hand across the body. Imagine trying to mount a horse from the right side with a sword hanging on your left side. The sword would be between you and the saddle and the chances are that it would get badly tangled with your left leg as you tried to swing it over the saddle and you might well end up by sitting on it. Mounting from the left creates no such problems. Consequently, both riders and drivers found it convenient to keep to the left in traffic.

At about the same time as I adopted my rein-coupling buckle, I had become convinced that the old-fashioned, and not very robust Balmoral Dogcart, was far from being the ideal vehicle for these competitions. In spite of fitting it with disc brakes (at least they still worked after going through water) and changing the back seats round, so that the grooms could face forwards, the springs also needed to be tied down to make them a bit stiffer for going across rough ground. However, the hubs still stuck out and the slightest contact with a tree, or turning over, inevitably meant a major rebuild.

It was while I was walking round the trade stands at Badminton that I came across a Mr Bowers, who was exhibiting newly built carriages. I asked him whether he could build me a carriage specially designed for competitive driving. I suggested a steel frame with a metal pole, and all metal wheels. It was to be a dual-purpose carriage, because there were mutterings that people who could afford two carriages had an unfair advantage. I explained that I wanted to have something that would look good for the presentation, dressage and cones and yet be robust

enough for the marathon. What I did not know at the time was that he contracted Michael Mart to build what I called the Bowers Dogcart, but which others referred to as the Iron Maiden. Michael Mart was later to become one of the leading specialist carriage builders for competitive driving.

There were two problems with the new carriage. By having stiffer springs and a metal, therefore more rigid, pole, there was not sufficient flexibility in the whole front assembly and pole to accommodate any up and down movement of the horses. The solution was to hinge the pole and attach a damping spring to stop it thrashing up and down. The other problem was that the wheels were made of steel and were much too heavy for the body. Good suspension for any vehicle depends on having low unsprung weight. In other words, the wheels need to be as light as possible in relation to the weight of the body.

I had paid a number of visits to the British Aircraft Corporation to see the new turboprop-driven Viscount and Vanguard, the VC 10 and Concorde, and, as a result I got to know the Chairman, Sir George Edwards, quite well. Aircraft engineers know all about light metals, so I thought I would ask his advice about some lightweight carriage wheels with tapered roller bearings and, above all, without hubs that stuck out some 10 cm. He told me that his experimental workshop could handle the problem quite easily and a short time later a splendid set of new wheels appeared and made all the difference to the suspension of the carriage.

Fig. 1.12 Driving the dual-purpose, all-metal Bowers Dogcart, known by some as the 'Iron Maiden', at Mellerstain in 1977. The carriage was built by Michael Mart. The original wheels were made of steel and proved to be much too heavy. Sir George Edwards of the British Aircraft Corporation very kindly had a set of aluminium wheels made at Brooklands, without prominent hubs. I used this carriage for several years until it became obvious that dual-purpose carriages were not the right answer. (*Robert D. Clapperton Photographic Trust*)

Results for 1974

EVENT	Dressage	Marathon	Cones	Pl/No
Windsor CAI*	7	7	6	7/16
Lowther	Retired			
Cirencester	4	4	7	4/7

Horses used: Buttercup, Castlegar, Cadogan, Rideau, Fort Steel, Solomon

* Concours d'Attelage International

Sir John Miller was the Crown Equerry from 1961–87 and was thus in charge of the Royal Mews at this time. He had learnt to drive a team of horses from the Mews, and I had persuaded him to enter for the first international event in 1969 to try out the new FEI Driving Rules. His enthusiasm for driving a four-in-hand soon got him elected to the Coaching Club, so I suppose it was inevitable that I should be elected to the Club sooner or later, and the invitation came in 1973. This introduced me to a completely different form of driving. There were some other 'combined driving' competitors in the club, but the majority were solely coaching enthusiasts.

Quite when amateurs began driving coaches is a mystery, but it is known that Oliver Cromwell, when he was Lord Protector, rather fancied himself as a whip. It is recorded that he had a very unfortunate experience when he used his whip on one of the horses he was driving, and the whole lot ran away with him. He was eventually thrown from the box, falling on to the pole and then on to the ground where he was dragged for some distance with his feet caught in the harness. To add to the confusion, he was carrying a pistol in his pocket which accidentally went off as he hit the ground. He must have been severely shaken, but he survived.

King George IV, when he was Prince of Wales, was a noted horseman and whip with a passion for speed. Thackeray records that it took the Prince only some four hours to drive from the Pavilion in Brighton to Carlton House in London, a distance of fifty-six miles (90 km).

The first of the driving clubs to appear was the Four Horse Club in 1808 and then in 1856 the Four-in-Hand Club was founded. The Coaching Club was founded in 1870 for coaching enthusiasts who could not get into the rather exclusive Four-in-Hand Club, and it is now the last surviving driving club of its kind in this country.

Nothing is simple in driving; every variety of carriage has its proper name and there are also a number of different kinds of coaches. The best known is probably the stage-coach. These vehicles provided the main form of long-distance public transport in the, roughly, eighty years between the improvement of the main roads, by Macadam, Telford and others, and the advent of the railways. The name comes from the stage, or distance, that a team of horses could be expected to pull a heavy coach at a reasonable speed. Depending on the type of going and the geography, most stages were between ten and fifteen miles (16–24 km), and it took the horses anything from an hour to an hour and a half at a fast trot. At the end of a stage the horses were changed at a posting inn with another team that would do the next stage. The first team of horses would then pull a coach back to the team's starting point, either in that afternoon or on the next day. The teams were changed very quickly, unless the change took place at a meal time, when the passengers were allowed refreshment. Unscrupulous innkeepers and stage-coach companies were known to make these stops so short that the passengers barely had time to get their teeth into any food.

At the peak of the coaching era, it was possible to get anywhere along the main roads of England at an average speed of about eight miles (13 km) an hour. A really fast team on a good road could cover ten miles (16 km) in the hour.

The Post Office ran a system of mail-coaches carrying the Royal Mail, but they also carried a few passengers. These mail-coaches were lighter and faster than the stage-coaches, and their coachmen prided themselves on keeping strictly to their schedule. While all other coaches had to pay a toll at toll-gates along the main roads, the Royal Mail coaches were allowed through free of charge. All coaches identified themselves to the toll-gate keeper by blowing a distinctive tune on their coach horns.

The rich owned their own coaches, known as park drags, for long-distance travel, although they were mainly used by the women, while the men rode their horses. They either hired teams of horses from innkeepers along the route, or, if they were regular travellers, they stabled their own horses with innkeepers or in their own stables. All public coaches were driven by professional coachmen until towards the end of the coaching era when it became the fashion for amateurs to 'take the ribbons'.

Current members of the Coaching Club own and drive all three types of the above-mentioned coaches.

The Club has a programme of meets at various places, followed by a drive to a chosen venue for a dinner or some other social gathering. The main event of the year is the Coaching Club annual drive and dinner. When I first joined the Club, the horses and coaches were boxed to a field near the roundabout at the entrance to Hampton Court. There, they were put-to and driven round to the garden entrance of the palace by their coachmen, where they waited till the owner-driver

29

Fig. 1.13 After I had been elected a member of the Coaching Club, I used to attend the Club's annual drive and dinner with my team put to the park drag from the Royal Mews. Here I am driving through Bushy Park before returning to Hampton Court for dinner. This event usually took place on the same Saturday as the Queen's Birthday Parade on Horse Guards. I had ridden Solomon in that parade in the morning and he was the off-wheeler in this team that evening. (*Author's collection*)

and guests had climbed on board for a drive through Bushy Park before returning to the palace for dinner. 'Climbed' is the appropriate word, because the majority of the passengers sit on the roof, and that is quite a long way up. In the old days, the expensive seats were inside the coach, but there was only a limited number: at most three facing forwards and three backwards. As the seats on the outside were cheaper, it was the origin of the term 'outsider'. The expression 'drop off to sleep' also has a coaching derivation; it is said to have originated as a result of passengers going to sleep on top of the coach and then 'dropping-off'.

I used to drive my horses to a park drag belonging to the Royal Mews. I cannot say that I ever became an enthusiastic coachman. Having started my career driving light and manoeuvrable phaetons and dogcarts, it was like stepping out of a sports car into a double-decker bus. I do not think my horses could have enjoyed it all that much either; they had to work really hard to move these heavy vehicles and, until they got used to the weight, this made them pull on their bits. It is also rather awkward for the driver because the box seat is perched above the rumps of the wheelers, which means that the reins have to go up to his hands from the terrets on the back pads almost directly below him. In an ordinary carriage, the reins go almost straight from the hand to the bits, so that the driver has a straight pull at arm, or shoulder, level. On a coach, the reins come almost straight up between

the knees of the driver and it is difficult, and tiring, to get a proper purchase on them. To make matters worse, carriage horses hate following other carriages. They seem to be obsessed with the idea that they must catch up with the carriage in front, and this makes them pull on the reins. The art is to drop back as far as possible without losing touch with the coach in front.

Since all the seats on the top of a coach are some twelve feet (3.6 m) above the ground, the anxiety about the possibility of rolling over is ever present. To make matters worse, coaches are so constructed that they have a very limited turning circle. If you, or the horses, try to turn too tightly, the chances are that you will break the main pole, and this usually means a major crash.

When I gave up driving horses in competition, I decided that it would be silly to drive a strange team of horses to a coach just once a year to the Coaching Club dinner. However, some bright spark knew that Sydney Smith owned a very smart small-scale coach designed for ponies, and suggested that I should borrow it for this annual event. Sydney very kindly agreed, but the problem then was to find the appropriate neck-collar harness, as I always drove the ponies in the breast-collar version. A further snag was that the collars have to be made to fit each individual pony. Micky Flynn discovered someone with such a set of harness, but he lived in East Anglia. This meant that he had to drive a box to Stow-in-the-Wold to fetch

Fig. 1.14 In 1974 I persuaded the Queen to have a photograph taken of us for a Christmas card, with Andrew and Edward, on the park drag from the Mews. It was taken from the George IV Gate of Windsor Castle, with the Long Walk in the background. (*Her Majesty the Queen*)

31

the coach, and then he had to make a trip to East Anglia for the harness. When the ponies were eventually put-to the coach, they reacted to this imposition with great patience, and I never had any difficulty keeping up with the horses. On many occasions the ponies came back looking immaculate, while many of the horse teams had got themselves into a muck sweat. It was this time-consuming business of getting everything together which eventually persuaded me to give up coaching altogether in 1999.

Chapter Two

Going International
1975–1980

I HAVE TO SAY THAT I was somewhat surprised at how quickly the sport gained popularity. Within only a few years it had attracted some fifteen four-in-hand competitors in this country. For example the following British drivers took part at the 1975 Windsor CAI. George Bowman, George Mossman (a much admired whip), Joe Moore (later to become Chairman of the BHS Competition Driving Committee), Alan Bristow, Jack Collinson, John Cowdery, John Parker (later to become Chairman of the British Driving Society), Major T. C. Morris (driving the Household Cavalry team), Albert Menaged, John Richards, John Miller and Cynthia Haydon.

At this point, I thought it might be an idea to explain what taking part in a driving event is like for a competitor. I am going to assume that all the decisions about which horses to take and how they will be put together for each phase have already been made.

A team driver can take five horses to an event, and since there are three phases (dressage, marathon and cones), it is necessary to find the most suitable combination of four horses for each of the phases. You may have a preferred combination, but all sorts of things can happen, which may cause you to choose a different combination at the last moment. Horses seem to be prone to all sorts of ailments, apart from choosing the most inconvenient moments to go lame.

Getting to an event involves having a suitable horsebox together with a trailer to take the dressage and marathon carriages and two sets of harness – a fine quality set for the dressage and cones and a working set for the marathon. The trailer is also designed with portable stabling on either side. This is usually constructed so that the sides unfold upwards to form roofs. Partitions are then fitted to form individual stalls. Unless the horsebox has ample accommodation for grooms, it is very likely that a caravan, with something to pull it, needs to be added to the establishment. All this has to be driven to the event and, as likely as not, it has to be set up in an uneven and frequently wet field, probably in pouring rain.

On arrival at an event, the first concern of the driver is to collect all the paperwork, and to discover any special conditions and the general layout of the whole event. In the early days, it was a custom for the Technical Delegate to preside over a meeting to brief the competitors, navigators and Chefs d'Equipe. This was no longer necessary when people became more familiar with the rules, and more experienced in the competition.

The next thing is to ensure that the horses are given adequate exercise in preparation for the first phase – the dreaded dressage, which is on the Friday of a three-day event. Then the starts and finishes of each of the five marathon sections, the sites for the ten-minute compulsory halts, and the positions of the obstacles have to be located. Having done all that, the time-consuming business of what is known as 'walking the obstacles' is next on the agenda. There are usually eight obstacles dotted about the landscape; each one consisting of up to six 'gates', lettered in the order in which they are required to be driven.

Fig. 2.1 Loading the ponies into the new horsebox at the Mews in Windsor Castle. The box can take six ponies, but competitors are only allowed to arrive at an event with five. Any four of the five can be used for each phase of the competition.

Most Fell ponies are very good about getting into and out of a box. There is nothing more frustrating than when a pony makes a fuss about getting up the ramp. The trailer for the carriages is on the left.

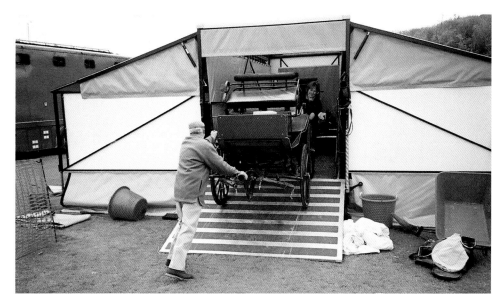

Fig. 2.2 Unloading the two carriages. The marathon carriage (*top*) and the best carriage (*below*) travel in the trailer, together with two sets of harness and a whole lot of other stable kit and the two 'Easy-rider' motorcycles.

Finding the best material for the tail-ramp was quite a problem. It needs to be robust and non-slip. (*Author's collection*)

The first problem is to find each obstacle's entry and exit flags and the positions of the lettered gates. You then have to figure out the best way of getting from one to the next in the right order. It may be easy enough to find the shortest way between gates, but it may not be the quickest way to get through it. Eight obstacles with, say, five gates in each, comes to some forty gates to be remembered. The only hope of getting through the obstacles correctly and quickly when the moment arrives is by walking the chosen route over and over again. There is nothing worse than suddenly seeing a better route at the last moment, and having to change your mental picture of the obstacle. One of the great sights on the Friday

Fig. 2.3 This is 'walking the obstacles' at Alnwick Castle in August, 2003 in ideal conditions! Glorious weather, and not another competitor in sight. An obstacle full of other competitors from different classes can be very distracting, particularly if you stop for a gossip. (*Author's collection*)

of an event is the picture of several drivers and their grooms endlessly walking round and round and to and fro in the obstacles. The natural temptation to stop and gossip with friends and rivals has to be resisted, or concentration will be lost and you have to start all over again.

This process of reconnaissance has to be interrupted to get ready for the dressage. This sounds easy enough, but, apart from the need to remember the sequence of the fifteen or so movements of the test, the driver has to bear in mind the individual idiosyncrasies of the horses. Leaders may be known to turn one way more easily than the other; one may have a horror of umbrellas among spectators when it is raining, or flapping flags in a wind. One wheeler may be known to 'fall-in' on corners more than the other. There are very few drivers who do not get a twinge of deep anxiety as they pass through the entrance to the arena at A. It is also very infrequently that a driver passes through A on the way out without feeling an immediate desire to shoot his horses and then to commit suicide.

I suppose some drivers must be able to sleep peacefully during the night before the marathon, but I suspect that most spend the time going over in their minds the routes through the obstacles. Getting through eight obstacles with your brain in replay mode is bad enough, but there is nothing more disconcerting than finding that you cannot remember which way to turn after gate C in the sixth obstacle. If your start time allows, you can go and have another quick look at the doubtful parts of some of the obstacles in the early morning, otherwise it is a question of getting the team together and checking the harness, ensuring that the time sheets for each of the sections are made out and clipped to a board and – very important – checking the time-of-day clock so that it coincides with the time-keepers' watches.

It is usually just as well to get to the start of section A in plenty of time; largely because there is always the possibility that something vital has been left behind. You watch the other members of your class being sent off at regular intervals and suddenly it is your turn for the timekeeper to count down the last ten seconds and send you on your way. It is then a matter of your navigator checking your progress against the kilometre markers against his stopwatch, and adjusting speed accordingly, making allowances for having to slow down going uphill and getting through tricky bits. Towards the end of the section, you have to start worrying about getting to the finish within the two-minute 'window'. There is then a short pause as you make your way to the start of section B, the first walk. Again you go through the agony of being counted down to the start. It is likely that your horses will have learnt about this countdown of the last seconds and become impatient about setting off. The walk only takes about ten minutes, but it is the longest ten minutes you have ever experienced in your life, and the effort to keep the horses going fast enough, without breaking into a trot, is seriously exhausting.

After what seems like an age, the finish looms up and you get in with a couple of seconds to spare – and start breathing again. Nothing is quite so welcome as the first ten-minute halt and an opportunity for the grooms to see to the horses and for you to stretch your legs and, possibly, have a cup of coffee. All too soon, you make your way to the start of section C and the countdown begins again. This is the fast section, and the experienced horses know what is coming. You have to get the horses going as quickly as possible and keep them going at a fast trot as you tick off the kilometre markers against the stopwatch. This time the window for arrival is only one minute. In the early days, making the time in this section was quite a challenge, but the maximum speeds were reduced, and it became just a question of timing.

Next is section D, the second walk, and it is just as trying as the first. The second halt is quickly taken up with attending to the horses, putting the buckles in the reins, so that the obstacles can be driven two-handed, and in a desperate attempt to go over the routes through the obstacles in your mind for the last time. Suddenly it is the countdown to the start of section E and then within minutes the first obstacle looms up and you get the feeling that you have never seen it before in your life. This is partly true because you have only seen it from the ground and now you are perched on top of a carriage with four horses in front of you, so everything looks different and a great deal more crowded. You are relieved to hear the quiet confident voice of your navigator muttering something about '... over to the right... left through A... sharp right to B... out and round the tree for C... go wide for D... swing left for E and OUT'. Phew, that's over, now for the second obstacle. It is to be hoped that they all go like that, but there comes the dreaded moment when either you or the horses make a mistake, your navigator loses his cool and you have to think quickly about how to make it right again. You then come out with a sinking feeling that you have made a mess of it.

Whatever has happened, there is a palpable sense of relief and achievement when you get to the end of the section. That may last until the horses have been taken out of harness and you are enjoying a late snack or a cup of tea, but then it dawns on you that you still have the cones to tackle the next day, and that you had better find out what time your class is on and when you can walk the cones course.

Learning the cones course is another test of memory, but it also includes deciding how to approach each pair of cones, what line to take for the box (a cone, or collapsible structure set within a three-sided enclosure) and any other multiple obstacles. There never seems to be enough time to do all this and to give the horses a short preparation through a couple of sets of practice cones, before going in to the collecting ring. The order of starting is in the reverse order of positions, so that the leader goes in last. You therefore spend time calculating how many points you can lose before you are overtaken, and you also calculate how many points the people ahead of you have to lose before you overtake them. Suddenly it is time to go into the arena and the bell rings as a signal for you to start. You hope all will go well, but there is always the chance that you will hear that ominous 'clunk' as you hit a cone. At the end of the course you try to catch a glimpse of the electronic timer to see whether you have managed to get round in the time allowed.

It takes a moment or two to get used to where you have finished and then you have to find your way to that place in the line-up for the prize-giving. Congratulations and commiserations to your neighbours; thanks for the prize – if any – and then off for a circuit of the arena before returning to the horsebox with a feeling of exultation, or a slight sense of disappointment and anticlimax. The horses are rewarded with a bite of grass and perhaps some sugar, then put away in their stalls; the grooms thanked and the process of packing up begins so that the whole circus can get away early the next morning.

My new carriage was ready for the Windsor event. This time there were only three foreign entries. It was won by Jack Collinson, driving Alan Bristow's team, followed by the enormous Kladruby team driven by Jiri Kocman from the famous stud in Czechoslovakia. This stud, which I visited many years later, used to produce the carriage horses for the Imperial Court in Vienna. George Bowman came third and I followed 10 points later.

This event is famous for John Miller's brave attempt to finish the marathon on three wheels. His referee describes what happened:

> The team was going splendidly, making excellent time, when just before reaching the brow of the hill, Sir John decided to take 'the short route'. It was a bold decision, just the sort of tactic you might try crossing Leicestershire on a 'quick thing'. If it had come off, it would have been brilliant, and would have saved a few vital seconds. Unfortunately it did not succeed – although plenty of things were about to come off. Calling on us to lean on the near side, Col. Miller swung his team sharply right-handed down the steep slope. I recall several spectators dashing across our path, which did not help, and then just before the water's edge, the leaders in our team ducked to the right. It was too much for the (antique) wagonette, which failed to make the turn back up the hill and crashed onto its near side spilling out Sir John, his navigator, John Marson, groom Mr. Long and the Referee. None of us was hurt. The near side rear wheel was smashed. By some miracle, which I was not exactly praying for, a woodcutter soon materialised with a saw, and quickly provided two birch branches. With hideous enthusiasm, volunteers led by Mr. Hendrick Haubroe from Denmark lashed the branches to the axles, leaving the wagonette listing to 45 degrees. The horses were harnessed again and Sir John – carnation button-hole still intact drove through the water and imperturbably completed Section C. Sadly, he failed to complete the course when the wagonette '… firmly declined to do any more mileage'.

Fig. 2.4 Sir John Miller with only three wheels on his carriage, Windsor, 1975. The nearside rear wheel has been replaced by a small tree tied to the carriage to act as a skid. This sort of damage was not infrequent in the days when people drove 'antique' carriages on the marathon. (*Author's collection*)

Oddly enough, Jack Collinson also lost a wheel during the European Championships later that year, but managed to finish the course on three. Soon after this the FEI changed the rules and carriages had to finish on four wheels.

A new event at Edinburgh appeared in the calendar, based on the Royal Highland Agricultural Society's grounds at Ingliston. The marathon took place round the golf course on the Morton estate. Although we did little or no damage, the golfers were outraged. I broke a leader bar in the walk section and had penalties for putting a groom down. I then broke a main bar towards the end of section E. Even then I managed to finish seventh out of fourteen.

Cirencester followed in July, where things went a bit better. It was at the end of this event that I got the unexpected invitation to be a member of the British team for the European Championships in Poland in August and my driving career entered a new, and wholly unexpected, phase.

The last national event of the season was at Lowther. Very sensibly, they had decided that an event in early spring in Cumbria was probably not a brilliant idea, and in 1975 the date was moved to the beginning of August, where it has remained ever since. There were only five entries. I managed to come second, although quite a long way behind George Bowman, largely as a result of going wrong in the dressage.

The sport had caught on in this country. New national events were being added to the calendar each year and local clubs were being formed; but there were many more participants in parts of Europe, particularly in Germany and Hungary, where every collective farm and horse stud seemed to have an international-class team of horses. If I had expected the sport to give me something entertaining to do during summer weekends, I was rudely awakened from this P. G. Wodehouse dream by the invitation to be a member of the British team for the next European Championships. These were due to take place at the end of August 1975 at Sopot, near Gdansk, on the Polish Baltic coast. George Bowman and John Miller were the other members. John Parker and John Richards were to have been the individual members but, in the end, they were unable to travel.

During my first reconnaissance of the course, I discovered, to my considerable consternation, that in section A of the marathon the course took us over the beach, into the Baltic and under a junior version of the Southend Pier. This was certainly not within the experience of my horses, whose contact, until very recently, with the countryside – let alone the sea – had been limited to processing up Ascot racecourse. I thought the only thing to do was to take the horses to look at the Baltic, one pair at a time. The sand was soft at the back of the beach and the first pair flatly refused to pull the carriage through it. My struggles and the efforts of my groom, David Saunders, to help get the carriage moving were observed with mystified interest by Polish sunbathers of various ages, sizes and sexes. We eventually got through onto the hard sand along the shore, but the little waves splashing onto the beach were altogether too much for the horses, and I had to retire defeated. At least we got through the soft sand without difficulty on the way back.

The same story was repeated with the second pair. I then decided to take the whole team to the beach. This time I got them onto the hard sand without trouble, but I could not persuade them that the little waves were harmless. I could get them to the very edge of the water, but every time a small wave hit the beach, they retreated daintily away from it. I was convinced that this would bring about the end of my career as an international, but, come the day, they dashed across the soft sand, straight into the water and under the pier as if they had done it every day of their lives. I was certainly relieved, but I was also – perversely – irritated with the horses.

The most time-consuming part of any driving event is the business of getting to know the course and the obstacles. The competitors were first introduced to the course at Sopot in a convoy of assorted vehicles. At one point the course went

Fig. 2.5 Paddling in the Baltic. Driving under the pier at Sopot near Gdansk, Poland in the 1975 European Championships. By great good luck, the sea was flat calm, with no little waves breaking on the beach to frighten the horses. The carriage was an antique phaeton from the Royal Mews. (*Zbigniew Kozycarz/KFP*)

through a large pond, or small lake, in a public park. The organizers had arranged for a cart with two horses to be driven through the pond so that we could see how deep it was and that there was no serious problem. However the cart had pneumatic tyres and I noticed that it seemed to bounce as it went over something in the middle of the pond. Everybody appeared to be happy with the demonstration, but I was a bit suspicious, so I came back later, and took off my shoes, socks and trousers and waded into the pond. Quite what the occupants of the Polish security car made of this is not recorded, but I soon discovered, by feeling around with my feet, that the source of the trouble appeared to be a huge boulder. I reported my find to the course builder, who quickly had it removed to the side of the pond, where, I have no doubt, it still rests providing a convenient seat for the weary.

Fig. 2.6 (*below*) This was taken on my return from the reconnaissance of the pond in the woods at Sopot, where I discovered a large boulder on the track under water. The course builder removed it before the event. (*Thomas A.G. Moore*)

Fig. 2.7 (*right*) Driving through the famous pond during the 1975 European Championships in Sopot, Poland after removal of the boulder. Notice the hoods with cup blinkers on the leaders. I borrowed the idea from the racecourse when it was the fashion to put such blinkers on racehorses. The wheelers are wearing ordinary carriage blinkers. Later on, I had blinkers made that buckled straight onto the bridles of all four horses. I argued that it would help the horses if they could see a bit more of the obstacles and avoid blundering into posts. (*Zbigniew Kozycarz/KFP*)

There were some thirty-one competitors from Poland, Hungary, Czechoslovakia, West Germany, Switzerland, the Netherlands, Great Britain, Sweden and Yugoslavia. The British team did reasonably well in the dressage: George Bowman collected 41 penalties, John Miller 46 and I was given 44 penalties, which put me in twelfth place. The best score was returned by Antoni Musial of Poland with 29 penalties. The next day produced some disappointment for the British team. John Miller went first and all was going well until he got to the second obstacle where, in his words:

> As we came up a steep bank, a bolt securing the top of the carriage to the bottom broke, with the result that the top of the carriage went forward and the wheels remained stationary, causing the axle to bend. At this point I was obliged to retire.

It was not John Miller's lucky year. I went next and got round safely, but at no great speed and together with a silly mistake in timing meant that I was placed twenty-first with 87 penalties. George Bowman was not at his best with a young team and could do no better than 69, which put him in tenth place.

I made a serious hash of the cones on the third day. One of my leaders – Buttercup – shied at the spectators and was unnerved by the sight of a small bridge. This resulted in my knocking down three cones in succession and a fourth one later on, which at 10 points each, plus some time faults, cost me 48.5 points. Even so, I moved up one place overall to twentieth. The Hungarians walked away with both the individual and team gold medals. Poland took the silver and Switzerland the bronze. The British team was placed sixth.

In those days, Poland was behind the Iron Curtain and I was shocked to see the queues outside food shops and the very meagre offerings in any of the shop windows. One evening we were invited out to a restaurant, where there appeared to be no lack of every kind of the richest food imaginable. We discovered that the majority of the customers were rich East German 'apparatchiks' on holiday.

RESULTS FOR 1975

EVENT	Dressage	Marathon	Cones	Pl/No
Windsor – CAI	8	8	3	4/16
Edinburgh	4	8	8	7/14
Lowther	5	2	1=	2/5
Euro. Champ. – Poland	12	21	27	20/31

Horses used: Buttercup, Castlegar, Rideau, Solomon, Niagara.

1976

The 1976 season was disappointing for me. It started well enough with a new event at Goodwood in Sussex, the home of the Duke of Richmond, but there were only three starters in the horse-teams class. Arthur Showell, the Queen's Head Coachman, with John Miller's team of Windsor Greys, had problems at the water and Alan Bristow was eliminated because the driver was given 'unlawful assistance' by his grooms during the cones.

This event was followed by the Windsor CAI*. Things started badly when, during a practice outing on a warm day shortly before the beginning of the show, I stopped the team in the water crossing, with the intention of cooling their legs. Suddenly, and for no apparent reason, Mexico, one of the leaders, plunged forward and broke the wooden leader bars. He then set off, taking the other leader, Solomon, with him. Solomon slipped and fell while turning onto the road; scraping his legs. Mexico was eventually found at the far end of the Home Park. There was nothing for it but to withdraw the team. John Miller had entered another team from the Mews, but was unable to drive it himself, and Arthur Showell had agreed to take his place. He very kindly offered it to me. There was just time to have a quick introductory session before the start of the competition. To my – and everyone else's – complete surprise, we did exceptionally well in the dressage and won it with a remarkable score of 26. I could only manage fourth place in the marathon. Compared to my horses, this team appeared to be twice the size and I had a bit of a struggle getting it round the obstacles. Never having driven it through the cones, I did even worse in that phase, however I still managed to make fourth place behind Emil-Bernhard Jung (Germany), George Bowman and Alan Bristow.

I did reasonably well at Edinburgh and Lowther, but while all my horses were sound again, I was not very happy with the way the team was going. So I was a bit anxious when I was invited to go as an individual entry to the World Championships at Apeldoorn in the Netherlands.

It is a wonderful place for such an event and it was beautifully organized. However, as far as I was concerned, nothing went right. I did an undistinguished dressage test and I was dogged by bad luck throughout the marathon. According to the note I made at the time:

> Broke a main bar in soft sand in D, but caught up the time. Twisted my knee quite
> badly as I had to abandon ship. Broke my whip just before the end of the Section.
> Got stuck in the first obstacle due to over-confidence and had to put the grooms

* CAI are the FEI initials for Concours d'Attelage International; CSI stands for Concours de Saut International (show jumping); and CCI stands for Concours Complet International (three-day eventing).

down. Sailed through the next obstacles only to break another main bar at a clattering wooden bridge. Both leaders broke away, but came back! Went on and through the next hazards, but broke a third main bar in soft sand just before the end. Tied leaders to wheelers with halter ropes. In spite of all this only 15 minutes late. Horses got upset in the 'U-shaped' obstacle and nearly bolted. Just managed to get them through the remainder of the course.

Imre Abonyi was the individual winner and the Hungarians took the team gold. The British placings were: George Bowman (5th), John Miller (19th), me (24th), Alan Bristow (26th) and John Parker (27th). Tjeed Velstra (30th) from Holland was eliminated in the marathon,but was later to become World Champion. The remarkable thing about this event was the huge number of spectators at the marathon obstacles and lining the course between them. I heard it estimated that some 30,000 people came to watch.

It was only much later that it occurred to me that I might deserve a place in the Guinness Book of Records as, possibly, the only President of any international sports federation who had competed in a world championship in a sport controlled by his own federation. At any rate, I found the experience highly useful when it came to discussions about the organization of international events in general. Several members of the Bureau had been international competitors in other disciplines, but I was the only currently active participant with experience of what it was like to attend events under FEI Rules.

RESULTS FOR 1976

EVENT	Dressage	Marathon	Cones	Pl/No
Goodwood	1	2	3	1/3
Windsor – CAI	1	4	8	4/8
Edinburgh	3	4	6	3/8
Lowther	1	4	3	4/6
World Champ. – Holland	15=	24	32	24/33

Horses used: Buttercup, Castlegar, Rideau, Solomon, Niagara, Merlin.
Horses used at Windsor only: Eagle, Rio, Santiago, Kestrel.

1977

The 1977 season started with a new event in Cumbria at Holker Hall, which was made much more enjoyable for me as I was invited to stay at the Hall by Hugh and Grania Cavendish. It is a glorious part of the world with much of the course overlooking Morecambe Bay. I think I must have been enjoying the scenery rather too much as I took the wrong course at the end of the marathon and was eliminated. The Goodwood event followed, but there were only two other competitors in my class. George Mossman collected a huge score and Alwyn Holder broke his carriage in the first obstacle.

There were twenty entries for Windsor, which was won by Emil-Bernhard Jung with me second. George Bowman lost two wheels as a result of cutting a corner on the marathon, and had to retire.

In June, seven competitors started at a new event in the Borders at Mellerstain, a magnificent house belonging to the Earl of Haddington. The dressage arena was just in front of the house, which provided a splendid backdrop. I was not enthusiastic about my test, but it must have been better than I thought, as I was 2 points ahead of George Bowman. Alan Bristow produced a new cross-country carriage for this event, which was obviously designed to withstand every kind of crash and mishap. So he was somewhat embarrassed when one of its wheels fell off at some stage of the proceedings, although not, if I remember rightly, while he was on the course. As usual, I blew it in the marathon and could only manage third place. Alan Bristow won, just 10 points ahead of George Bowman.

There was another new event at Nostell Priory in July. The house is impressive, but the site was not ideal and it was not repeated. I was second to George Bowman in the dressage and kept that place throughout. Alan Bristow's team was driven by his Head Groom, Charlie Mouron, but he developed cramp in his arms while driving the cones and had to retire.

I was unable to get to Lowther because of Jubilee-year events, but I sent David Saunders, who would succeed Tommy Thompson as my Head Groom, with a pair of my horses. He was unfortunate to break the pole during the marathon, but he finished the course.

The first National Championships took place in the middle of September at Goodwood. I won the dressage, but then dropped to second place behind Alwyn Holder. Meanwhile, George Bowman and Alan Bristow had gone off to the European Championships at Donaueschingen in Germany. George Bowman had problems at the first obstacle when his leaders jumped a tree trunk and one of his wheelers ended up lying on it and he had to retire. Alan Bristow's team refused at the U-shaped obstacle in the cones and was eliminated.

RESULTS FOR 1977

EVENT	Dressage	Marathon	Cones	Pl/No
Holker	1	E	4	4/4
Goodwood	1	1	1	1/3
Windsor – CAI	3	2	7	2/15
Mellerstain	1=	3	3	3/7
Nostell Priory	2	2	1=	2/5
National Champ. – Goodwood	1	2	2	2/4

Horses used: Buttercup, Castlegar, Solomon, Niagara, Mexico, Merlin.

1978

The 1978 season again started with an event at Holker. It was the first event for my new (Dutch) horse, Piper. Just how I managed to cope with him for nine years I will never know. He was a dedicated puller and even pulled when going downhill. He was also one of those dreaded horses, who think they know best and inevitably get it wrong. I finished third out of nine, but it was not a particularly distinguished performance. This was followed by the usual Windsor event, which attracted six foreign drivers and was won by Tjeed Velstra from Holland with a team of black Friesians. George Bowman tipped up, but still managed second place, while I spoiled a good start by making nonsense of the U-shaped obstacle in the cones course and let Alan Bristow through to third place by 3 points.

The Scottish International was at Mellerstain in July and I only just managed to keep ahead of the Swedish driver, Colonel Bengt Blomquist, in spite of a series of misfortunes and a disastrous cones round. George Bowman won and Jack Collinson came second.

The highlight of the season was the invitation to join the British Team for the World Championships in Kecskemet in southern Hungary. Hungary was still in the 'comrade' world with a Russian garrison in the town, and the stay was a very interesting experience. John Miller and I were comfortably accommodated in the guest house of a collective farm a few miles outside the town. I had expected the 'comrades' to be egalitarian, but I discovered there were at least four messes for different ranks with John Miller and me eating together apart from the others. After some negotiation, we combined with the senior managers and the security team, who were clearly surprised by this display of egalitarianism by the dreaded capitalist aristocrats.

There were some thirty-seven entries and I was surprised, but quite pleased, to have been placed equal sixth with George Bowman in the dressage, but as I had won the presentation, my combined score put me in second place on the first day. That was about the end of my satisfaction, although I was very pleased to have the great and late Imre Abonyi as my referee for the marathon. During the walk sections, I was doing my best to get the horses to walk as quickly as possible, but Abonyi kept saying 'go on, go on' and when I pointed out they were trotting, he said 'never mind, go on!'

Fig. 2.8 A sand dune on the marathon course of the 1978 World Championships at Kecskemet in southern Hungary. Sitting next to me as referee is past World Champion Imre Abonyi. He was very helpful on the walk sections and helped right the carriage after we overturned on the wigwam obstacle. (*Fritz Widmer*)

I got stuck against a tree in the first obstacle and succeeded in bending the pole, but it was not bad enough to put me out, and I only collected 7 penalties. Real disaster struck in obstacle 3. It was a very simple obstacle and consisted of a traditional Czikos (Hungarian cowboy) reed wigwam and a tall pole with a lever for getting water out of a well; all inside a square wooden fence. Enclosed within the fence were a number of sheep and some enormous white Hungarian cattle with horns like those on Highland cattle. The course through it only required the driver to steer a figure of eight. The animals must have been resting quietly when the previous competitors came through, but one of these great cows decided to lumber to its feet just as my leaders came round the wigwam. This was altogether too much for Piper, who shot forward and then sideways and pulled the carriage up the sloping side of the wigwam. The inevitable result was that we turned over.

Fig. 2.9 The Czikos reed wigwam obstacle on the marathon at the World Championship at Kecskemet in 1978. It may have looked like a nice soft reed building but it turned out to have a hard centre, which caused me to tip up when the leaders dragged me onto it after spooking at a large Hungarian cow. The offending white cattle can be seen in the background. (*Fritz Widmer*)

Fortunately the Iron Maiden lived up to her name and no serious damage was done and the horses did not run away. We had the carriage upright again very quickly and were on our way in no time. The only problem was that a turnover in an obstacle cost 60 penalties at that time. The outcome was academic after that, but there was also some confusion about the scoring generally.

Things did not improve much on the third day when one of my leaders got a bit overexcited in the cones and slowed me down a bit. I also hit a cone, which gave me a score of 23.5. I ended up in twenty-ninth place, but this placing plus George Bowman's ninth place and Alan Bristow's nineteenth, was enough to give the British team the bronze medal, but only after Zygmunt Waliszewski of Poland took the wrong course, which cost Poland an otherwise certain silver medal. The whole event was dominated by the Hungarians, who finished with five drivers in the first six places. Their gold medal team consisted of Gyorgy Bardos, Sandor Fulop and Jozsef Papp. Tjeed Velstra of Holland, having abandoned his Friesians for Dutch Warmbloods, managed to achieve fourth place. The German team of Michael Freund, Ernst Fauth and Georg Knell won the silver medal.

Since the Hungarians could not bid for the next World Championships in 1980 having won twice in succession, the option went to Germany, but they decided not to bid for it, so, in due course it was allocated to Great Britain.

The season ended with the National Championships on Smith's Lawn in Windsor Great Park in September. I was second in the dressage, third in the marathon, but then made another mess of the cones and let Alan Bristow through yet again, although I still finished in third place.

Tommy Thompson decided to retire at the end of this season. I think he had had quite enough of taking the whole party on those long journeys across Europe to championships, most of which seemed to be behind the Iron Curtain. He had been with me for the best part of six years and I could not have done without him in those early days. He was succeeded by David Saunders, who had learnt almost everything he knew about managing horses from Tommy.

Fig. 2.10 Major Tommy Thompson had been Riding Master in the Household Cavalry before joining me in 1972 as my Head Groom with the Cleveland Bay team from the Royal Mews. He did sterling work for six years, which included getting the whole circus of five horses, two carriages and two sets of harness across Europe through the Iron Curtain several times.

The horses are in breast-collar marathon harness, which I bought in Hungary. The carriage is the dual-purpose Iron Maiden and we are getting ready for the marathon at Goodwood in 1977. (*West Sussex Gazette*)

RESULTS FOR 1978

EVENT	Dressage	Marathon	Cones	Pl/No
Holker	1	3	2	3/9
Windsor – CAI	3	3	11	4/18
Mellerstain	2	4	9	3/11
World Champ. – Hungary	6=	32	28=	29/37
National Champ. – Windsor	2	3	5	3/7

Horses used: Castlegar, Solomon, Merlin, Piper, Polka, Samuel.

1979

Although it started quite well with a third place at Holker and a second at Windsor, 1979 was a dreadful year. I would rather draw a veil over my results at Mellerstain, Lowther and the National Championships. At Mellerstain I recorded:

> Everything came unstuck in the cross country! It rained, the horses pulled, I made mistakes in every obstacle, fell off the carriage and nearly got run away with down the hill (my Referee bailed out!). I had just mentioned to him that one of my leaders – Piper – always pulled downhill, and looking round I saw that he had gone. It was only later that I discovered that he had chased after the carriage and got onto the back step. Needless to say, all this was seen by, or gleefully reported to, his friends, who ribbed him unmercifully.

Years later I paid a visit to a hunter class at the Royal Highland Show. When the judge had been introduced, he asked me whether I remembered him. I was completely stumped until he reminded me that he had been my referee on that famous occasion.

At Lowther, I hit a tree in the second obstacle and broke the pole. I think I had forgotten that I had a spare with me and I am not sure that I wanted to be reminded of it. I was prepared to call it a day, but my referee – the 'sporting judge' who I had tipped out in 1974 – urged me to fit the spare pole and continue. Anyway I finished the course with a hatful of time faults, but even then I was not last as three drivers had been eliminated and I did do a clear round in the cones.

I had been selected to drive at the European Championships at Haras du Pins in Normandy at the end of August. We all set off from Windsor at the crack of dawn on 27 August to catch the ferry from Portsmouth to Cherbourg. I was towing the grooms' caravan, and as it started swaying at anything over about 40 mph (64 kph), it was not one of my most enjoyable experiences. We arrived in the late afternoon to be greeted with the news that my uncle, Lord Mountbatten, had been assassinated at his holiday home in Ireland. I only discovered later that a bomb had been detonated in his fishing boat and that Nicholas, one of his twin grandsons and his son-in-law's mother, Doreen, Lady Brabourne, were also killed and that the others in the boat, his daughter, Patricia Brabourne, and her husband, John Brabourne, had been very badly injured. As soon as I could arrange for an aircraft to pick me up at Caen, I set off for home.

This dreadful year was rounded off by an awful performance at the National Championships at Windsor. I managed to uproot the post in the middle of the second obstacle and one of my grooms fell off the carriage. Then one of my leaders (Merlin) refused to go into the water for the first time ever. I had to go out of the penalty zone in order to try again and succeeded in crashing over a barrier. The real disaster was reserved for the last obstacle when Merlin pulled everything against a post in the last gate. The traces broke and the horses bolted until they came to a halt in a gorse bush. I was eliminated.

I had been driving the Iron Maiden for several years as a dual-purpose carriage for all three phases, but I had come to the conclusion that it was not such a good idea after all. The reason being that the carriage had to be clean and sparkling for the presentation, which meant that if I wanted to exercise the horses before the event started, I became extremely unpopular with my grooms, who had to clean it all again for the presentation. By this time Michael Mart was building some very handsome 'classic' phaetons, with all the modern improvements like aluminium wheels, disc brakes and without prominent hubs. I had ordered one of these at the beginning of the season and I used it for the first time for the dressage and cones at these National Championships.

At the end of this season, I decided that I really needed a purpose-built marathon carriage incorporating all the improvements that various drivers had tried out. I bought a standard Mart undercarriage with aluminium wheels, independent trailing-link suspension and disc brakes on the back wheels. I then asked the brilliant mechanical engineer at Sandringham – George Bushell, ex-Fleet Air Arm – to build a superstructure for it. When he had fitted the box seat, footrest and dashboard, he suggested that I try it out for comfort before he completed the back part of the carriage. During the trial outing, we just placed a couple of planks across the back springs for David Saunders and George Bushell to stand on. I was very happy with my end, so it only remained to decide how to finish the back end. During the trial we noticed how easy it was for a groom to get off and on to the planks over the back of the carriage while it was moving, rather than the more usual way, from the side. One of the disadvantages of getting in and out from the side is that the step is between the front and back wheels. Any slip and there is a good chance of falling off and the danger of the unpleasant experience of getting a foot through the spokes of one of the wheels. We therefore decided to construct the back rather like the back of a chariot, with a step across the back of the carriage and then a platform between the rear wheels. There was enough room to install a locker on each side, which could also be used as seats for the grooms, and another locker behind the box seat for all the various gear and spares that need to be stowed somewhere on a carriage. This open-back design was the first of its kind and the prototype for virtually all present-day marathon carriages.

Fig. 2.11 'The daddy of them all'. The purpose-built cross-country carriage by George Bushell, the Sandringham Estate Mechanical Engineer in 1980. The undercarriage with aluminium wheels came from Michael Mart. The novel feature of the design was the open back, which allowed the grooms to get on and off much more easily – and safely – than the traditional access from the side. (*Alf Baker*)

Fig. 2.12 A close-up of the arrangements behind the box seat. The little drawer is handy for spare gloves, keys, rein buckles and other odds and ends. The space immediately under the drawer contained halters and halter-ropes, spare reins and other bits of spare harness. The locker below was used for wet weather clothing and other kit needed by the driver and grooms. It also served as a platform for the Head Groom to whisper helpful instructions to the driver in the obstacles. (*Alf Baker*)

One of the problems with getting round obstacles, particularly posts and trees, is the danger of getting one of them between the front and rear wheels. The FEI rules specify that no part of a carriage may protrude beyond the wheel hubs, but a strengthened mudguard covering the front and rear wheels, just inside the width of the hubs, does ensure that nothing can get firmly stuck between the wheels. The other vulnerable place is the space between the splinter bar and the front wheels. There is no complete answer to this, but a partial solution is to angle the end of the splinter bar backwards and downwards so as to keep anything from getting into that slot, although this too may not stick out beyond the hubs of the front wheels. The most vulnerable place of all is between the backsides of the wheelers and the splinter bar. Unfortunately, it is virtually impossible to prevent a post getting into this space and, if it does so, it becomes extremely difficult to get the horses back and away from it without putting the grooms down.

At about the end of this season I also came to the conclusion that the traditional blinkers tended to obscure the horses' vision. Unless very carefully fitted, traditional blinkers are inclined to close over the eyes. I thought it might be a good idea to give the horses, particularly the leaders, a better view. After all, they were being invited to find their way through these complicated and tight obstacles and, it seemed to me, the more they could see, the more likely they would be

Fig. 2.13 I had these cup blinkers made to replace the racehorse hoods, which were cumbersome to fit under a driving bridle. Blinkers should not really be necessary at all, indeed Army horses have never worn blinkers. I suspect they were introduced during the coaching era, when young, badly trained horses were pressed into service. Their value is that they help to concentrate the attention of the leaders on what is in front of them, and prevent the wheelers from seeing the whip waving about behind them. I once drove a team of Haflingers in a cones competition without any blinkers. (*Author's collection*)

to avoid hitting posts or rails. Blinkers are not absolutely necessary anyway. They were never used in the Army and I suspect that they came into use during the stage-coach era, when it was desirable to get young horses into work as soon as possible. Blinkers prevented them from seeing the coachman's whip and any distracting activities on either side. Driving through obstacles does result in the whip being waved about quite a lot, as drivers manoeuvre the reins. I hit on the idea of borrowing those hoods with cup blinkers, which are sometimes used on racehorses. They seemed to work quite well, so I had some made to go under the bridles. I still believe in them, but as few other competitors appear to have taken to using them, I can only assume that there is some doubt about their value.

Results for 1979

EVENT	Dressage	Marathon	Cones	Pl/No
Holker	1	3	3	3/7
Mellerstain	2	4	9	7/11
Lowther	1	9	1	6/9
National Champ. – Windsor	2	8=	3	6/8

Horses used: Castlegar, Solomon, Merlin, Piper, Samuel, Frederick.

1980

When we first started competition carriage driving in this country, I think every one of us used standard English neck-collar harness. It is very efficient, from the horse's point of view, since the traces connecting the wheel horses to the carriage run from the collar direct to the splinter bar and the whole weight is taken on the horse's shoulders without interfering with his breathing or the movement of his legs. It is undoubtedly very smart, but there are three disadvantages with this form of harness. In the first place, it is rather heavy, secondly each horse needs to have his own perfectly fitting collar, and thirdly it needs to be taken apart each time it is taken off to be cleaned.

When I first saw the Hungarians at championships in Europe, I noticed that they all used breast-collar harness. In this system there is effectively one strap running from the roller bolt on the splinter-bar, round the breast of the horse and back to the other roller bolt. Obviously, there are other straps necessary to keep it in the right place on the horse's shoulders. If it is fitted too high, it interferes with the horse's breathing, and if it is too low it interferes with the front legs. The main advantage is that the whole harness is much lighter and, with appropriate adjustment, it can be made to fit any horse of a similar size. Furthermore it can be put on and taken off in one piece.

However, while it is possible to connect a neck collar through the traces directly to the splinter bar, without causing any problems for the horse, if you do the same with a breast collar, the movement of the shoulders within the collar causes the shoulders to rub against the stationary collar. To avoid this, a swingle bar needs to be fitted to the front of the splinter bar, which allows the collars on the wheelers to move freely with the action of the horse. I decided to get a set of breast-collar harness from Hungary, as I thought the saving of weight would be a great advantage to the horses on the marathon. It also meant that I did not have to use the best collar harness for everyday exercise work.

I used both the new carriages (the dressage/cones phaeton and the marathon carriage) in the 1980 season, and I was very pleased with them. Indeed everything went a lot better in that year. I started with a third place at Holker in glorious weather and then came second – again – at Windsor out of seventeen starters. I accumulated several time penalties in section C, which I attributed to the fact that the horses were on their home ground and saw no serious reason to exert themselves unduly, especially when the course took them away from home. Unusually, I managed the only double clear round in the cones.

Mellerstain was deeply disappointing, as I should have won. The trouble started when I got the loop of my whip over my head just as I began the serpen-

Fig. 2.14 Holker Hall in 1980. The course was excellent, the weather was glorious and the horses went beautifully. Altogether a rare combination. This photograph was used on the dust cover of the book *Competition Carriage Driving*. David Saunders is on his favourite perch as navigator and Brian Stanley is helping to keep the carriage upright – or 'back-stepping' as it came to be known. Brian went on to manage the Stud at Hampton Court. (*K.G. Ettridge*)

tine in the middle of the dressage test. In the struggle to get it clear, I managed to lose track of the test and succeeded in putting in an extra loop. I then had to go back and do the movement again. This cost me some extra penalties for going wrong, and for exceeding the time allowed for the test. However, George Bowman, unusually for him, collected 31.5 penalties in the cones, which put me just 11.5 points behind him in the overall totals. In other words, but for that nonsense with the whip, I might have beaten him, and thirteen others!

The weather at Lowther was dreadful, but it did not prevent me from getting a surprisingly good dressage score. The going was so bad for the marathon that sections A and B had to be cancelled. George Bowman won – as usual – with Alwyn Holder second and I followed 9 points later after doing the second-fastest clear round in the cones. There were fifteen starters including two teams from the United States: Mrs Tippet's team was driven by Jimmy Fairclough and Mrs Hewitt's team by Peter Munt.

One of the very enjoyable social occasions during the early Lowther events was the invitation to the team drivers from Albert Menaged and his wife to an evening party at their house on an island at the top end of Derwent Water near Keswick. They produced a lavish buffet dinner and this was followed by some splendid jazz from Mick Potts and his amateur band. Eileen Bowman revealed an unexpected talent, when she joined the band to belt out 'Johnny Come Home' and other jazz classics.

In September the World Championships came to Windsor. Forty-two teams turned up from eleven countries and the procession from the Mews up the Long Walk to Smith's Lawn for the opening ceremony was a spectacular sight. I thought it would be a good idea to invite all the competitors and officials to a party at the castle on the Saturday evening and I persuaded Mick Potts to bring his band to play for the assembled company. I think he played for three or four hours non-stop and I was led to believe that there were several dancers who never left the floor while he was playing.

George Bowman came third in the dressage with 42 (plus 7 for presentation) points, I followed with 45 (plus 5), which put me in sixth place, but poor old Alwyn Holder (the third member of the British team) could only manage 63 (plus 9), which put him twenty-eighth. By this time the system for calculating the national team scores had been changed from taking the best two overall scores, to adding together the two best dressage scores, then the two best marathon scores and finally the two best cones scores. The overall team score was the sum of the two best scores in each of the three phases. However, a team member had to complete all three phases for any of his scores to count for the team total. This meant that, after the dressage, the British team was in second place with 99, behind Hungary with 96.

Fig. 2.15 The Bushell carriage in use at the 1980 World Championships at Windsor. David Saunders had taken over from Tommy Thompson in 1979, and is standing on his navigating perch. His right foot is on the mudguard, which was designed to prevent posts getting between the front and rear wheels. Brian Stanley is on the back step ready to help the carriage stay upright in sharp corners. The obstacle in the picture is the sandpit. You got into it over what seemed like a precipice, and it needed strong and determined horses to drag the carriage through the deep sand. It caused quite a lot of grief among the competitors. (*Findlay Davidson*)

The marathon was fully reported by *Country Life* and I can do no better than quote from Gordon Winter's article of 18th September 1980:

On Saturday the most hairy of the eight obstacles was a slalom course in water [southern end of Virginia Water] between concrete bollards; a steep sandpit leading down between concrete bollards, a turn at the bottom and up again between bollards, then a turn across the steep sandy slope and down again between bollards; and the final and most difficult hazard of all, known as the Maze. Not surprisingly, vehicles were overturned and on occasion wrecked so that they could not proceed. All over the course the air was rent by cries of drivers (most of them, perhaps fortunately, in languages we could not understand), and by the sound of splintering wood either in the obstacles or the vehicles.

The Marathon and the obstacles are designed to sort out the excellent from the good, and on Saturday they certainly had that effect. They left the two main contending nations, Hungary and Britain, still closely interlocked. By the end of the day, however, the arithmetic was beginning to look markedly in Britain's favour. By Saturday evening, the leading scores ran like this. Hungary: Bardos, 79 penalties; Muity, 173; Fulop 230 (a high penalty score for a former World

Champion, but he wrecked his vehicle in the dreaded Maze*. The Hungarians also had Fintha, with only 126 penalties, but unfortunately for them he was entered as an individual and could not count for the national team. Britain: George Bowman, 85; Holder 114; Prince Philip, 239 (after an expensive misadventure in obstacle 7, the Garden Pens; the Royal Mews horses are really too big for this game). Taking the lowest pairs, the scores were Britain 199, Hungary 252. Next came the Poles with 338, and no other nation was in serious contention…This meant that Britain began the last Phase with 53 points in hand, or the equivalent of 5 cones between the two drivers, Bowman and Holder, assuming that both the Hungarians went clear. When their turns came Holder and Muity each scored 10 penalties, leaving the relative position unchanged. So everything lay between the last to go in, the two leaders, Bowman and Bardos. Bowman, who went in first, kept his penalties down to 20, and that was good enough. Britain had regained the World Driving Championship, last held by us in 1974. Bardos duly went clear, deservedly retaining his individual world championship, with Bowman taking Silver and the Dutch driver, Velstra, the Bronze.

In point of fact, we had already won the team gold before George Bowman went in, because my score was 10 penalties, which meant that it was Alwyn Holder's and my scores, which counted in this final phase. In the overall individual placing, Alwyn Holder came fourth and I was placed twenty-first.

RESULTS FOR 1980

EVENT	Dressage	Marathon	Cones	Pl/No
Holker	2	3	2	3/9
Windsor – CAI	2	5	1	2/17
Mellerstain	9	2	1	2/13
Lowther	2	5	1=	3/15
World Champ. – Windsor	6=	25	8	21/42

Horses used: Castlegar, Solomon, Piper, Frederick, Kiel.

It was at about this time that I came across an old book of carriage designs and I noticed illustrations of what were called 'equi-rotal' carriages. The normal four-wheeled carriage is built with the body and the back wheels fixed together, while the front axle is attached to the forepart of the body on the underside of a turntable. The pole is fixed to the front axle, which means that when the wheeler

* He lost a wheel.

horses are turned one way or the other, the front axle and wheels follow the pole, thus steering the carriage. The equi-rotal system worked like a two-wheeled carriage with the back part attached to the front part by a hinge, like a trailer, or gun and limber. This struck me as an interesting idea for a marathon carriage, but I thought I had better do some research before building one.

I was due to attend an Olympic Congress – as President of the FEI – at Baden-Baden. The FEI had decided to hold a Bureau (Executive Committee) meeting at the same time. During a break in the Congress, I looked for, and found, a toy shop in the town. My idea was to buy one of those toy kits, which could be assembled into various wheeled vehicles. I explained to an attentive shop assistant roughly what I had in mind; she inquired about the age for which it was intended, and was somewhat taken aback when I answered 'about sixty'. Anyway, I found what I wanted and went back to my hotel, where I asked the floor waiter whether he could find a couple of empty wine or champagne bottles for me. He duly obliged, and I set about putting the kit together in equi-rotal fashion. I was happily sitting on the floor of my room pulling this model round the champagne bottles when all the members of the Bureau walked in. I had completely forgotten that I had invited them to the meeting in my room that afternoon. I am not certain that they were entirely reassured about the mental state of their President, even after I had explained the reason for this eccentric behaviour.

I eventually had the old Iron Maiden converted to equi-rotal, but it was not an unqualified success. I found it was more difficult to prevent it hitting posts on the inside of a turn. George Bowman had also tried an equi-rotal and he had come to the conclusion that the trouble was that you were effectively trying to drive a team from a two-wheeled vehicle. The difference is that, with a four-wheeled carriage, the wheel horses of a team move across to one side as they turn the front axle and wheels. This means that the outside wheeler gets further away from the driver, while the inside wheeler gets closer. The point is that it is necessary to hold off the wheelers when turning a corner so that they do not cut the corner by turning at the same time as the leaders. 'Holding off' means that you have to shorten the rein to the outside wheeler until the wheelers are past the gate post, or whatever it is that you are trying to get round.

In a two-wheeled vehicle, the driver goes round with the wheelers, as it were, so that in order to hold off you have to take in a lot more of the outside wheeler's rein. This is not at all easy to do when driving two-handed, and if you do not, it is inclined to allow the wheelers to turn too soon, with predictable consequences. Some pairs' drivers continued to use this equi-rotal type of carriage for a time, but then they faded from the scene.

CHAPTER THREE

ENTER THE PONIES
1981-1983

ALTHOUGH I WAS competing regularly with the horses, I continued to drive a team of Fell ponies at Balmoral. I used the ponies to keep my hand in, and to practise the dressage test while the horses were making their way to a championship or international competition abroad.

When I became President of the FEI, it was the practice for world championships for the three disciplines (show jumping, dressage and three-day eventing) to take place separately during the even years between the Olympic Games. What were known as 'Continental Championships' (Europe, North America etc.) took place in the odd years. Driving was added to the list of FEI disciplines in 1969, and since then, long-distance riding, vaulting and reining have been added, although none of these is an Olympic sport. For a time, each of these disciplines was entitled to have its own World Championships in the even years, but then the FEI decided to organize the World Equestrian Games for all its disciplines in one place. These were to take place in the even years between the Olympic Games. The only driving class included was that of horse teams. The first of these Games took place in Stockholm in 1988.

The Olympic disciplines then have what amounts to World Championships again at the Olympic Games in the other even year. This leaves the Olympic Year for the driving classes, and the other non-Olympic disciplines – other than horse teams – to have their separate championships.

As driving was not an Olympic sport, the introduction of the World Equestrian Games, made little difference. In any case, since most of the driving nations were in Europe anyway, the championships took place in Europe and the same

Fig. 3.1 The team of Fell ponies beside the Long Walk at Windsor in 1992 during the second halt before starting section E (the obstacle section). The painting is by Barrie Linklater. It shows Tom and Carrick in the wheel being cooled down by Michael Muir, and Dawn and Lady in the lead being washed down by David Muir (Jun). 'JJ' Reep is shown riding the spare pony, Ebony. They were not there at the time, but I had them added in to get the whole team into the picture. In the background is the formidable Karen Bassett driving her team of Native British Spotted Ponies. The carriage is a smaller version of the Bushell horse-teams carriage made by Michael Mart.

competitors attended both the World and Continental Championships. The first appearance of a national team of horse teams from the USA was at the World Championships at Windsor in 1980.

Driving causes quite a problem for the FEI. All the other disciplines are only concerned with one 'class' of competitor, although there are various championships for different age groups. The problem with driving is that there are eight classes, that is: singles, pairs, tandems and teams of horses, plus the same for ponies. Needless to say, all these classes have ambitions to have their own championships.

The idea of having a major championship for each of the eight driving classes separately, or to have them all at once, all in the same year, is somewhat daunting, and I suspect that it would not be practical. At the time of writing, apart from the World Equestrian Games and World Championships for teams of horses, there are World and Continental Championships for singles and pairs of horses, and European Championships for teams of ponies. Then in 2003, the FEI introduced joint championships for single, pairs and teams of ponies.

It is perhaps stretching a point to suggest that I started serious competitions with ponies in 1981, but I did drive a pair of Fell ponies at a small event at

Fig. 3.2 Lady (*above left*) and Ebony (*above right*) taken in 2003 at the ages of 23 and 25 respectively, in happy retirement at Balmoral. (*Author's collection*)

Balmoral that summer. It was won by that indefatigable and enthusiastic pony driver, Sydney Smith, with a very smart pair of Hackneys, and I managed to scrape into second place. I designed the four obstacles, including one near the Gelder Farm buildings, which required the groom to dismount to open and then shut a gate.

The only other obstacle I have ever designed was used once at Lowther. The rules say that the entry and exit flags must be 20 m from the first and last gates of the obstacle and, 'The track through an obstacle must never exceed 250 m on the shortest route between the Entry and Exit Flags…'. My suggestion was that the entry flag, gates A and B, and the exit flag should be in a straight line (20 m + 250 m + 20 m = 290 m long; the idea being that people should have a chance to gallop through it as fast as possible. I enjoyed it, but it was not all that popular with some other competitors and has not been repeated!

To go back to Sydney Smith. She had been a pupil of the great Hackney expert, Cynthia Haydon, who drove a team of Hackney horses in the early days of combined driving and was rarely defeated in the dressage. For many years Cynthia also generously volunteered her services as a driving dressage judge and gained a reputation for the caustic comments on her judge's sheets. She was a stickler for correctness and was not at all in favour of the new two-handed system of holding the reins for the marathon and cones. She believed strongly that all teams should be driven in the traditional one-handed coaching method.

There came a time when Sydney Smith thought she would like to drive a team of Hackney ponies and she asked me to show her how the two-handed system worked, but she insisted that it had to be done without Cynthia Haydon finding out. I took her into a field on the other side of the main road during an event at Scone Palace, but even then she had to look over her shoulder every now and then in case Cynthia Haydon had popped her head over the hedge and caught her trying the system.

You may well ask why I ever contemplated driving Fell ponies in competition. Tommy Coombs, a seasoned four-in-hand whip and a frequent judge and commentator at driving events, once wrote 'who would ever think of driving Fell ponies in a dressage test', or something to that effect. I agree that it is a fairly novel idea, but, it seems to me, this attitude misses the point. I believe that his view derives from the fallacy of comparing ridden dressage with driving a set of compulsory figures at different paces in a carriage behind a single, or multiple, turnout of horses or ponies. In the ridden version, it is the horse who has to perform the paces and movements under the control of the rider's legs and hands. Instructions by voice are not allowed. In the driven version, the horses have to pull a carriage without anyone on their backs while the only aids available to the driver are the reins, whip, and the discreet use of the voice. What a rider can do to collect a horse under saddle, a driver cannot do from the box seat. In any case, the pleasure of driving is to have a willing, obedient and above all, light-in-hand single or multiple turnout. Driven dressage in my opinion, should be more a display of lightness and accuracy in the whole test, than the shape and movement of a single horse going through a series of athletic exercises.

It is also worth bearing in mind that the dressage competition for drivers is only one of the three phases in a combined driving event and that, as far as penalties are concerned, the marathon is considerably more important and, usually, very much more fun for the competitors.

Anyone who has watched pony classes will have noticed that the majority of ponies competing are either Welsh or Welsh crosses. It is true that Karen Bassett drove and won with a team of Shetlands in her early days, and later did very well with a team of Native British Spotted ponies, but she was an exception. The reason I chose Fell ponies was simply that we use these ponies at Balmoral to carry stags (and hinds) off the hill during the stalking season. This is the traditional practice in most deer forests in Scotland, although, until the outbreak of war, most estates hired local farmers to provide their working Garron, or Highland, ponies for that job. After the war the number of ponies on farms dwindled away to nothing as more tractors came into use and we had to do the job with our own ponies.

The Queen had a Fell riding pony (Gypsy) when she was young and the pony's temperament suggested that the breed would be highly suitable for carrying stags.

Some local Highland ponies were also acquired and then, during a State Visit to Austria, the Queen was given two Haflinger mares, so that the present team of about twenty stalking ponies is made up of these three breeds.

If I remember rightly, the first team of ponies that I attempted to drive, was composed of the most reliable of the stalking ponies, rather than a well-matched team all of one breed. When I got a bit better at it, I tried out teams of the three breeds and came to the conclusion that the Fell ponies were the most suitable. I found the Highlanders willing, but lacking in 'sparkle'. The Haflingers might have done the job, but they seemed to have a will of their own and if it did not coincide with my intentions, a crisis inevitably ensued. In some respects they were too clever by half. They would learn something very quickly, but it then became a habit and difficult to break. On some occasions, while I was driving them on the estate roads at Balmoral, they would suddenly pull in at a lay-by and stop of their own accord. It was somewhat disconcerting, but I realized that they had acquired this habit on stalking days, when they had to wait at various points along the road for a signal from the stalker that they were needed to fetch a stag from the hill.

Later on, I was interested to discover that, when all the stalking ponies were turned out after the stalking season at Balmoral, they developed a 'pecking order' at feeding time. First came the Fells, followed by the Haflingers, with the Highlanders a polite third.

For a time, we also used Haflingers for forestry operations. With special harness and a set of chains, they were employed in towing logs from where they had

Fig. 3.3 Haflinger and Highland ponies carrying hinds at Balmoral. (*Balmoral Estate*)

been felled to the roadside. The ponymen soon discovered that the ponies learned what was expected of them very quickly. Once the pony had been shown the route, one of the ponymen waited by the log to be moved and attached it to the pony when it arrived. The other waited by the road to release the log, whereupon the pony went back on his own for the next one.

The history of the Fell pony is interesting. It is said to date back to when the Romans were building Hadrian's Wall between Newcastle and Carlisle. They used local native ponies to carry the construction materials, but they were rather small for the job. There were several mercenary units raised in Frieseland involved in the construction of the wall, and these had brought some horses with them. These Friesian horses were then, as they are now, black and quite big and, when crossed with the native hill ponies, the product was what we now know as Fell ponies. Once established as a breed they continued to be used as pack animals in the hill country of the Lakes and Borders and, when they were used for driving, they showed a considerable turn of speed. Friesian horses are still popular in Holland. Tjeed Velstra started his competition career with a team, but he gave them up after the European Championships at the Haras du Pins in France when they 'blew up' during the marathon.

Fig. 3.4 A Highlander dragging a log during forestry operations at Balmoral. The pony is being led by David Muir (Jnr) who succeeded his uncle (also David) as my Head Groom for the pony team. (*Kit Houghton*)

1981

Since the dates for Holker had been moved to June, the 1981 season started with the Windsor event in almost continuous rain. I came in second for the third time – to George Bowman this time. Considering I was driving three new horses in their first full competition, I was more than satisfied, particularly as my team was the only one to complete a double clear round in the cones in pouring rain and in an arena that had become a sea of chocolate mousse. The three new horses were Lady Isabella, Brown Owl and Harrier, all home-bred Cleveland/Oldenburg crosses, and they remained in the team until I gave up the horses in 1986.

Windsor was followed by a new event at Scone Palace, near Perth, the home of the Earl and Countess of Mansfield. The weather was just as wet. I was just beaten by Peter Munt in the dressage by a couple of points – owing to a botched rein-back – and there were fewer than 10 points between the first three at the end. Peter Munt just managed to keep ahead of George Bowman and I came third.

One of the features of these early competitions was the entertainment provided by the organizers or initiated by the driving community itself. It is not a very big community and people get to know each other quite well in the stable-field 'village'. It is really like a peripatetic weekend party and all the horses and ponies have come to accept the curious social habits of their owners.

Wynn Colville, who organized the Scone event, had engaged the services of an excellent caterer, and on Saturday evening he arranged a barbecue and a disco in his large tent in the stable field. The whole party staying at the palace came along for the evening and, after dinner, I invited my hostess to sample the disco. This was going on at the far end of the tent in appropriately subdued lighting and at the usual decibel level. As I walked in, I noticed what looked like pots of plants of some sort dotted all over the grass dancing area, and I thought what an original form of decoration. It was only when we started dancing, and my eyes adapted to the lower light level, that I realised that the 'plants' were long grass growing around fairly fresh cow-pats. Later, I tactfully suggested to Lord Mansfield that, if there was to be another event at Scone, he might move his cattle out of the stable field a bit earlier in the year.

My horses had health and fitness problems at Holker, but they managed the best dressage score (28) since I drove the Mews team in 1976, but I got stuck in obstacle 4 and then had two cones down. Finishing fourth was not bad considering George Bowman finished some 120 points ahead of me and 90 ahead of Christine Dick, who came in second.

Since persuading the Royal Windsor Horse Show to organize an international driving event, it had been my ambition to get some of the other agricultural shows to do the same. The first to agree was the Norfolk Show at Norwich. (The only other show to be persuaded to run a driving event was the Royal Highland at Ingliston with the marathon on the Earl of Morton's estate at Dalmahoy, but that only lasted for one year.) The problem for these shows was that the only suitable arena for the dressage and cones competitions was the main arena, and consequently these displaced other ring events, which attracted rather more interest from the public.

However, the event at the Norfolk Show at the end of June was a great success, at least from my point of view. I managed to achieve my first proper win – after eight years (George Bowman was not present)! My dressage was spoiled by one of the leaders putting a foot outside the arena, but, luckily for me, one of Peter Munt's wheelers got a leg over a trace, although even then I only beat him by 2 points. The marathon course was laid out at Stephen Vincent's Wramplingham Hall estate and it proved to be a very good one, although section C was rather shorter than it should have been, and this caused timing problems. This was definitely not Peter Munt's happiest event. He had just had a new cross-country carriage made for him, only for it to break in half in the first obstacle, leaving the back wheels standing while the team shot off with the front wheels, leaving the occupants all over the place and quite badly shaken.

I had an unnerving experience at the start of the marathon. As stated, in order to achieve greater control of the horses in the obstacles, I had developed a system of buckling the two nearside reins together and the two offside reins together, and holding the leader reins over my index fingers, with the wheeler reins under my little fingers and the buckles in the palms of my hands. As I was approaching the first obstacle, I noticed that the horses were not responding to the reins in quite the way I expected. I looked down, and to my horror I saw that I had picked up the reins upside down, so that the wheeler reins were on top and the leaders underneath. I only just managed to sort them out before getting into the obstacle.

On Sunday, the horses managed a double clear round in the cones, which put me about 20 points ahead of Christine Dick in second place, followed by John Parker, 1 point behind her. Micky Flynn, later to come to work for me when I was driving a team of Fell ponies, was driving Alan Bristow's team of grey Hungarians and finished seventh.

In July, I entered for a new event at Tatton Park on the outskirts of Knutsford. It had belonged to the Egerton family, but had since come into the hands of the National Trust, which let it to the local authority. Its claim to fame was that the park was used by the Army during the war as a dropping zone for trainee parachutists from what was then RAF Ringway – now Manchester Airport.

The main arena was reasonably flat and most of the marathon course was brilliant, although some parts were very bumpy over grass tussocks. Thanks to mistakes by George Bowman, Peter Munt and Christine Dick, I managed to hold on to an early lead in the dressage and win for the second time running. Needless to say this never happened again, although it did get me into the team for the European Championships in Switzerland in August, which took place at Zug on the Zuger See just south of Zurich in attractive countryside, and proved ideal for the championships.

Fig. 3.5 The presentation phase at Tatton in 1981. The judges inspected the horses, harness, carriage, grooms and driver in minute detail and allocated marks out of ten. These were added to the dressage score and then converted to negative points. (*Clive Cooksey*)

Thirteen countries – including Spain for the first time – were represented by thirty-nine competitors. My new marathon carriage attracted quite a lot of attention as the European press had been commenting on the unsightly 'battle-wagons' that had been built, or adapted, specifically for the marathon. One of the common design solutions to the problem of protruding hubs was to attach what looked like round metal 'shields' to conventional wheels. These covered the wheels from the rims to the hubs. They may have worked, but they looked awful. Then there was a variety of very obvious bumper bars around the carriages, which gave them an ungainly air. Oddly enough, no-one had thought of my open-backed 'chariot' design with combined mudguards and bumper bars. I am not claiming that my carriage was particularly elegant, but at least it looked a lot neater and tidier. Several continental carriage builders later copied the design.

Presentation took place at nine in the morning in pouring rain, but the horses took it very well. We managed equal seventh place (4 points behind the leader) in the dressage, in rather better weather conditions. With my team of relatively big horses (most of them were over 17 hh) I was always inclined to take the longer routes in the marathon obstacles and try to make up for it by going faster. The problem is that the bigger the horses, or ponies, the longer it takes to accelerate if they have had to slow down or stop. I got a bit too enthusiastic in two of the

Fig. 3.6 Tackling one of the obstacles in my new marathon carriage in the European Championships at Zug, Switzerland, August 1986. It was at the bottom of an old quarry and provided a great view for the spectators who crowded round the top. (*Findlay Davidson*)

Fig.3.7 A continental carriage showing the extra spokes fitted to prevent the hubs from getting caught behind a post in a marathon obstacle. Other carriages had what looked like circular war shields over the hubs, with their rims attached to the rims of the wheels. Both solutions were very unsightly compared to the hubless wheels made by the British Aircraft Corporation for my 'Iron Maiden'. (*Jack Watmough*)

obstacles and incurred time penalties for overshooting. Otherwise all went well and I finished in thirteenth place, 1 point behind Peter Munt. George Bowman did brilliantly to finish second behind the Hungarian World Champion Gyorgy Bardos. We all managed clear rounds in the cones, but, thanks to mistakes by two Swiss drivers, Peter Munt and I moved up two places and the British team came away with the bronze medal. Looking back through the score sheets, I see that we should have had the silver medal. Peter Munt and I both scored 40 in the dressage, while George Bowman collected 47. This meant that the British score for the dressage was 80. If this score had been added to the team score for the marathon (Bowman 15 and Munt 37) and with nothing to add for the cones, the total would have been 132, instead of 139 shown on the score sheets. Since the Polish team, in second place, had a total of 137, we would have beaten them by 5 points.

The season was not quite over as the National Championships were at Windsor in mid-September. I was a bit disappointed with my dressage score, but, while Lady Isabella could be brilliant, she was a bit of a prima donna and on this occasion she was not quite in the mood. However the real disaster came in the marathon obstacles. I hit a wheel against a tree and bent the pole. I had to get the grooms down and manoeuvre the carriage against a tree and push the horses across to bend it more or less straight. I then hit another tree in the last obstacle and only managed to wriggle free after 4½ minutes. John Richards had a problem in the cones, while I managed a clear round and moved up into fifth place out of

Fig. 3.8 The British-team drivers at the 1981 European Championships at Zug in Switzerland. One of my grooms, John Morgan, is behind my right shoulder, Anne Munt is on my left with her husband Peter next. George Bowman is on the right. We managed to come third, for the bronze medal, although I suspect there was a muddle in the scoring and we should have come second, 5 points ahead of Poland. (*Author's collection*)

ten. It was a disappointing end to an otherwise successful season. The dressage was consistently good and I only had two cones down in the year. On top of that I had the unusual experience of winning no less than two events.

Results for 1981

EVENT	Dressage	Marathon	Cones	Pl/No
Windsor – CAI	2	4	1	2/16
Scone	2	3	3=	3/6
Holker	2	6	4	4/8
Norwich	1	1	1	1/10
Tatton	1	3	1	1/8
Euro. Champ. – Switzerland	7=	14	1=	10/39
National Champ. – Windsor	3	6	1	5/10

Horses used: Castlegar, Solomon, Piper, Brown Owl, Lady Isabella, Harrier.

1982

A new event at Stanmer Park near Brighton started the 1982 season. The property stretches from the Brighton to Lewes road in the south to the top of the Downs in the north. It is an archetypal English country estate and house, which had belonged to the Pelham family. The fine eighteenth century house sits at the foot of the Downs with a garden on the south side. The front of the house faces onto a cricket ground, with the church and farm buildings beyond. The stables and a walled garden are tucked away behind the house. It was compulsorily purchased from the family of the Earls of Chichester by the Brighton Corporation soon after the war. Some years later the first buildings for the newly established Sussex University were built in the southeast corner of the estate, while the park continues to be used as a public park and the rest is farmed. The only flat part of the estate is along the main road and is normally used by the University as playing fields. It is borrowed by the organizers of the driving event for the dressage and cones arenas.

The main house was used by the university as administrative offices while its own buildings were going up. When the university moved out, the house – in spite of being a Grade I listed building – was left in a dreadful state. It so happens that the present Lord Chichester is a friend of mine and I thought he might be interested to watch a driving event and also to see what had happened to his family seat. When he had had a look inside, he was horrified and set about trying to get the house put back into reasonable order. He eventually managed to get a preservation trust formed. This succeeded in repairing the roof and doing some other urgent work before the Brighton Corporation decided to take charge of the house itself. I saw no signs of further activity the last time I competed there.

Things started quite well in the dressage, but come Saturday morning, Piper, one of my regular leaders, was obviously unwell and I had no option but to put Lady Isabella in the lead for the first time and hope for the best. We got through the first two obstacles remarkably well, but the water in the third caused serious problems. The water was in a circular, concrete-lined dew pond, and I had great difficulty in persuading Isabella to get her feet wet and that piled up quite lot of time penalties. A flapping advertisement in the fourth obstacle was more than she was prepared to take, but we eventually scraped through. I added to the problems when I went wrong in the seventh. This may look like a pretty dismal performance, but five others did a lot worse and I was surprised to find that I was not all that far behind Alwyn Holder and Peter Munt. Unfortunately for him, Peter Munt hit four cones and let me through to second place.

In 1979, David Saunders had persuaded me to write a book, which eventually came out under the title *Competition Carriage Driving*. It was intended as a guide

Fig. 3.9 This carriage is a modern steel-framed and aluminium-wheeled facsimile of a classic phaeton. The only clue to its modern manufacture is that the wheel hubs do not protrude. I used this carriage for dressage and cones. The Cleveland Bay horses in this photograph taken at Stanmer Park near Brighton in 1982, made up what was probably the best team I ever had. Lady Isabella and Brown Owl are in the lead with Solomon and Castlegar in the wheel. They are in traditional English neck-collar harness. (*Alf Baker*)

for people who might be thinking of taking up the sport. All it did was to set out my experience of horses, carriages, harness, horseboxes and the competition in general. He then successfully persuaded the TV documentary company Thames International to make a video based on the book and they spent the first part of the 1982 season putting it together. They started with the Brighton event, and Lady Isabella's refusal at the water features in an early sequence.

On several occasions I took the cameraman with me on the carriage for a training run. One of the problems about driving at Windsor is that if you want to get into the Great Park from the Home Park, you have to cross the Albert Road as you drive out on the Long Walk. The cameraman got down when we reached the Albert Road to take shots of the team crossing the road. It was only when David Saunders saw the rushes that he noticed that, as we waited to cross the road, the leaders had followed the *Highway Code* and turned their heads together first to the right, then to the left and then to the right again.

The Windsor CAI followed in mid-May in the usual way and, by one of those infrequent strokes of luck, I actually won the event (for the first and only time, after coming second four times in succession) in front of the cameras. Peter Munt

was second and Jan-Erik Pahlsson of Sweden, third. George Bowman had turned over in the seventh obstacle and Emil-Bernhard Jung was thrown out in the fourth.

For various reasons, I was unable to take the horses to Scotland in May, so I thought I would enter the team of Fell ponies for an event at Scone Palace. This was my first competition in the pony-teams class and the opposition looked quite formidable: the two Bassett sisters, Karen with Shetlands and Pippa with Welsh ponies, would come to dominate the class within a few years, before going over to horse teams; Mark Broadbent, who later successfully turned his hand to carriage building; Claudia Bunn, daughter of Douglas Bunn of Hickstead fame, who later turned to tandems and then to teams of horses; Tony Barnard and Richard Oddie, whose tall frame towered above his small ponies.

The ponies looked marvellous and, on the whole, they behaved impeccably. I thought a fourth place in the dressage the first time out, in spite of Bramble hanging his head and Carawich trying to bite the leaders' bottoms whenever they came within range, was quite an achievement. The weather could not have been better, but the carriage was 130 kg overweight. The heat also got to the ponies and there was not much I could do to speed them up in the obstacles. In the cones, I had two

Fig. 3.10 As Piper was unfit for the marathon, I took a chance and put Lady Isabella in the lead. All went reasonably well until we got to the water obstacle in this circular concrete dew-pond. Lady Isabella did not like the look of it, and it took me quite a while to persuade her to get her feet wet. She is the offside leader and is still looking highly indignant in the photograph. (*Alf Baker*)

Fig. 3.11 I am receiving the trophy from the Queen for winning the 1982 Royal Windsor Horse Show event. David Saunders is sitting with me on the box seat, Brian Stanley is holding the leaders, and John Morgan's head can just be seen behind the Queen. The carriage is the Michael Mart modern phaeton. (*Findlay Davidson*)

down and 20 penalties for time, which suggests that the ponies were pretty weary by then. Karen Bassett won, with Mark Broadbent in second place followed by Tony Barnard in third, and I came fourth. The other three entries had all got themselves eliminated.

Tatton Park came next for the horses in early June, and by now I realized that I had a really good dressage team. I won this phase fairly easily, but, needless to say, I threw away the advantage in the marathon where the leaders went the wrong side of a tree in the second obstacle and I dropped to third place. I then hit one cone, which lost me another place. I subsequently discovered that the measurement of my track width (in those days the cones were adjusted for each competitor's track width measurement) had been given as 136 cm instead of 156 cm. In that particular competition the allowance over track width was 40 cm, which meant that I only had 20 cm to spare, or 10 cm either side of the wheels.

Holker came in the middle of June, and my horses had all been involved in various State occasions. I rode Solomon in the Queen's Birthday Parade (Trooping the Colour) in the morning, and I then had him in the team for the Coaching Club Meet and Dinner at Hampton Court that evening. On top of that, all the horses had two days in the carriage procession up the racecourse at Ascot. However, I still managed to win the dressage, but they were obviously unsettled. I was not fast enough – as usual – in the marathon and George Bowman got 2 points ahead of me. We both did clear rounds in the cones, so I kept my second place.

The whole of the Norfolk Show event had now been moved to Wramplingham at the end of June. I won the dressage again, but the heavens opened on Saturday and we got caught in a thunderstorm ten minutes after starting. The going was very heavy and the unfortunate Household Cavalry team lost a wheel in the second kilometre. The eight obstacles were 'diabolical', according to my record, and only four of the eight competitors managed to finish at all. I had to leave for Holyrood before the cones, but David Saunders was allowed to drive the team and collected 7 time penalties. We finished second but some 90 points behind George Bowman.

I was very pleased to be invited to join the British team for the World Championships at Apeldoorn in Holland in September but, meanwhile, in July I entered the ponies for an event at Floors Castle on the Tweed near Kelso, belonging to the Duke of Roxburghe. It is set in glorious Border country, but it is challenging going for competitors.

Having done my research on the equi-rotal carriage, I had decided to borrow one to try out with the ponies at Floors. It was not a great success, as I had to get a groom down in one of the obstacles to pull the back end clear of a post. However, everything else went well for me, and the ponies behaved beautifully. The others were not so lucky. Mark Broadbent had to retire as a result of his ponies being spooked by a covey of partridges getting up under their feet. Richard Oddie also had to retire and both Bassett sisters accumulated a lot of time penalties in section E. So, to my – and I suspect to everyone else's – amazement, I succeeded in winning.

As the horses had to set off for Holland at the beginning of August, I also entered the ponies for Lowther. This time I managed to win the dressage. All went remarkably well in the marathon, apart from a small problem in obstacle 4, where I hit a tree with a front wheel. This pulled the leaders round the tree, and one of the buckles on one of the leader's coupling reins went back through the terret and stuck there until I had to get a groom down to free it.

The position before the cones was that Mark Broadbent was leading with 144, with me 7 points behind on 151. This meant that he could not afford to hit a cone (each cone down cost 10 points at that time), but he could have some time faults. I got round without touching anything but had 0.5 time faults. He sailed round the course without a problem until about three cones from the end, one of his leader traces came unhooked from the bar. It dangled through the next couple of cones without touching anything, but then at the very last pair it flipped up and knocked the ball off the top of the cone. That cost him 10 penalties and let me through to an unexpected win.

The World Championships took place on the Royal Estate at Apeldoorn in Holland, which happened to be the place where Kaiser William ended his days in exile after World War I. The whole event was very well managed and the facilities could not have been better. The countryside is rolling woodland on sandy soil, and ideal for such an event. The country house, Het Loo, was built by William and Mary, who later became King and Queen of England after the departure of James II. There is also a small medieval castle on the estate, known as the Little Loo, which Queen Beatrice had restored and made habitable, and which she very kindly allowed me to use during the championships.

There were thirty-eight competitors from sixteen nations and eight national teams. The British team consisted of George Bowman, Alwyn Holder and me, with Alan Bristow and Peter Munt as individual entries. When we went to walk the obstacles, I was somewhat dismayed to find that the third was in the semi-flooded bottom of a sand quarry, with a series of sailboards tied to posts with their sails hoisted. Drivers were required to drive in and out between the boats. I had a nasty feeling that Piper would not take kindly to the flapping sails, so I managed to borrow a couple of these boats and placed them on a path near the Little Loo and took the horses to look at them. Fortunately, they were rather more tolerant than I had expected, but I was still not entirely confident that there would not be a major crisis when they encountered the real thing. In the event, they went through the obstacle without a moment's hesitation.

Deirdre Pirie, who was responsible for introducing competition carriage driving to the USA, James Fairclough, also in the US team, and I shared first place in presentation with 3 penalties each. The dressage was won by the German driver, Bernd Duen, with 28. Velstra was in second place with 31. Leo Kraaijenbrink came third on 34 and I followed in fourth place with 38. George Bowman had 47, and Alwyn Holder 54. This put the British team into fourth place, equal with the USA.

In those days, grooms were allowed to run behind the carriage during the

Fig. 3.12 On my way into obstacle 3, the sand quarry, at Apeldoorn, Holland, August 1982, to face the dreaded flapping sails of the sailboards. The rather tense expressions give away the anxiety. You may notice that I am wearing a leather belt and a small apron. The idea of the belt was for the groom to hold it when there was a chance of my being tipped out. The apron was in token compliance with the rules, which required competitors to wear hats, gloves and aprons. The original purpose of aprons was to keep the leather reins from rubbing against the trousers. It was a good idea, because the traditional way of getting a proper grip on leather reins was to rub them with beeswax. Without an apron, this would have rubbed off onto the right trouser leg. (*Findlay Davidson*)

trotting sections of the marathon. At one stage in C – the fast section – my grooms got down to run up a short hill, but it was sandy and they had great difficulty in catching up. Velstra and I were the only two competitors to do all the sections without any time penalties. For once I did reasonably well through the obstacles and only had one hiccup in the fourth. It involved doing two similar circuits and Piper decided to do the first circuit again, which meant that I had to go round yet again to get it right. One of the remarkable features of these championships was the size of the crowd round the marathon obstacles. Rumour had it that some 30,000 spectators had turned up to watch the proceedings.

After the marathon, George Bowman was in fourth place, I had dropped to seventh, Alwyn Holder was eleventh and the team moved up to third place. George Bowman and I did clear rounds in the cones, so he retained his fourth place

Fig. 3.13 Each phase of the 1982 World Championships at Apeldoorn in the Netherlands attracted large numbers of spectators. The grandstand for the cones looks to be full as I try to negotiate the U obstacle. I managed a clear round and finished sixth overall and the British team collected the bronze medal. (*Findlay Davidson*)

overall and I moved up a place to sixth. The team retained its third place after Holland and Hungary and we won the bronze medal. These championships proved to be the high point of my international career.

The season was not quite over yet, as I had entered for the National Championships at Windsor in late September. I got the best dressage score of my career of 24, but things went rather downhill after that. I very nearly turned over in the first obstacle, a groom fell out and we bent the pole. I went on for a bit, but it was obvious that we had to try to straighten the pole and this caused some time penalties. Things went better after that and I only dropped to third. I managed a clear round in the Cones and just stayed ahead of Christine Dick who was only 3 points behind.

Results for 1982

EVENT	Dressage	Marathon	Cones	Pl/No
Brighton	1	3	1=	2/6
Windsor CAI	1	4	1=	1/17
Scone (ponies)	*4*	*5*	*5*	*4/7*
Tatton Park	1	6	3=	4/12
Holker	1	2	1=	2/8
Norwich	1	2	2	2/8
Floors (ponies)	*4*	*1*	*3*	*1/7*
Lowther(ponies)	*1=*	*2*	*1*	*1/5*
World Champ. – Holland	4	12	1=	6/38
National Champ. – Windsor	1	4	1=	3/10

(I see that I won the dressage with the horses in every national event of that season.)

Horses used: Solomon, Piper, Brown Owl, Lady Isabella, Harrier.

Ponies used: Bramble, Roy, Martin, Carawich, Rosie.

1983

The 1983 season started in frightful conditions at Brighton, and, to make matters worse, the horses were giving me serious trouble before the event. While practising for the dressage, I noted that all the horses pulled, Harrier turned too easily, Lady of Man turned too late, Lady Isabella would not turn to the right and Brown Owl jogged throughout. Typically, they went really well in the test and scored 31, which put me 20 points ahead of Peter Munt. In the marathon, we had to climb to the top of the Downs twice in pouring rain and in deep mud. I also had to stop to tighten a back spring, which was working loose, and collected 33 time penalties. This dropped me to second place behind Alwyn Holder. At least I did a clear round in the cones and retained second place. We later discovered a crack in the back axle, which could well have been due to the dreadful going.

The Windsor CAI followed in May, and again the going was badly affected by the rain. I managed to win the dressage again, but this time by only 5 points from George Bowman. Velstra stormed round the marathon in 66, while it took me 112. George Bowman had a groom down in one of the obstacles, so at that point we were equal on 144 with Peter Munt on 152. I had one cone down, which let Peter Munt through to third place, while George Bowman ended up in second place to Velstra.

At the end of May, I brought the ponies down from Balmoral to compete at Scone. I arrived from a State Visit to Sweden just a couple of hours before the dressage. We were not very good, but I was still third, just 5 points behind the leader. After the marathon, I was 11 points behind Richard Oddie, who was in the lead and 10 behind Claudia Bunn. A lot was going to depend on the cones. I was clear in the cones but had 2 time penalties. Claudia Bunn went in next and had one cone down and 7.5 penalties for time, so I moved up a place. Richard Oddie then went in and hit one cone and added 34.5 for time, so I moved up to first. As a bonus, I was awarded the Maxwell Prize for the best performance by a competitor over sixty!

Holker was a chapter of disasters. Isabella had a swollen face due to a sting, so I had to put Piper in. I also had to leave out Solomon. In spite of that, they did quite well in the dressage. I managed to win by 8 points from George Bowman. Solomon had to stay in London so that I could ride him in the rehearsal for the Trooping of the Colour on the Saturday. This meant that I had to use a helicopter to get back to London on Friday, but by using the helicopter again after the rehearsal, I was able to get back just in time for the marathon on the Saturday afternoon. The going was again very heavy and by the time we got to section E, my horses were exhausted. I collected 14 time penalties in C and a further 24 in E. Alan Bristow's team was driven by Micky Flynn and only had 2 penalties in D, the walk section. Michael Gilbey and George Bowman had to retire. Micky Flynn was eliminated in the marathon, and the Household Cavalry was going *hors concours* anyway, so only three finished the course. Alwyn Holder won fairly easily and I followed some 40 points behind. Third place was filled by Keith Farnhill, a great character known as the 'Bradford Messer'.

Holker had a rather unusual water obstacle. It was long and straight, but both the entry and the exit were quite steep and narrow. It looked as if a bulldozer had been used to widen a ditch running across the park. Quite a lot of the horses found this rather unattractive and tried to avoid going into the water by climbing up the steep bank, with the inevitable result that the carriage turned over. On one occasion, as I was approaching this obstacle, I was hailed by an anxious Cynthia Haydon and told that the last four competitors had overturned at the water. I am not quite sure what she expected me to do about it, but I did not get to it in a state of brimming confidence. Fortunately, my horses behaved impeccably and we splashed through in style.

The Norwich event had been dropped, but I managed to persuade a very reluctant Julian Loyd, the Sandringham Land Agent, to agree to an event at Sandringham with the sponsorship of the Norwich Union. The going is always good on the sandy soil and there are enough tracks to be able to vary the marathon course each year. About fifty acres of the estate is let to the Norfolk Lavender Company, and taking the course through the lavender in full bloom seems to be very popular with competitors, provided, I assume, they did not suffer from hay fever.

As I had got to know the estate quite well from the box seat by then, I undertook to suggest the route for the marathon course – other than section E and the obstacles – and I have done it ever since. I do this in January when I have time to drive around looking for possible tracks. I try to vary the course each year, but since the distances have been reduced the options are more limited. For instance section A used to be anything up to 10 km, whereas it is currently limited to 7 km. It used to be just possible to arrange for a ten-minute halt to be at a pub, but this cannot be done anymore. Inevitably, main roads have to be crossed and it requires quite a lot of juggling to get each section to finish so that the road can be crossed between the end of one section and the beginning of the next. The places for the ten-minute halts also need to be selected so that they are accessible to support teams. Many people seem to think that Norfolk is flat. True, there are no mountains, but the country is rolling and on a hot day, the hills can be quite demanding.

This first event attracted 123 entries, which was rather more than could be handled, so there had to be a ballot to reduce the numbers to ninety, although all sixteen horse teams were accepted.

I just managed to beat George Bowman in the dressage by 1 point, but he beat me in the marathon by 13 points. Owing to the misreading of a stopwatch, I was given 21 penalties in the sixth obstacle, but as I had someone taking a video recording, I was able to prove that I should only have been given 15. I had one cone down to George Bowman's clear round, so he won by 24 points, I was second and Peter Munt third.

While all the marathon courses at other events were splendid for the drivers, I had come to the conclusion that we ought to try to make them more spectator-friendly. At my suggestion we laid out the course so that sections A, C and E started, and B and D finished, in the main arena. Unfortunately, in later years, when the whole show became a country fair, we had to vacate the arena to allow ring events to take place. The other innovation was to build all the obstacles in section E fairly close together in a line with the course looping out into the woods in between. It proved to be quite a success with the spectators, if not with all the drivers. The obstacles have remained in the same area ever since.

At the beginning of July, I got the ponies down again from Balmoral for the event at Floors. Martin had a touch of colic and so I had to bring in Laddie, but his inability to stand still and Bramble's habit of lurching backwards at the rein-back lost me several points in the dressage. In the marathon, Rosie's inclination to trot in the walk sections and to canter in the trot sections added another 21 unwanted penalties. However, they got me through the obstacles very smoothly but, even so, Albert Metcalf got 20 points ahead. The ponies did brilliantly in the cones and recorded the only double clear round in both the horse-teams and pony-teams classes. Albert Metcalf had one cone down and 1 penalty for time, which was not enough to prevent him winning fairly easily, and I came in second.

Tatton Park took place later in July in very hot weather and hard going. John Richards won the dressage with 33 points, David Brand was second with 36, I came next with 37 and George Bowman was fourth with 38. My score was rather worse than usual thanks to Isabella showing a bit of temperament. Anyway it was all much too close together for my liking. It was still very close at the top after the marathon. George Bowman went round in 62, I managed 66, Alwyn Holder was breathing down my neck with 67 and John Richards was on 71. Mine was the only team to get through all four sections on time. The obstacles were wide open, but they were all on slopes and six singles turned over in the sixth by going too fast. Everything depended on the cones, and I was much relieved to do a clear round and keep my second place, 3 points behind George Bowman and 1.5 ahead of John Richards.

At Lowther, things started really well for me with a dressage score of 25, 6 points ahead of George Bowman. After the marathon, I was 9.5 points behind George Bowman and 9.5 ahead of David Brand. This meant that if I could do a clear round in the cones, which I did, George Bowman would have less than one cone in hand. In the event he had a really disastrous round. He hit a cone on the way onto the bridge, even though they were much wider apart than the ones on the rest of the course, then slipped off the bridge and missed the entry to the box which constitutes a refusal, and finally demolished the box and damaged his carriage. All this cost him 71 penalties and dropped him to sixth place.

Quite by coincidence, the organizers had transferred the cup for the pony-teams class to the horse-teams class. I had won the cup in 1982 with the ponies and now, a year later, I won the same cup with the horses. At the time of writing, I think I am still the only driver to have won Lowther with a team of ponies as well as with a team of horses. In both cases it only happened because of mistakes by the driver in first place before the cones.

One of the features of the 1983 Lowther Trials was the inclusion of a freestyle, or kur, dressage competition, where competitors were required to choreograph their own dressage routine set to music. It sounds simple enough, but I discovered that it requires a great deal of preparation. Having decided to have a go, the first thing I needed to do was to establish the rhythm of the horses' hoof beats at the walk and at collected, working and extended trots. I thought I would also try a canter, in case it proved possible to fit it into the test. To do this, I took out a single horse and dangled a tape recorder from the dashboard. I then tried to find pieces of music that corresponded roughly with the recorded rhythms. Next, I had to devise, and time, a sequence of movements so that I could record appropriate music for the correct time for each movement. I then had to practise the sequence of movements and try to get them to fit the timing of the pieces of music. It worked – more or less – and, if I recall correctly, I won the competition for horse teams. I remember that the Household Cavalry team driver had designed a performance that ended with the team cantering up the centre line to halt in front of the judges at C. The driver in question – who had best remain anonymous – was not noted for his control over his horses, and when the judges saw his team breaking into a canter down the centre line of the arena and coming straight at them, they prudently scattered in all directions.

I went up to Balmoral after the Lowther event, to find that some local enthusiasts had organized a one-day event at Tarland and, as the ponies were there, I thought I would have a go. The weather was glorious and the obstacles were quite demanding, but the ponies were totally unmoved. I won the dressage and the cones, but Wynn Colville got ahead in the marathon. The third entry in the class was Leslie McRonald with a tandem.

As there were no international championships in 1983, I was persuaded by David Saunders to enter a CAI at Tjoloholm in Sweden in August. It was in a marvellous setting in the private park of a remarkable house built by a very successful Scottish/Swedish businessman in a sort of Scottish baronial style. It had not been lived in for some time, but, in spite of these limitations, Colonel Hans Skioldebrand, the Swedish equivalent to our Crown Equerry (Sir John Miller), Ulf Kronberg and their wives somehow made it more or less habitable and invited John Miller, Brian McGrath and me to stay there. The wives provided all the domestic help – including dressing as parlour maids at dinner time – and made us very comfortable and gave us no end of entertainment.

One of the problems was that the plumbing system upstairs had ceased to function and the nearest supply of water and washing facilities were in the lavatories in the basement, provided for use when the house was opened to the public. Our hosts had very kindly rigged up a temporary shower and I later discovered that they had put up a notice to say 'Reserved for The Duke of Edinburgh'. Unfortunately, John Miller and Brian McGrath got there first and removed the notice. After that it was a matter of first come first showered. It was all rather cramped and provided some quite unusual challenges to the business of washing.

I thought I had started well by doing quite a good dressage test, but Colonel Bengt Blomquist decided that my wheelers had not been sufficiently on the bit and marked me down; despite this, I was fourth. David Brand did well to come in equal second with Waliszewski of Poland. We went round the marathon in great style and I recorded the same score as George Bowman, but dropped to sixth. I managed a clear round in the cones, while Jan-Erik Pahlsson and David Brand both had a cone down. This let me through to a very satisfactory fourth place overall.

The weather was glorious throughout; the marathon attracted the presence of The King and Queen of Sweden and Prince and Princess Bertil, and a surprisingly big crowd of spectators. It was altogether an unusual, but a most enjoyable, event.

The final event for the year was the National Championships at Windsor. I managed to win the dressage by one point from John Richards and David Brand, but that was about the end of my good fortune. All went well in sections A and B of the marathon, but section C took the team back towards the Copper Horse (the big equestrian statue) and the girls simply did not want to do anything so silly as to trot fast away from home. Things were made worse as Solomon tried to do all the work and kept breaking into a canter, and so, for the first time that year, I had time penalties. However, that was relatively unimportant compared to what happened in the water obstacle. Solomon started to plunge and succeeded in getting his front legs over the swingle-trees. We struggled out of the water with Solomon hopping on his back legs, whereupon Lady of Man, the leader in front of him, started to kick and, needless to say, hit Solomon several times in the face. As Solomon was obviously quite badly injured, and Lady of Man had suffered several cuts, that was very definitely that. I had to retire and I was also unable to drive the cones the next day. It was a very disappointing end to what had been quite a successful season.

Results for 1983

EVENT	Dressage	Marathon	Cones	Pl/No
Brighton	1	2	1	2/8
Windsor CAI	1	6	1	4/18
Scone (ponies)	*3*	*3*	*1*	*1/7*
Holker	1	2	1=	2/6
Floors (ponies)	*2*	*2*	*1*	*2/4*
Sandringham	1	3	2	2/16
Tatton	3	2	1=	2/12
Lowther	1	2	1=	1/13
Tjoloholm	4	5=	1=	4/18
Tarland (ponies)	*1*	*2*	*1*	*1/3*
National Championships	1	Retired		

Horses used: Solomon, Piper, Brown Owl, Lady Isabella, Harrier, Lady of Man.
Ponies used: Bramble, Roy, Martin, Rosie, Laddie.

This was the tenth anniversary of my first competition. It was one of the busiest years and in many ways the most successful so far.

Chapter Four

My Last Three Years with the Horse Team
1984-1986

IT SHOULD BE FAIRLY obvious by now that if I had a talent for dressage and was fairly reliable in the cones, I was not a huge success in marathons. However, thanks to the system for scoring team results, I always had a chance of being selected for championships in the hope that I might do well in the dressage and cones, while the other two members of the team needed to have a talent for the marathon. Fortunately, the selectors could always rely on George Bowman's talent in all three phases. His success rate both at home and abroad for well over thirty years is quite remarkable.

The season did not start all that well. At the first Windsor Park Equestrian Club event of the season, I have very distinct memories of coming to the first obstacle (composed of a series of logs, originally built for the National Championships the year before) with a certain amount of apprehension. I had decided to give Lady Isabella – a wonderful-looking horse but quite scatty – another chance in the lead, but at the sight of all the logs, she started to pull. There is nothing more calculated to ensure a disaster than a pulling leader in an obstacle. Inevitably, the worst occurred, and we turned over. Fortunately the horses stopped, nothing was broken, and there were no injuries, so I decided to try again – and we turned over again. This time I ended up with my leg trapped between the seat-back of the box seat and one of the logs. Even more fortunately this time, the horses stopped, but not before I appreciated that my leg had been quite seriously bruised and I came to the conclusion that it was time to go home.

In mid-April I took part in a CAI at Duerne in Holland, and ended with the National Championships for the ponies on Smith's Lawn in Windsor Great Park in mid-September. I was fortunate to be selected for the World Championships for horse teams at Szilvasvarad in eastern Hungary in mid-August.

Starting the season with an international event was quite daunting, although I had virtually the same team as in the previous year. The only other British entries, in a total of twenty-eight, were Alwyn Holder and David Brand. Duerne is not far from Eindhoven and I was accommodated in great comfort by Mr Martien van Doorne, the head of the DAF Company. The event was based at a very smart equestrian centre, managed by Tjeed Velstra.

I was surprised, but pleased, to have made third place in the dressage after Velstra and his fellow Dutchman, Leo Kraaijenbrink, driving Friesian horses, but I was not able to keep it up. All went reasonably well in the marathon until we got to obstacle 3, where I was taken the wrong side of a tree before I could stop the leaders and, in getting out, Piper got a trace wrapped round his leg and I had to put a groom down to sort it out. At least we got home within seconds of the time allowed and I was relieved to find that I had only dropped to twelfth place.

The team went brilliantly in the cones with one of twelve clear rounds. It was still the custom at that time to run a drive-off against the clock for those who had done clear rounds. However, the overall placing was decided by the first round of the cones, so the drive-off made no difference. On this drive-off, Bernd Duen started with a time of 148 seconds, I went in and took 153 seconds, then Velstra came in and squeezed between us with 149. Alwyn Holder went in last and stormed round in 133 seconds.

Brighton followed at the end of April with thirteen entries. A score of 31 in the dressage (2 for presentation, plus 29 for the test) gave me a good start over Christine Dick in second place, but things went downhill after that. I thought the obstacles were very tight and as the posts were not dug-in properly, many of the obstacles were under constant repair. To add to that, my horses were much stronger than usual and getting through the obstacles was a real struggle. George Bowman went round in 70, while I could only manage 174. That dropped me to sixth, but even after hitting two cones I went up one place as the Household Cavalry (Hywel Davies), in fifth place after the marathon, collected 26 in the cones and dropped to seventh.

Brighton was followed, as usual, by the Windsor CAI. Things started badly. To begin with, one of my grooms got drunk on Thursday evening and fell off a ledge outside his room above the Riding School and broke his pelvis. Then Lady Isabella appeared to be slightly lame, but after being reshod, she seemed much better and the show vet allowed her to go in the dressage.

In those days, the kilometres were not marked on the course and I liked to find some feature at the end of each kilometre by which to time my progress. For this purpose I had a kilometre tripmeter fitted in my Range Rover, but it chose this occasion to stop working properly, and, to cap it all, the video camera broke down.

I had better explain. Round about the time I started driving, I acquired a video camera, with the intention of recording the antics of the horde of press cameramen, who had come to dog our lives at Sandringham during and after the Christmas holidays. I tried it once, but the next thing I heard was that they had complained to the Chief Constable that they were being harassed! I found a better use for it when I persuaded a friend to film my dressage test so that I could get a better idea of what the horses were doing and so that I could identify and correct mistakes. I then thought it would be fun to have a record of a complete event by getting my passage through as many of the obstacles recorded and then to record the cones competition.

One of the first, and more or less willing, volunteers for this task was Brian McGrath, at that time my Private Secretary. He was, and still is, an avid and wildly partisan follower of all competitive sports and a highly dedicated and competitive golf player, and, as he would be the first to admit, he is not averse to a bit of gamesmanship. In some ways he was an ideal choice for the job, but his very enthusiasm, coupled with a certain incompatibility with things mechanical or electronic, had its drawbacks. On one occasion he walked from one obstacle to the next without realizing that he had not switched the camera off and there is quite a long sequence showing his feet stepping through the grass. Needless to say, he then switched the camera off, just as he wanted to record my negotiation of the next obstacle.

When he first started to record my driving competitions, he must have been unaware that these cameras also recorded sound. Either that, or his enthusiasm got the better of him at moments of tension or anxiety. At any rate his candid comments about what I was doing, while they enlivened the record, he sometimes felt were a bit embarrassing for him. I am sure he was considerably relieved when I discovered that my driver, David Key, was prepared to undertake this task without giving vent to his feelings – and holding the camera still while filming. Brian may have given up operating the video camera, but it has certainly not dampened his involvement in the sport. His comments are just as pungent, and they are recorded if he happens to be standing within earshot of the camera. Chewing his handkerchief is a sure sign that he is deeply anxious about the outcome and, in certain tense finishes to the cones competition, he has been known to look the other way altogether. How his nervous system has managed to survive over twenty years of driving events is beyond me.

To revert to the Windsor event: things improved when the competition started. I managed to win the dressage with 25, which put me 5 points ahead of George Bowman and 6 points ahead of Tjeed Velstra in a total field of ten natives and eight foreigners. The team went well, but not fast enough in the marathon. I was 40 seconds late in section C largely because of Blantyre's inclination to canter. At the beginning of E, I drove over a dead branch, which broke with a loud crack and spooked the team. One half of the stick flew into the air and came down on Harrier's back. The other half went under the carriage and managed to sever the hydraulic pipe to the brakes. Fortunately, none of the obstacles was on sloping ground so I could manage without brakes. Tjeed Velstra got round in the ridiculously low score of 49 compared to my 90, however only ten teams managed a score of less than 100. I went clear in the cones but collected 7 time penalties and ended up in seventh place, one place behind Micky Flynn driving Alan Bristow's team of grey Hungarians.

The ponies came down to Scone at the end of May, where I found three other pony teams: Claudia Bunn, Richard Oddie and family, and the Colvilles from Islabank. Claudia Bunn won the dressage with 3+37. Oddie came second with 2+51 and I trailed with 4.5+52. This was not altogether surprising as I had not seen the ponies since January. I pulled up 1 point on Claudia in the marathon. Richard Oddie did some very fast times through several of the obstacles. In obstacle 5, for instance, he scored 17 while the rest of us were in the 30s, but he collected time penalties in sections B, C and D, which dropped him to third place.

Although I did the fastest clear round of the day in the cones for the two teams classes and Claudia Bunn had one cone down, she was too far ahead to be caught. The Colvilles were going *hors concours*.

The next event was with the horses at Holker, and I was rather keen to do well in the hope of being selected for the World Championships later that year. I was just beaten by George Bowman in the dressage by 2 points. The marathon was hard uphill work in section A and the speed for C was 19 kph. Only Micky Flynn and I managed to do it within the time allowed. The obstacles were big and open, which encouraged speed, but not too much. Michael Gilbey turned over in obstacle 5 and Alwyn Holder nearly went the same way. Micky Flynn drove a brilliant marathon, 4 points faster than George Bowman, to pull up to second place and I went down to third by 0.3 points! Lex Ruddiman and I were the only two to do clear rounds in the cones. Micky Flynn had bad luck to hit two cones and get 2 time penalties, which let me back into second place. I very nearly made first place when George Bowman hit the last cone and the ball jumped into the air, but it dropped back into its hole! This is plainly visible on the video. The prospects for selection for the World Championships looked reasonable.

Fig. 4.1 The grounds of Scone Palace near Perth run down to the Tay and provided a splendid setting for a driving event. The event in May 1984 was the first of the season for the ponies and they went very well through the cones to record the fastest time in their class. (*K.G. Ettridge*)

I had a good start at Sandringham with a dressage score of 31, just 3 points ahead of David Brand and 5 ahead of George Bowman. All was going well in the marathon until Harrier fell as we were crossing the Anmer Avenue and was dragged 18 m before I could pull up.

Some years previously, Deirdre Pirie (who was responsible for introducing competition carriage driving to the USA) had the brilliant idea of connecting the wheeler traces to the splinter bar and the leader traces to the swingle-trees with snap shackles designed for yachts. The problem with the traditional fastenings is that they are almost impossible to get off when under tension. This meant that whenever a horse fell, the traces had to be cut, and that was the end of that. I decided to adopt these snap shackles and I set off towards Old Windsor, where I remember seeing a yacht chandler. He knew exactly what I needed, but had none

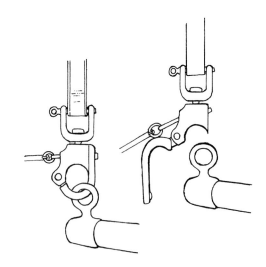

Fig. 4.2 Originally designed for use in yachts, this shows how snap shackles work. By pulling the toggle on the left, the shackle can be opened, even when under tension. This means that, when used to connect traces to a carriage, the traces need not be cut in emergencies. The shackles are fitted to the ends of the traces to connect the wheelers to the splinter bar, and the leaders to the swingle-trees at the end of the pole. I also use similar devices to connect the pole straps on the wheelers' collars to the end of the pole, and on the connecting strap between the leaders.

in stock. He produced the goods a couple of days later and I have never regretted the decision to use them. Apart from proving their worth in this instance, they made harnessing-up and unharnessing very much quicker and easier.

It took only a few moments for the grooms to trip the shackles on Harrier's traces and poll strap and she was up and ready to go. She was hardly marked as her outside trace had taken the worst of the scraping and we were able to continue. The only problem was that we had to make up three minutes in the last 4 km. We just made it, but I think the extra effort slowed them down in E; but then no-one made the time in E and I was just 5 seconds slower than Micky Flynn. In the end, I only dropped to third behind David Brand and George Bowman. Micky Flynn had pulled up from sixth to fourth. There were five clear rounds, of which mine was the fastest, so I retained third place. I was beaten by George Bowman in the drive-off by 2 seconds.

Only a small party of six went to Floors in July and, again, the horses went brilliantly in the dressage to put me 5 points ahead of George Bowman. He and I were the only two to do the times in all the sections of the marathon, but he went a good deal faster through the obstacles, so we changed places. I took the easiest routes through the obstacles, but I dropped a rein in obstacle 3 and Piper made mistakes in the water and in 8. I just managed to stay ahead of John Richards by 5 points. The cones course was really awkward and everyone had time penalties. I had 5.5 plus a cone down, while George Bowman had 8 and John Richards 15.5 time penalties. Altogether it was a very good competition and I also received the welcome news that I had been selected for the team in the World Championships.

Sandringham was one of the places where there was usually some sort of Saturday evening entertainment. I remember one major occasion organized by the irrepressible horse-pairs driver, Joe Pullen, which mirrored an event on the Royal

Yacht Britannia. On long voyages and on special occasions, the crew of the Britannia used to organize a concert party consisting of a series of acts, as in a variety show. At one such party, I was somewhat perplexed to see what looked vaguely like a squad of guardsmen march on to the stage whistling 'Colonel Bogey'. They seemed to have enormous faces and very short bodies and legs. It took a moment or two to appreciate that their 'faces' were, in fact, their upper torsos, with their nipples made up to look like eyes, and their navels to look like mouths pursed as when whistling. They hid their arms above their heads in their bearskin caps. It brought the house down.

In the show at Sandringham, a group of five such large-faced creatures marched onto the makeshift stage, but their enormous hats were modelled on the green and yellow baseball caps worn by George Bowman's grooms. The only other difference between the Guardsmen and this lot was that two of the latter appeared to have pop-eyes, and it was a moment or two before people realized that they were females; an interesting twist that also brought the house down!

Floors was the last event before the horses set off for Hungary for the World Championships in August (which took place shortly after the Los Angeles Olympics). The horses had to travel to the far east of the country, and this took them the best part of a week. The British team consisted of George Bowman,

Fig. 4.3 I attended the Olympic Games in Los Angeles in 1984 in my capacity of President of the International Equestrian Federation. The last event was the team jumping competition, which took place in the specially built arena on the Santa Anita racecourse. On race days, the racecourse uses six Shire horses to pull the starting gates into position, and on the day before the final event, I was persuaded to drive the Shires into the arena with the medal winners' platforms on a low loader. I had never driven six horses before, but they behaved immaculately in front of a crowd of some 30,000. (*Author's collection*)

Micky Flynn, driving Alan Bristow's team, and me. The individual British entries were John Richards and Alwyn Holder.

Tom Coombs reported on the Championships for *Horse and Hound* (my comments are in italics).

Over 200 people from Great Britain, almost 100 from the USA and a select party from Australia joined about 30,000 others from nearly every country in Europe at a new stadium in the village of Szilvasvarad in the foothills of the Bukk mountains in North East Hungary…*[As far as I was concerned, I arrived to be told that Piper's incipient navicular had made him noticeably lame and therefore effectively out of contention].* Presentation was judged early on the first day and with Prince Philip sharing the lead with George Bowman and heading the Dutch World Champion Tjeed Velstra, the Hungarian champion Gyorgy Bardos and the only lady driver, Deirdre Pirie from America, by one point, the 46 competitors from 12 nations endured an opening ceremony involving endless speeches laboriously translated into three languages. *[I can vouch for that because, as President of the FEI, I was one of the speakers.]* Prince Philip held his lead with a remarkably good dressage score of 28 until the last competitor on the second day, Gyorgy Bardos, achieved a world record one of 22. Bardos's team mate, Laszlo Juhasz, who was to be the new world champion, beat George Bowman's score of 32 by 3 points and the Hungarian team headed the British by 4.

Germany was now lying third, largely on the strength of Bernd Duen's dressage score of 29 and America and Poland shared fourth position.

Velstra scored 29 in dressage and of the other British competitors, Alwyn Holder scored 38 and John Richards and Micky Flynn…each scored 49.

Mental exhaustion towards the end of the nine hour session may have contributed to some eccentric judging. Judging results were not always consistent *[they very seldom are!]* but an examination of their scores reveals no nationalist bias. *[When I looked up the scores given by the individual dressage judges, I saw that Jeno Varady, the Hungarian judge, had given Bardos only 9 less than the maximum, compared to 26, 30, 22, and 23 by the other judges. My equivalent scores were 24, 34, 30, 31 and 20 (from Varady). There is no doubt that Bardos was the rightful winner in spite of the apparent favouritism of the Hungarian judge.]*

The 24 km (approximately 15 miles) marathon included an overall climb of 700ft and an equivalent descent. Long and very steep hills in all three trot Sections were only just negotiable by very fit horses on good going, and a threat of rain caused anxiety which was justified by a thunderstorm in the morning of the Marathon day.

Anxiety turned to alarm when the first starter, 18-year-old Georg Gschwander from Austria lost control down the steepest hill. His father, travelling as groom, got his foot through a wheel in his efforts to help and was dragged for some 30 yards.

Dreadfully injured, he was flown to hospital in Vienna, where he was still critically ill at the close of the trials.

This was the worst accident in any driving trials to date and it need not have happened if the driver had heeded advice to retire when his brakes failed because of a fractured hydraulic pipe earlier in the course. *[This was indeed a very unpleasant descent and the brakes made little difference on the wet ground – the wheels simply locked and slipped. I was hardly in control most of the way down. There was an obstacle at the bottom of the hill and it was only when I went back to watch the last competitors through that obstacle that I looked up the hill and remember wondering why there had not been many more accidents.]*

Seven marathon obstacles commemorated the seven world championships. The first five were ingeniously designed and very well built, and their severity was largely attributable to the gradients immediately before them as well as in them.

Fig. 4.4 This was the obstacle at the bottom of the very steep hill at Szilvasvarad in the 1984 World Championships in Hungary. This obstacle was also on a slope, which creates special problems for drivers, because the lead horses are generally encouraged to help to pull the carriage up hills. This means that as soon as they are turned to go uphill through a gate, they are inclined to pull the end of the pole round and the inside front wheel of the carriage hits the post. The picture shows that I have left it to the very last moment before turning the leaders uphill through the opening. (*Author's collection*)

[Obstacle 3 was a simple figure of eight through charcoal-burning clamps, but it was at the top of a steep hill and I could only get my horses to walk round it. It was here that George Bowman got a connecting rein buckle caught in a terret, which caused the leaders to go round in circles. It was eventually cleared by a groom walking out along the pole, In order to avoid penalties for having a groom down in an obstacle. He then broke a trace in 4.]

Obstacle 6 was not sensibly conceived and incorporated low rocks and boulders with sharp edges, which could have seriously damaged the legs of any horses trying to jump them. All drivers negotiated it with due caution and escaped injury.

Obstacle 7 in the main arena was a floor of new wooden planks surrounded by a low rail with gaps on two opposite sides, with two iron lamp posts in the middle of it. The requirement, in effect, was to drive a complete circle round one or other of these, and this unspectacularly simple test was only made virtually impossible when the rain made the flooring as slippery as an ice-rink.

Eight horses fell on this surface until the rain stopped at midday and Tjeed Velstra was eliminated when he had three horses down and could not extricate them within the time limit.

Unnatural and grossly unfair, because its surface varied from one competitor to the next, this obstacle was imbecile in its conception. *[I quite agree. Fortunately, some sand was put down before I got there, but even so, I had to be very careful.]*

Bardos and Juhasz each scored 50 Marathon penalties and the next best was Mick Flynn's 59 for Britain. *[Micky had no time penalties in any of the sections, whereas I had 55 and George Bowman 48 in E. Micky moved up from thirty-second to fifth.]* Bill Long, driving for Mr Finn Caspersen, added only 62 for the American team and Thomas Erikson and Jan Eric Pahlsson recorded 72 and 74 respectively for Sweden.

George Bowman was in difficulties in Obstacle 4 and prudently slow through Obstacle 7 to return a score of 130 *[eighteenth]*. Prince Philip drove consistently but rather below his best speed for 136 *[nineteenth]*. Alwyn Holder scored 173 and John Richards 204. *[In spite of all these dramas, I noted in my account – 'it was a very good course with the obstacles nicely varied and all on slopes with a good balance between the tight quick routes and the longer easier ones.']*

The obstacle competition started on day four, with the Hungarians 63 points ahead of their nearest rivals the Swedes, and the Americans 18 points behind them heading the British by four.

An excellent obstacle course in the main arena produced only six clear rounds and an exciting finish when Bardos had two cones down and was overtaken by his team mate Juhasz who thereby became the new World Champion.

Prince Philip's 10 faults *[Lady Isabella kicked a cone]* and Bowman and Flynn's 20 each were better than most and put the British team just ahead of the American one for a final bronze medal, with Sweden taking silver and Hungary winning the gold by a distance.

The first five individual places went to Hungary, but Mick Flynn covered himself with glory by becoming the best non-Hungarian driver in 6th place, and Bill Long also competing in his first international trial, was only 5 points behind Mick to take 7th place for America.

An interminable closing ceremony with more long speeches over-ran its own time-table by nearly three hours and spoiled our enjoyment of the attractive displays by the Hungarian herdsmen and dancers. *[It was indeed a great trial and I remember that it was four hours from the moment I got on the box seat until I returned to the stables. I have had a horror of closing and prize-giving ceremonies ever since!]*

Fig. 4.5 Waiting around during the endless prize-giving ceremonies at the Hungarian World Championships in Szilvasvarad, 1984. George Bowman, with his wife Eileen, is receiving a commemorative piece of pottery. (*Author's collection*)

Best party was given in the British camp by the British ladies, helped by Mrs. van Opstal, wife of the Dutch driver. They catered for over a hundred guests of all nationalities. *[Eileen Bowman organized it and produced huge quantities of steaks, while Mrs. van Opstal, an Italian by origin, produced gallons of spaghetti.]*

Fig. 4.6 The medal-winning teams at the end of the 1984 World Championships in Hungary. The Swedish team is on the left with their silver medals. The gold-medal winning Hungarians (in the middle) are Bardos (individual gold) on the left, Juhasz in the middle and Fulop on the right. The British bronze-medal winning team is lined up behind Joe Moore, our Chef d'Equipe. George Bowman is immediately behind Joe Moore, with Micky Flynn in the middle. Micky had driven a brilliant marathon, with Alan Bristow's horses, to come third in that phase, and eventually sixth overall. (*Findlay Davidson*)

It was a major undertaking to attempt in a large, but fairly remote, village and, apart from the opening and closing ceremonies, the whole event was very well organized and took place in wonderful country. The local enthusiasm was remarkable. The arena was almost full for the less-than-lively business of judging the presentation, and for every session of the dressage from early morning until late afternoon. There were large crowds at every obstacle on the marathon and the arena was again packed for the cones competition on the Sunday.

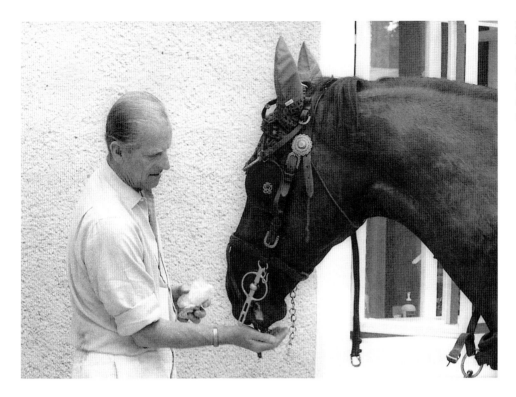

Fig. 4.7 I made a habit of giving sugar lumps to the horses on return to the stables after every outing. This is Brown Owl after the marathon at Szilvasvarad. She always acknowledged this reward by rubbing her head against my shoulder. (*Author's collection*)

On the Saturday evening, the local municipality entertained everyone to a reception in what had been the country house of the previous landowners, the Pallavicini family. I was intrigued to discover that Prince Pallavicini himself was present at the reception and when I asked him whether he remembered the place, he pointed to a window in the upper floor and said 'that was my room as a boy'. It turned out that he had leased the deer stalking on his old estate on several occasions while Hungary was still behind the Iron Curtain. Several other previous landowners, now living in Vienna, were also present. One of the other guests was Bert de Nemethy, who had done so much for the American international show jumpers as trainer and Chef d'Equipe. He had been invited to be Chef d'Equipe for the USA driving team as a way of letting him get back to his native land.

Talking about the US team reminds me of the time when Finn Caspersen (Chairman of the Board of the Beneficial Corporation) was registering his team, he put himself down as 'owner-groom', this concept was alien to, and completely flummoxed, the 'comrade' Hungarian officials and it took him some time to explain the position.

On return from the gruelling experience of the championships, and the long journeys there and back, the horses were turned out at Hampton Court for a well-earned rest. However, I thought I would enter the ponies for the National Championships at Smith's Lawn in Windsor Great Park in September. I was surprised

Fig. 4.8 Finn Caspersen on the back step of his carriage with his team driven by Bill Long. When he described himself as 'owner-groom' it caused some head-scratching among the Communist officials in Hungary in 1984. (*Alf Baker*)

to find myself lying third after the dressage, as I had not expected to do very well. Claudia Bunn was in the lead and Mark Broadbent in second place. I had trouble with Bramble in the early sections of the marathon, as he would break into a canter when he should have been trotting, and trotted when he should have been walking. Nonetheless, I ended up second to Mark Broadbent as Claudia Bunn was eliminated in section C. I was very impressed by the way the ponies went round the obstacles and how fit they were at the end of what was quite a long, tough course. Furthermore, I was the last to go round and, as the going was quite soft in places, the ponies really had to work hard. They went brilliantly through the cones in a very fast time, and, although I hit one quite hard, the ball stayed on. Mark Broadbent won the drive-off by 3 seconds.

Fig. 4.9 I gave the horses a break after the World Championships in Hungary and brought the ponies down from Balmoral for the 1984 National Championships on the Polo Grounds at Smith's Lawn in Windsor Great Park. At the end of the cones phase, there was a drive-off against the clock for those who had managed clear rounds in the final phase of the combined event. The cones are placed further apart, which allows most of the course to be driven at a canter. As you can see, the weather was not brilliant that year. (*Stuart Newsham*)

RESULTS FOR 1984

EVENT	Dressage	Marathon	Cones	Pl/No
Duerne CAI	3	15	1=	12/29
Brighton	1	6	5=	5/13
Windsor CAI	1	10	10	7/20
Scone (ponies)	*3*	*1=*	*1=*	*2/4*
Holker	2	3	1=	3/16
Sandringham	1	5	1=	3/16
Floors	1	3	2	2/6
World Champion. – Hungary (team bronze medal)	2	21	8=	18/45
Nat. Champion. (ponies)	*3*	*2*	*1=*	*2/9*

Horses used: Piper, Brown Owl, Lady Isabella, Harrier, Lady of Man, Blantyre.

Ponies used: Bramble, Roy, Martin, Laddie, Dawn, Ebony.

1985

In 1985 I entered the horses for eight events and the ponies for one and, since there were no championships in this year, I took the horses to Sweden for a CAI at Flyinge at the end of the season. Meanwhile, the grooms and I had thoroughly enjoyed the event at Duerne the previous year and, as it is fairly easy to get to Holland, we decided to have another go there in the early part of the season. In retrospect, I rather wish I had not gone. We had a string of disasters beginning with Peregrine going lame. As I had intended to drive him in the wheel with Harrier in the dressage and in the lead with Brown Owl for the marathon, this was quite a blow, but worse was to follow. It became obvious that Lady of Man had come into season, which affected her, and the team's, performance. The dressage was not as bad as it might have been, considering the incessant rain, soft going and flapping flags round the arena, and a slip by Brown Owl while reining-back.

Unfortunately, there was more rain the next day, but Lady of Man was in a thoroughly awkward mood and shied at everything. She was so bad that, before section E, I put her in the wheel and moved Harrier to the lead. Harrier did her best in an unfamiliar position, but a combination of deep going, Lady of Man and driver error, caused a minor stick in obstacle 2, a major one in obstacle 5, and errors of course in 4 and 7. At least I did not have to retire, which was the fate for four other drivers. Only Tjeed Velstra, who won very easily, and one other competitor managed to get through all sections without time penalties. The only small consolation was that I did one of thirteen clear rounds, and the second fastest time in the drive-off – 5 seconds behind Bernd Duen of Germany.

Brighton was next in late April, where I did reasonably well to win the dressage with Peregrine in the wheel for the first time. I was always just that much slower than George Bowman and Alwyn Holder in all the obstacles. I got stuck in obstacle 7, when we went over a post, which got stuck in front of the splinter bar. Releasing the snap shackle on a trace got us out without having to put a groom down, but we had to replace both pole-straps on the way to obstacle 8. I had also lost the brakes, which meant going rather slowly in 8. By that time I was about 30 points behind George Bowman and Alwyn Holder, but the next driver, Nick D'Ambrumenil with the Household Cavalry team, was 130 points behind me. Things improved a bit when I did a fast clear round in the cones. Not brilliant, but it could have been much worse.

The Windsor CAI came round again in early May, but this time with only nine entries. I just got ahead of Alwyn Holder by 1 point in the dressage. It was the first time out for Barn Owl, who went with Brown Owl in the lead. I had Peregrine in the wheel for the marathon and he rather let the side down by breaking pace in

Fig. 4.10 (*left*) and 4.11 (*below*) The water obstacle at the 1985 International Event at Duerne in the Netherlands was a sort of concrete tank with decorated drums forming the gates. It looks as if I have gone the wrong side of a gate. It is quite a good illustration of the value of buckling the reins together. The weather is obviously wet and the leather reins would have been much too slippery to pull-up like that if they had not been joined together. (*Findlay Davidson*)

section C, which resulted in 9 time penalties and 5 referee's penalties. Not that this made much difference, as Alwyn Holder was some 30 points ahead. Unusually for him, George Bowman was eliminated in obstacle 1. Meanwhile Bill Long, driving Finn Caspersen's team, with the owner as one of the grooms, fairly stormed round the course to finish some 20 points clear of Alwyn Holder. Bill Long eventually won by 12 points from Alwyn Holder, I finished in third place 30 points behind, and John Richards came in fourth some 110 points later. There had been a lot of rain during the show, and, by the time we got into the main arena for the cones, the whole place was a sea of soft grey mud.

I always enjoyed Holker and this time everything seemed to come together. Before the event started, we were all invited to drive across the Kent Sands over the north end of Morecambe Bay from Silverdale to Grange-over-Sands. It was a route used by the stage-coaches between Lancaster and Ulverston to save the long haul round the top of the Bay at Stainton. There is still a Queen's Guide, whose job it is to mark the safe route across the quick sands after every high tide. There is an eighteenth-century story of a passenger who arrived at Ulverston to inquire when the next coach was due to leave for Lancaster. He was informed that it depended on the state of the tide. He was then told about the risk of quick sands, so he enquired whether anyone was ever lost on the crossing and was told 'Oh no, they always get washed in by the tide'.

Fig. 4.12 Before the event at Holker Hall in May 1985, a party of intrepid drivers drove across the north end of Morecambe Bay from Silverdale to Grange-over-Sands. The Tetley Walker Brewery Company were sponsors of the Holker event and their dray joined the expedition just before we got to Grange-over-Sands. The Queen's Guide, Cedric Robinson, is sitting beside me. Brian McGrath's head appears between us. (*Author's collection*)

The Queen's Guide came with me on the carriage and about twenty pairs and singles joined me in this unusual adventure. We were fortunate to have glorious weather and it attracted a huge crowd of onlookers, many of whom escorted us in trailers towed by tractors and, as we were also accompanied by a helicopter, the noise was deafening. The Queen's Guide warned everyone not to follow in each other's tracks, but once we had got across the freshwater stream at Silverdale, the sands dried out and the going was very good. It was quite a curious sensation to be driving a carriage on what should have been the sea and to view the landscape as if from a boat. The general noise upset the horses and they pulled my arms out all the way across, and the experience did nothing to settle them down for the dressage the following day.

In spite of that excitement, I see that I was given a very generous dressage score of 20, which broke the record set by Bardos at Szilvasvarad. The judges mark each movement out of 10 and, at the end, the marks are added together and divided by the number of judges. This figure is then multiplied by a co-efficient – usually 0.8 – to get the total in the correct proportion to the average marathon scores. On this occasion the three judges between them gave me eight tens and twenty-three nines. They also gave me seven sevens and one six. This was made more satisfactory because I had not seen the horses for three weeks and did not know how they would go.

Things did not start brilliantly in the marathon. I hit an iron gate and got the leaders either side of a tree in section A. I then had a few time penalties in the first walk and a few more in the fast section, C. We got round the obstacles somehow, while George Bowman was thrown out and Alwyn Holder got stuck in obstacle 2. I finished some 10 points ahead of George Bowman, which were later reduced to 7 after I had 3 time penalties in an otherwise clear round of a really nasty cones course. At least I had the unusual experience of winning. A great bonus was that we had brilliant weather throughout the weekend.

At the beginning of July, I was able to get the ponies to Floors for their only outing in 1985. It was the first time out for the two mares, Dawn and Ebony, and they performed very well in the wheel. The dressage was spoiled by Roy, who was never able to get the point of this performance, and by the two new girls, who made a mess of the rein-back. All went reasonably well in the marathon, except that we collected some 16 time penalties in the walks. As I was nearly the last to go, the tracks had become quite badly poached, and the ponies had a hard time dragging the carriage through some of the muddy woodland rides. They scuttled round the cones in the fastest time, although I hit one. I remained in third place, out of four, throughout the event.

Nine horse teams turned up at Tatton for a two-day event on the following

Fig. 4.13 One of the great features of driving events is that many of them take place in the grounds of some of the stateliest 'stately homes'. Floors Castle, the home of the Duke of Roxburghe, looks across extensive meadows down to the Tweed. One year, after dinner, I managed to pull a 1.8 kg (4 lb) sea trout out of the river. (*K.G. Ettridge*)

weekend. The dressage and cones were on Saturday and the marathon on Sunday. George Bowman had another convincing win from Alwyn Holder. I was very annoyed to be 33 seconds late in the walk section, but I came in third overall, some 24 points behind Alwyn Holder and nearly 100 ahead of John Richards.

Lowther started well enough with a 4 point advantage over George Bowman after the dressage. I took things carefully in the obstacles, but in obstacle 3 Piper decided he knew best and took us past one of the gates and, as we were pointing downhill, there was no way I could get them back. I was therefore eliminated, but I went on to do the other obstacles without any serious problems. No less than six of the eleven competitors were eliminated, and six had to put grooms down in various obstacles. John Richards had a dreadful time. He had time penalties in all the sections, he was eliminated in obstacle 6, and had to get his grooms down in obstacle 7. George Bowman won, Mark Weston came in second and Micky Flynn, in spite of having to put one groom down in obstacle 6 and both of them down in 7, was not far behind in third place. As I was effectively out of it, I left on Saturday for Cowes and David Saunders took the team for a clear round in the cones.

There being no championships in this year, I managed to get a place in a CAI at Flyinge in southern Sweden, where twenty-three drivers from ten nations assembled for the Swedish Championships. The Swedish programme described it as '*Internationella Fyrspannstavlingar och Svenskt Masterskap*'. It went on to explain:

The historical roots of Flyinge can be traced back to the 12th century. Flyinge was then a fortress for the cavalry of the Danish Archbishops. When southern Sweden was conquered by the Swedish King Carl X Gustav, a royal stud was founded in 1661. Ever since, riding horses have continuously been bred at Flyinge.

After almost 320 years of government administration, the responsibility for Flyinge was handed over in 1983 to a foundation…In Flyinge stables, you will find more than 50 licensed stallions – 4 Thoroughbreds, 1 Anglo-Arab, 1 Standardbred Trotter and the remainder Swedish Warmbloods.

Fig. 4.14 The Stud at Flyinge where the *Internationella Fyrspannstavlingar och Svenskt Masterskap* was based in 1985. (*National Stud of Sweden*)

I was fortunate to be invited to stay with Baron and Baroness Malte Ramel in great comfort in their ancient, and spectacular, moated Hviderup Castle.

I was intrigued by my invitation to a buffet supper at the Warren Hastings Meadow. I am afraid I have completely forgotten the reason for this connection with Warren Hastings, the first Governor General of India. The event was sponsored by Volvo and I suspect that this was largely due to the fact that the Chairman of the company, Mr. Pehr Gyllenhammar, was at that time President of the Swedish Equestrian Federation and a member of the FEI Bureau.

I drove the same team as at Lowther and I thought they went better than ever in the dressage, but I was just beaten by 1 point by Zygmunt Waliszewski of Poland, who eventually won the event. I took things quietly in the marathon and dropped to eleventh, but I was one of only five to do section C within the time. However, having one of five clear rounds in the cones took me up two places. Alwyn Holder finished just ahead of me in eighth place. It was a very happy event in an exceptionally friendly atmosphere.

The Sandringham event was moved to September to coincide with the first World Horse-Pairs Championships. It was a bit chaotic, but it all ran more or less to time. After a string of wins, the dressage judges put me in second place. Even so, I see that I got five nines, fourteen eights, eight sevens, twelve sixes and four fives. Things did not go brilliantly in the marathon; Piper – yet again – thought he knew best in the first obstacle, and then I overshot in obstacle 4 and went through gate C before B and failed to correct it, so that was the big E (elimination) for me. Alwyn Holder was also eliminated in obstacle 4 and then went on to be eliminated again in 5. The King's Troop entry driven by Major L. C. Tar, was also eliminated and Richard Oddie retired. I ended up seventh out of nine. This was a rather disappointing end to the season.

RESULTS FOR 1985

EVENT	Dressage	Marathon	Cones	Pl/No
Duerne CAI	6	21	1=	21/26
Brighton	1	3	1=	3/7
Windsor CAI	1	3	1=	3/8
Holker	1	1	2	1/8
Floors (ponies)	*3*	*3*	*3*	*3/4*
Tatton	1	3	3	3/9
Lowther	1	E	1=	6/11
Flyinge CAI	2	14	1=	9/22
Sandringham	2	E	5	7/9

Horses used: Piper, Brown Owl, Lady Isabella, Harrier, Lady of Man, Peregrine, Barn Owl.

Ponies used: Roy, Martin, Laddie, Dawn, Ebony.

1986

I went back to Duerne again in April 1986, but it again turned out to be a bad mistake. Just before the dressage, the brakes failed on the best carriage and then seized solid. We drained the hydraulic system, which freed the system, but then I had no brakes. I also had a new horse – Condor, another home-bred – who had very little experience. To add to my problems, Isabella was in one of her moods. I was quite relieved to get as far up as eighth. The marathon was a total disaster. In the fourth obstacle, the leaders managed to get either side of a tree and I had to put one groom down in obstacles 2, 7 and 8, and both grooms down in obstacles 3 and 5. That cost me 70 points alone. Harrier was in the wheel, but even so she managed to get her head the wrong side of a tree going downhill in deep sand and broke quite a lot of harness in the process. All that took a lot of time and I ended up with 271 penalties in the obstacles and 64 time penalties. When added to my dressage score, I had accumulated the massive total of 384. Bill Long, the American, and Alwyn Holder had even worse problems. Alwyn Holder accumulated 382 before the cones, but he had three cones down to my one plus 4 time penalties, which moved me up to twenty-third. Long finished on 652. Velstra won easily on 114 in spite of having two cones down at the end.

Fig. 4.15 There is always the risk of going wrong or getting in a muddle in an obstacle. More often than not, it is due to a driver error or lapse of memory. Such mistakes can usually be corrected, even though it may cost several penalties. However, escape from some situations can be very difficult. In this case, I have gone wrong going downhill in deep sand. Under these circumstances the wheelers cannot be expected to push the carriage back and the only hope is to get one or both grooms down to see if they can solve the problem. In this case a wheeler (Harrier) has her head the wrong side of a post and David Saunders is doing his best to get it back. (*Author's collection*)

There were fourteen starters at Brighton, and this time I did a very much better dressage test to lead Alwyn Holder by 9 points, Peter Munt by 10, Micky Flynn by 18, and George Bowman by 19. However, George Bowman flew round the obstacles in 80, while it took me 107. Micky Flynn made it in 100. Bill Long (driving Finn Caspersen's team) went even faster than George Bowman with only 67 penalties in the marathon. After the debacle at Duerne, I was very pleased with the horses, although Barn Owl twice refused to go between flapping plastic advertisements for the sponsor – The Anglia Building Society.

The cones course must have been worse than it looked. Not one driver had a clear round. George Bowman collected 9 time penalties, while Bill Long managed to trap a cone under his carriage, which knocked down three more before it was dislodged and he then hit two more. I had three cones down plus two time penalties, which got me into fourth place, just 2 points ahead of Micky Flynn. Seven drivers had a score of more than 200. When there are problems like these, getting a good score in the dressage can come in very handy.

There was no CAI at Windsor in 1986 as the World Championships were to be at Ascot in August. If there was a national event, I have no record of taking part in it. I could not go to Holker, as my horses had a virus. So my next outing was at Floors in mid-July, where I ran into some trouble even before the event. While I was exercising the team on the Friday, Peregrine pulled off a shoe and cut his foot in the process. It was a two-day event, and on the Saturday morning he could hardly walk, so I had to put Harrier together with Isabella for the first time since Hungary. I won the dressage, but only by a whisker from Peter Munt. Luckily, the team went very well across country and Munt was only 17 points ahead. I managed to pull back 4 points in the very tight cones course and just managed to stay in front of Micky Flynn by 10 points. Not one of the seven drivers managed a clear round in the cones.

At some events everything comes together, then, just when you think you have cracked it, everything falls apart. It was certainly the latter case at Sandringham in July. I did a dreadful dressage test to trail Micky Flynn by 11 points and Alwyn Holder by 7. The marathon course must have been quite difficult because not a single driver got through all sections without penalties and everyone had time penalties in E. My times through the obstacles were about average, but I collected 66 penalties for being slow in both walks and in E.

The cones course must also have been more difficult than usual, since there were only three clear rounds. I had one cone down and 3.5 time penalties, which put me sixth in that phase and seventh overall. It looks like a dreadful result, but there were only 11 points between fourth and seventh places. Alwyn Holder won easily and Micky Flynn came second.

On this dismal form, and not having attended sufficient qualifying events, it was not altogether surprising that I was not considered for the team for the World Championships. I only got in as an individual because the host nation is allowed rather more individual entries than the visitors.

On the weekend following the Sandringham event, there was a new event at Hoghton Tower, between Preston and Blackburn. The Tower is a medieval castle perched on top of a hill and is owned by the de Hoghton family. Sir Bernard and his Italian wife kindly put me up in great comfort, but I did feel that I was living in a different age.

Hoghton Tower has two claims to fame. It seems that Shakespeare took refuge there with his former schoolmaster after getting into trouble with the authorities in Stratford-on-Avon. There is speculation that he wrote one of his plays there, as the stage directions exactly fit the layout of the Great Hall. It also appears that James VI of Scotland (James I of England) stayed at Hoghton at some stage in his reign. Legend has it that he was so impressed by the quality of the loin of beef he was offered for dinner, that he knighted it with his sword and ever since a loin of beef is known as a sirloin.

The Hoghton Tower event was organized by Joe Pullen, when sponsorship by the Ben shipping line for the Tatton event failed to materialize. The facilities and layout were not altogether ideal, but it was a very entertaining experience. There were only six entries, but George Bowman was one of them and he won without much trouble. He got 1 point ahead of me in the dressage, although neither performance had much to recommend it. The horses went well through the obstacles, but I made a silly mistake in obstacle 4 and was much too slow in 7. I also had 12 time penalties in section E. Together, these extra points put me behind Mark Weston. Both he and Lex Ruddiman did better than George Bowman in the marathon, but not enough to catch him. Although I did a clear round in the cones, I ended up 20 points behind Mark Weston and 30 behind George Bowman.

I did not think it was a good idea to take the horses all the way to Lowther the weekend before the World Championships, so I took the ponies there and we had a very jolly event. There were seven entries and, considering it was their first time out that year, I was quite pleased to make fourth place in the dressage. Unlike Welsh ponies, Fell ponies are not built for dressage, but, if you can keep their attention and drive them accurately, they can do quite well. The marathon course must have been fairly tough, because no-one went clear on time through the five sections. Only Mark Broadbent and I had no time penalties in section E. He flew round the obstacles in 63, while it took me 116. At least I got through them without disaster, unlike Araminta Winn and Claudia Bunn, who both came unstuck.

Fig. 4.16 Sometimes things go smoothly in an obstacle and all goes according to plan. My referee, Admiral Sir Anthony Synnot RAN, looks on calmly while David Muir, on the back step, is keeping a wary eye on a post of an obstacle at the Lowther event in 1986. (*Author's collection*)

Araminta Winn hurt her leg quite badly and drove the cones phase with it strapped up. No-one did a clear round and I ended up in second place.

My referee on this occasion was Admiral Sir Anthony Synnot, RAN, who had lately been Chief of the Australian Defence Staff, and who had also been in my Term at Dartmouth in 1939. This somewhat unlikely coincidence was due to the fact that his wife had taken up driving and they were spending a season in England. On this occasion he was not needed to 'back-step' for her and was, therefore, free to referee.

The World Championships at Ascot followed, but they turned out to be a disaster for the home team. Micky Flynn had been selected to drive Alan Bristow's team, but Alan Bristow had a typically silly row with the jury about some triviality and withdrew his team in a huff. We all felt very sorry indeed for Micky Flynn, who really deserved to drive in these championships. In addition, sadly, one of George Bowman's horses developed azoturia after section A and he was unable to go on. This completely destroyed any hope of the British team doing well.

I had great difficulty deciding which team to put together for the dressage. In the end I accepted David Saunders's suggestion of Lady Isabella and Peregrine in the lead with Harrier and Condor in the wheel. It worked rather better than I had expected. My name came out first in the draw, and so I was first into the dressage arena in the Silver Ring of the Ascot Racecourse. Whether this early draw was lucky or not, I do not know, but the fact remains that I had a surprisingly good score of 36. By the end only six of the forty entries did better.

In the marathon, I had a hold up at the water obstacle as Condor refused to go in at the first attempt. I then had a problem in obstacle 7 with a wheel behind a post. I eventually finished twenty-fourth in the marathon, but adding the dressage score lifted me four places to twentieth.

Fig 4.17–21 (*see also pages114–115*) A series of photographs of my efforts to get through the water obstacle at the 1986 World Championships at Ascot. The first picture shows the leaders trying desperately to avoid getting their feet wet on the way in.

Everything went fairly
smoothly after that through
a tight and complicated
obstacle.

This picture shows the party leaving the obstacle with relief.

There were fifteen clear rounds of a very nice cones course, but I had to put in a scratch team for this phase, as Barn Owl was judged to be lame at the vet's inspection. Unfortunately, I hit one cone, but I still went up two places and finished in eighteenth place. Peter Munt managed fifteenth place and Alwyn Holder came in twentieth. The best performance by a British driver was Mark Weston's thirteenth place overall, which was a really brilliant performance by a relative newcomer.

Tjeed Velstra was the overall winner with the remarkable score of 94. He was followed by another Dutchman, Ijsbrand Chardon on 98 and Laszlo Juhasz of Hungary on 112. The team medals went to Holland, Hungary and West Germany. The USA came fourth and Britain was fifth, only 1.7 points ahead of Switzerland and 1.8 ahead of Sweden. It was a very disappointing event for the home team, but otherwise it was a splendid competition and a wonderful culmination of my fourteen-year career driving a team of horses. It also happened to be the end of my twenty-two years as President of the FEI.

I had been contemplating giving up the horses for some time. I had reached, what I thought at the time, was the grand old age of sixty-five and I was certainly the oldest competitor on the international circuit, but it was also partly due to my grooms falling out with each other.

The big Cleveland Bay x Oldenburgs from the Royal Mews quickly accepted the demands of these FEI driving events, and needless to say, while I paid for all competition expenses, they were always available for public duties when required. Every year they did their stuff at Ascot and any other duties required of them in London. Indeed, David Saunders, my Head Groom, drove Lady Isabella and Brown Owl in the carriage processions to and from St Paul's for the Wales' wedding. Of the twenty-four Bays in that procession, I had driven eight in competition. In addition, I rode Solomon in the Trooping the Colour Parade for six years and then Brown Owl for a further three years. I think it was generally acknowledged in the Mews that my horses went all the better for their experience in competition. At any rate, as far as I was concerned, I was not giving up driving altogether as I fully intended to continue with the Fell ponies based at Balmoral.

I had discussed with David Saunders the idea of him running a driving school/centre at Sandringham and actually had some stables built for him at Appleton, but he was almost immediately invited by the American millionaire, John Kluge, to drive a competition team for him and his wife. They then moved David and the horses up to Mar Lodge, not far from Balmoral. This was not a brilliant idea; the winters in that area can be very rough and it is miles from the

Fig. 4.22 Lady Isabella was home-bred, and although she was a bit temperamental, she had the most graceful action and was the envy of many other competitors. She completed six years with my team before going back to the Mews and routine public duties. (*Royal Mews*)

Fig. 4.23 Brown Owl was another home-bred mare and one of the nicest horses I have ever come across. She did six seasons with my team, usually in the lead alongside the temperamental Lady Isabella. After giving up the horse team, I rode her for the Trooping of the Colour for another three years. With all the experience of international events, walking up the Mall between applauding crowds, and standing watching the Birthday Parade on Horseguards caused her no anxieties. (*Royal Mews*)

Fig. 4.24. I had been riding a horse provided by the Royal Mews for the Queen's Birthday Parade (or Trooping the Colour), but the time came for Bachelor Gay to retire, and I had to find a replacement. I was very fond of Solomon and I thought he had exactly the right temperament for such an occasion. As it turned out, I was fortunately right, and he served me faithfully for six years. I used to ride him for the parade in the morning and then put him in the team for the Coaching Club Annual Drive and Dinner at Hampton Court Palace in the evening. (*Royal Mews*)

nearest national driving events. As it happened, the Kluges got divorced quite soon afterwards and David was given a week's notice to get rid of the whole horse establishment and leave his house. Later on, he went to America. Brian Stanley went to Hampton Court Stud to help David Saunders's father and eventually to take over from him as manager. John Morgan went back to the Mews. Many years later I was to use the Appleton stables for the ponies.

Fig. 4.25 The artist, Terence Cuneo, had a thing about mice, and always managed to include one somewhere in all his paintings. When he heard about my driving a team of horses, he produced this charming cartoon of a mouse driving a team of ferrets. (*The Cuneo Estate*)

All my horses went back to the Mews and continued their State duties. I hope that sometimes, while drowsily munching their hay behind the bars of their comfortable boxes in deepest London, they remember trotting over Askham Fell at Lowther in sluicing rain, or down sunny country lanes at Sandringham, or perhaps of galloping through the cones in a drive-off somewhere behind the Iron Curtain in Europe.

RESULTS FOR 1986

EVENT	Dressage	Marathon	Cones	Pl/No
Duerne CAI	8	23	15	23/29
Brighton	1	5	7	4/14
Floors	1	2	2	2/7
Sandringham	3	7	5	7/11
Hoghton Tower	2	4	1=	3/6
Lowther (ponies)	*4*	*2*	*2=*	*2/7*
World Championships	7	24	16=	18/40

Horses used: Brown Owl, Lady Isabella, Harrier, Peregrine, Barn Owl, Condor.
Ponies used: Roy, Martin, Dawn, Ebony.

Years (horses)	14
Total competitions	80
First place	6
Second place	18
Third place	15
Fourth place	14

Championship medals	1978 World Team Bronze
	1980 World Team Gold
	1981 European Team Bronze
	1982, 1984 World Team Bronze
Best place in a championship	1982 – 6th

Cleveland Bay horses used from 1973 to 1986:

	Dates
Buttercup	73–77
Doric	73
Castlegar	73–81
Cadogan	73–74
Rideau	73–76
Fort Steel	74
Solomon	74–83
Niagara	75–77
Mexico†	77
Merlin	76–79
Eagle*	
Rio*	
Santiago*	
Kestrel*	
George	76–77
Piper	78–85
Polka	78
Samuel	78–79
Frederick	79–80
Kiel	80
Brown Owl	81–86
Lady Isabella	81–86
Harrier	81–86
Lady of Man	83–85
Blantyre	84
Peregrine	85–86
Barn Owl	85–86
Condor	86

Twenty-eight horses (twenty four Bays, four Windsor Greys)

* Arthur Showell's team of Windsor Greys borrowed for the
  Windsor CAI, 1976.

† Went to the Prince of Wales as a hunter.

Grooms employed with the horses:

	Dates
Maj. W. L. Thompson, Head Groom	73–78
Ron Steer	73
R. Grigg	73–74
David Saunders	74–78
Head Groom	79–86
Ian Garnett	74–75
Gerald Smith	74
Hugh Murphy	75–78
J. Stanford	75 (Sopot only)
D. Thompson	76
Martin Harding	76–86
Brian Stanley	79–86
Roddy McDonald	79
John Morgan	79–86
Corporal 'Yogi' Howe	80 and 82 (Hungary)
William Oram	81 and 82 (Hungary)
Mark Schofield	82–83
David West	86

CHAPTER FIVE

OVER TO PONIES

1987–1990

DAVID MUIR (SEN) had been the Head Ponyman at Balmoral for several years. He had played a big part in putting the original team of Fell ponies together and training them for competition. Since 1980, David, together with his son Michael and his nephew David, had been to all the competitions with the team of ponies, and so they had some experience of travelling and of all the business involved in these driving competitions. However, life became a good deal more complicated for them from 1987. We were to travel to eight competitions in all, and the team would need to be based at Windsor for the season.

This turned out to be rather more than David Muir (Sen) was prepared to take, and I was left with an awkward problem. In the end I decided to invite his nephew David to take on the post of Head Groom. His father had emigrated to America, and David was born and did his early schooling there, but he had then come back to Scotland to stay with his uncle at Balmoral. He was a little laid-back and his sense of responsibility in those days was not one of his strong points. However, he had helped out with the ponies during the stalking season and, when I took him on as a groom, he showed quite a lot of enthusiasm for the competitions. It was a gamble, but it paid off. He must have been in his early twenties and I had to teach him to drive a team, but he turned out to have a talent for organization. I soon discovered that I could rely on him to get the whole show to an event in good order and without leaving anything behind. I gave him several books on stable management, which he studied with great care, and, what was almost more important, he was always calm and patient with the ponies and never lost his cool with the other grooms.

I decided to continue the practice of bringing the whole organization down to

Fig. 5.1 The 'best' carriage for the ponies went through several design changes. The wheels and undercarriage came from Mark Broadbent and the first edition was designed to be dual-purpose. The box seat remained the same but the back seat for the grooms could be lifted off for the marathon. It worked quite well, although it was not popular with the grooms when they had to clean it after an exercise run before the dressage. This photograph shows Mark 2 with a fixed back seat. Mark 3 retained the original undercarriage and wheels, but I got a local blacksmith in Tarland, near Balmoral, to build a new top for it from a design I had seen in a book of nineteenth century carriage designs. (*Stuart Newsham*)

Sandringham in January. I hardly recognized the ponies when they first arrived from the cold Balmoral winter. They were all as round as barrels and extremely hairy. I should not really have been surprised since they had spent the winter in the open in Scotland, and in a part of Scotland with a reputation for cold winters. The grooms had a hard time getting them into presentable shapes, but gradually the ponies became more recognizable, as bags of hair were groomed off them, and progressive exercise improved their figures. They were quite fit and going well together by the time they arrived in Windsor in early February.

There is a considerable difference between driving a team of horses and a team of Fell ponies. The whole turnout of the ponies is obviously smaller, and they take up less room in the obstacles, but their centre of gravity is lower, which means they can be turned more sharply. I remember watching Mark Broadbent the first time he drove a team of horses at a club event at Windsor. He had been a successful pony-team driver and had become used to pulling the leaders round sharply in the obstacles. When he tried to do the same with the horses, the two leaders simply fell over.

There was also a marked difference in the temperaments between the horses

Fig. 5.2 Photographs to illustrate the evolution of the 'best' carriage for ponies:

1. (*above*) Dressage version of the original dual-purpose carriage.
2. (*above right*) Marathon version of the dual-purpose carriage.
3. (*below*) Following on from the intermediate version, as shown in Fig. 5.1, this current version was developed. (*Author's collection*)

and the ponies. I found the ponies to be far less 'twitchy' in tense situations. The horses were more inclined to panic, whereas the ponies accepted the problem and tried to help me to get out of trouble. There is always a risk of getting the leaders either side of a post in an obstacle. The horses did not like this, but the ponies were capable of twisting like eels to get the right side of the post. They also seemed to recover their composure more quickly after some drama and were generally forgiving. On the whole, they seem to be more intelligent.

I also had exactly the right venue at which to practise and get the ponies working as a team. Back in the 1960s, I had started the Windsor Park Equestrian Club (WPEC). It was based on an idea I picked up from Douglas Bunn at his establishment at Hickstead. I had been to watch an international event there, when I was President of the FEI, and I had noticed people jumping in some outlying arenas. When I asked him what was going on, he explained that he had started a club for local enthusiasts, and allowed them to use an arena for a modest rent. The members paid an annual subscription and an entry fee for whatever competition they wished to enter, and this money was used to cover costs and as a sweepstake to provide rosettes and small prizes. There was no provision for spectators.

I thought this was a brilliant idea, and it seemed to me that something along these lines could be started on Smith's Lawn in Windsor Great Park. I had already started a polo club on the main part of the Lawn, but there was still plenty of room on the other side of the road. I took the idea to Sir Michael Ansell, who agreed and said he knew just the man to start it. People found it very difficult to say 'no' to Mike, and in no time a committee was formed, Col. Frank Beale had been appointed Director, and the club was in business by the following summer. It now has over a thousand members and runs a two-day meeting every month through the summer. It has three, and sometimes four, jumping arenas, about six dressage arenas and a driving area on the Cannon Ground just below Cumberland Lodge. The Great Park has plenty of room for a variety of marathon courses.

I find these club events extremely valuable pre-season indoctrination, particularly for newcomers to the team. I divided the ponies into two pairs for the March event and put a complete team into the April and early May meets, in an effort to find suitable combinations of the ponies for the three phases. To give an idea of the problems I was having, this is what I wrote in my account of the first event:

> I thought there might be a chance of a decent Dressage team if I put Tom and Bramble together. Dawn can't stand her son Tom; Roy and Tom argue all the time and Martin is not much better with Tom. Ebony has been a pain in the neck all the time, and is no good in the lead anyway.

Brighton loomed up in mid-May 1987, and I see that I put Martin and Dawn in the lead with Roy and Ebony in the wheel for the dressage. To my great surprise, we won this, beating the Bassett sisters, but the success was short-lived. All the fitness training at Sandringham had not prepared them for the very tough course at Stanmer. We had to climb to the top of the Downs twice, once in section A and again in E. By the time we got to the obstacles, they were not all that enthusiastic and we were much too slow. In addition, we had time penalties in E. At least we had a clear round in the cones and finished third. There was an embarrassing moment when my track width was measured after the cones. It turned out that it was 4 cm too narrow. I was using the Mark 3 pony carriage, which had been built by the blacksmith at Tarland, near Balmoral, and I can only imagine that he must have reduced the track width.

I had to use the same team at Windsor and I won the dressage again, but I had time penalties in both walks in the marathon. It made little difference as I was eliminated at the end of section E for not having the leader traces attached to the end of the pole. It happened on my way out of obstacle 3, when the shackle holding the swingle-trees to the end of the pole just came off, but fortunately the

Fig. 5.3 All the early season training and preparation, walking the obstacles and the agonies of dressage and cones are forgotten when you can drive a good team through this sort of countryside in Stanmer Park in good weather. (*Author's collection*)

ponies stopped. I thought I had stopped outside the obstacle, but, judging by the 86 penalties I was given, it must have been inside. Quite forgetting a new rule about having to finish with the traces attached, I got the grooms to take the swingle-trees off altogether, and tie the leaders' traces over their backs. We then went on to drive the remaining obstacles without the leaders being attached to anything, other than by the reins – and in quite respectable times too!

John Robertson and Richard Carey were also eliminated and John Bennett retired. I had a clear round in the cones, so I ended up sixth, but with an eliminated score. Karen Bassett won fairly easily with Claudia Bunn in second place.

The next 1987 event was at Islabank in mid-May on a farm belonging to the Colville family. Wynn Colville had been an enthusiastic pony-team driver and was the main organizer of the event in the grounds of Scone Palace. Sadly, he had died suddenly of cancer the previous year, but his widow, Deirdre, and her sons decided to continue with the event, taking over the Scone dates when that event lost its sponsor.

It was only while I was driving around the course in my car that I realized that Islabank is no distance from Meikleour. I had known the owner, Lord Lansdowne, for some years as Balmoral is just over the hill beyond Blairgowrie. As the course went past his front door, I stopped the car and decided to call on him. The front door was locked, but I knew the way in through the gun-room. I gave a maid a dreadful fright as I passed her in the corridor. She thought his Lordship was in his study, as indeed he was, and was somewhat astonished to see me walk in. He had agreed to allow the course to go over his estate, but I am not sure that he fully appreciated what it was all about, although he was well acquainted with the Colville family. When the event was repeated over the next few years, he very kindly invited me to stay with him. It is a charming house set in beautiful grounds right on the banks of the Tay, just above where it is joined by the Isla. One of the features of the place is a very tall beech hedge along the road from Perth to Blair-gowrie. The story goes that there was no-one around to trim the hedge during the 1745 Rebellion and, by the time they came back, it had grown too high for any-one to be able to trim the top. At one time the local Fire Brigade used to bring one of its extending ladders in order to trim it.

Mine was the only pony team at this event, so I was put together with the three horse teams. This was reduced to one – George Bowman – when Lex Ruddiman withdrew and Paul Gregory retired. Meanwhile, I was getting rather desperate about finding the right combination of ponies for the dressage. This time I put the two girls, Dawn and Ebony, together in the lead with Martin and Roy in the wheel. It worked, and I managed a score of 38 – one of the very few occasions when I scored less than 40 with the ponies. There was a bit of a panic before the presen-

Fig. 5.4 Beech hedge,
Meikleour House,
Perthshire.
(*The Meikleour Trust*)

tation as my grooms had forgotten their bowler hats. They wore these with Balmoral tweed jackets and moleskin trousers. We all normally wore deer-stalkers for
the marathon, so I told them to put them on for the dressage. I was told by the
judges later, that they preferred the deer-stalkers, and I heard that even Cynthia
Haydon approved of them! Several years later, hard hats were made compulsory
for the marathon, but my grooms have been wearing deer-stalkers for the dressage and cones phases ever since. I use mine when it is raining.

Fig. 5.5 Selecting the right sort of clothing for the pony team in the dressage and cones phases was quite a problem.

I thought that top hats for a fairly bucolic outfit would have been a bit over the top. I settled for a Norfolk jacket in Balmoral tweed, with an apron of the same material, and a bowler or straw hat. I put the grooms in Balmoral tweed jackets and moleskin trousers with deerstalker hats. I was encouraged when Cynthia Haydon approved.(*K.G. Ettridge*)

I did not make the times in either walk, but I did manage to beat George Bowman through the obstacles (another extremely rare event) but he had had a problem in obstacle 1. I had two cones down while he had a clear round, but I still managed to stay ahead of him.

Karen Bassett and Andy Mills were the only other pony teams at Holker at the end of May. A good presentation mark and not a bad dressage test gave me a useful lead of 17 over Karen Bassett, but she caught up to within 5 points by the end of a very tough marathon. Andy Mills got lost in section C, and I was nearly pitched out of the carriage. Karen Bassett did her usual fast clear round in the cones, which left me with just one cone in hand. The spectators appreciated the nail-biting finish. I just managed a clear round of the cones, although I was one second over time, which gave me 0.5 time penalties and I just kept my first place.

Because of the Derby, Trooping the Colour and Ascot, I have never been able to compete in June until the very end of the month, so my next event was at Floors. This time there were no other pony teams, and I was again added to the six horse teams. It must have been owing to the lack of opposition, or concentration, but I went wrong in the dressage (after all these years!) which added 5 points to my score. However, I was interested to see that only about a dozen competitors in all the other classes had managed a dressage score of less than 45. The ponies did brilliantly through the obstacles and were fastest of the teams through obstacles 2 and 6. They also managed a clear round in the cones, and I was only 8 points behind George Bowman's overall score, which would have put me second if I had been competing in the horse class.

Sandringham attracted five pony teams, but it was a pretty disastrous event for three of us. Fell ponies very seldom go lame, but Roy was certainly not sound after the dressage, and I had to leave him out for the rest of the competition. The dressage standard was low enough to let me win it with 47. I had time penalties in all sections, and poor Dawn got a nasty shock when she was confronted with a cardboard cut-out of a cow in the second obstacle. I then went wrong in obstacle 5 without appreciating my mistake, so I was eliminated. Karen Bassett lost a wheel in obstacle 7 and had to retire. Richard Carey had to retire in 8. This left Claudia Bunn to win easily with John Robertson in second place some 120 points behind. Even on an eliminated score and two cones down, I finished in third place.

Lowther came next with only four pony teams entered and, as far as my records go, it was the first appearance of Georgina Frith in the class. She later went on to win the European Championships three times running. On this occasion she came in last. I was 0.2 points behind Claudia Bunn in the dressage, and I could not match her times in the obstacles. Only a better dressage score saved me from being beaten by John Robertson. Both Claudia Bunn and I had 1 time penalty in the cones and she won the whole thing by 20 points.

The season normally ended with Lowther, but in 1987 I entered a pair of ponies for a one-day event at Thornton Castle, the home of the Thornton-Kemsley family. The castle is not far north of Montrose, and within easy reach of Balmoral. There were four entries, one of whom was Philippa Gammell from Glenisla, who later took to pony teams all too successfully. Things started badly when I suddenly realized that I had practised the wrong dressage test and then Dawn and Bramble decided to pull my arms out. Section A took us past the big houses at Fasque and Fettercairn; the former owned by the Gladstone family. Philippa Gammell got 9 points ahead of me in the marathon, and then I hit two cones while she only toppled one. Driving back to Balmoral, David Muir found that the Sherpa van, with which he was towing the trailer with the ponies, did not have enough traction to pull it up the very steep Cairn-a-Mount road. He eventually had to take the ponies out and walk them up the steepest bits of the hill and then put them back in again. Otherwise it was a very pleasant end to the first full season with the ponies.

The ponies then had about six weeks off before the stag-stalking season started in October, and continued working through the hind-stalking season until December. After that they only had a short break before going down to Sandringham again in January. The stalking season is quite hard work for the ponies, although no speed is involved. Stalking parties usually leave for the hill at about nine in the morning and there are two ponies allocated to each of the beats. The ponies, led by two ponymen, leave the stables at about the same time having been told by the stalker where they are to go to await further orders. In the pre-electronic era, when the stalker needed the ponies to pick up a stag, he would signal by lighting a small heather fire. This indicated to the ponymen where to bring the ponies to pick up the dead stag. The stag then had to be strapped to a special deer saddle and carried down to the nearest road. It is obviously very important to ensure that the stag is securely strapped, as there is nothing worse than to have the stag, or the saddle, slip with the risk of the antlers spiking the pony.

Since the invention of two-way radios – walkie-talkies or 'jabber-boxes' – things are much easier. The stalker can now keep the ponymen informed about his position and intentions. Some of the beats are quite a distance from the stables, which means that, at the end of the day, the ponies are turned out in a field as near as possible to the beat. They spend the week there and only come back to the castle stables for the weekends. The ponies get to know their beats remarkably quickly, and they have such an unerring homing instinct that the ponymen frequently turn them loose at the end of the day and let them find their own way back to their field.

On one of the beats at Balmoral, the ponies are kept not far from a public car park and visitor centre. One evening, when a ponyman was bringing back a stag, he was questioned by an elderly visitor who wanted to know what had happened to the stag, to which the resourceful ponyman replied 'It's a case of lead poisoning', to which the visitor responded 'Aye, there's a lot of it about these days'.

RESULTS FOR 1987

EVENT	Dressage	Marathon	Cones	Pl/No
Brighton	1	3	1=	3/4
Windsor	1	E	1=	6/9
Islabank	1	1	2	1/3
Holker	1	1	2	1/3
Floors				1/1
Sandringham	1	E	2	3/5
Lowther	2	2	1=	2/4
Thornton (pair)	1=	2	4	2/4

Ponies used: Bramble, Roy, Martin, Dawn, Ebony, Tom.

Looking at these results, I notice that I did surprisingly well in the dressage. I say 'surprisingly' because Fell ponies, with their hairy legs, long manes and tails and rather upright paces, are not usually considered by dressage judges to have the ideal shape or movement for this curious competition. Incidentally, there is a convention that native ponies are not clipped and their manes and tails are not pulled to give them a smarter look. I get the impression that foreign dressage judges do not quite know what to make of them. They have to admit that the ponies do the figures accurately and willingly enough, but they do not see the rather exaggerated movement in the collected and extended trots, which they are accustomed to seeing in Welsh ponies. It says a lot for the temperament and patience of the Fells that they can be encouraged to do these exercises with any enthusiasm at all. They certainly cannot manage the extraordinary effortless floating paces of the Cleveland Bay x Oldenburg horses, which I used to drive. These big graceful horses may not have been ideal for the marathon obstacles, but they must have been the envy of all the other team drivers when they were in the dressage arena. I hope the other drivers were consoled by the thought that, whatever score I managed in the dressage, they always had a very good chance of overtaking me in the marathon.

It was partly because I was getting a bit irritated by this apparent prejudice against dressage by hill ponies, that I wrote a small book called *Driving and Judging Dressage*. It seemed to me that it was about time that driven dressage was seen as a discipline in its own right, and not just as a poor relation of ridden dressage. I also felt that it was important to appreciate that dressage is a challenge to both drivers and judges.

One of the interesting features of the pony-teams class was the gradual build-up of competitors from 1987 onwards. I noticed, in particular, the very considerable improvement in the standards of driving in all three phases, which started about this time. It was also noticeable that the Europeans were taking to this class and by 2003 they had come to dominate it.

1988

By the time the 1988 season started, the Bassett sisters were really finding their feet, although they also had their occasional disasters. Karen Bassett, in particular, seemed to be plagued by unreliable wheels.

We went off to Australia in early spring so that I missed Brighton and my first event was the Windsor CAI, although at this stage there were no foreign pony teams involved. There are always difficulties with driving mares, and Dawn chose the week before this event to become awkward. Fortunately, the ponies did a very good dressage test, which gave me a useful lead of 9 points over Pippa Bassett and 12 over Karen Bassett.

Fig. 5.6 Karen Bassett driving her team of Native British Spotted Ponies at Holker Hall in 1986. She had been driving ponies since her teens, and she was very difficult to beat with this team. She eventually moved to the horse-teams class and has been quite successful with her impressive team of Trakehners in international competitions. (*Alf Baker*)

After that Dawn's co-operation ended. She did as little as possible and Roy was too idle to go on his own, so that the two leaders flapped about on loose reins and I could not stop them going wrong in the seventh and eighth obstacles. The wheelers did their best, but ran out of steam by the fourth obstacle. At least we made all the times, including the walks. The only reason that I managed to get into second place overall was that Pippa Bassett took a wrong turning in obstacle 3 and was eliminated. John Robertson also went wrong in the same obstacle, which let Richard Carey move up into third place, although his overall score was 418.

At the end of May we were up in Scotland for the Islabank event on the Colville Farm near Coupar Angus. This time I stayed with Lord Lansdowne at Meikleour. The weather was glorious, the arena was flat and the marathon course was good. Part of it took us over the golf course at Rosemount, just outside Rattray, and I suspect the members of the club were not too pleased. The only other pony-team competitor was Caroline Musker. It was a fairly close competition, although it was just as well that I managed a reasonable dressage test, and got through the obstacles without any dramas, because I hit two cones and Caroline only had 5 time penalties. There were six horse teams taking part, and I was somewhat mortified to see that five of them got round the obstacles faster than I did.

When I started driving ponies, it always seemed to me that I was going faster than the horses, but this was obviously an illusion. I think this is caused by the fact that the carriage is smaller and you sit nearer the ground. Furthermore, the ponies' legs and, therefore, their paces, are shorter; a horse doing a normal trot covers a lot more ground than a pony doing the same pace. This means that the ponies need to trot as fast as they can, or canter where possible, in order to keep up with the horses through the obstacles.

Holker followed in early June, and this time there were five pony teams, including the Bassett sisters, and the new face, at least to me, of Nicholas Saphir. Again, it was just as well that I did a reasonable dressage test as I was slower through the obstacles than the other three. This was partly due to getting stuck in obstacle 1. Pippa Bassett was 0.3 ahead of me after the marathon, so things were a bit tight before the cones. However, she obligingly hit two cones, including the very last one and, as I only had one cone down, this let me finish in second place behind her sister Karen.

I had taken on a new groom at the beginning of the season, but after the event at Holker he was offered a full-time job at the Mews in London and took himself off without saying a word to David Muir or myself. As it happened, David had seen his cousin, Paul, at Islabank, who had helped out with the ponies at Balmoral for a couple of years. Paul told David that he was out of a job and would be delighted to come back to the ponies for the rest of the season. So I now had three Muir grooms again.

I went to Floors at the beginning of July to find that I was the only pony team present. I was asked whether I would mind joining the horse-team class, as it would make life easier for the timekeepers. This meant doing section A at 15 kph, instead of 14 kph; B at 7 kph, instead of 6 kph; and C at 19.5 kph, which is pretty fast even for horses, and above the present limit. To my great surprise, I was only 30 seconds late in the two walks and 19 seconds late in C. By this time I was feeling rather confident that I might be able to compete with the horses in the obstacles. In fact I was fastest through obstacle 1 and third fastest through 2, but then disaster struck in 3, where I hit a tree rather too firmly and bent the pole, and the near front wheel was skewed outwards. There was nothing for it but to retire. Fortunately the ponies were not affected by the mishap, and we managed a double clear round in the cones.

David Saunders was driving the Kluge team of horses, and had the misfortune to turn over in obstacle 7.

To compensate for this rather dismal performance, the weather was glorious and I was invited to have a go at catching a sea trout in the Tweed after dinner. It was a magical evening, and I had the satisfaction of landing a 1.8 kg (4 lb) sea trout just as it was getting dark.

The Sandringham event was held on the first weekend in July. This time there were eight competitors in the class. Karen Bassett had the misfortune to lose a wheel in obstacle 6, the water obstacle, for the second year running. I made a mess of obstacle 4, but the ponies went really well through all the obstacles, and I found myself in the lead with 11 points in hand before the cones. Luckily I managed a clear round and had the satisfaction of winning in front of the 'home crowd'.

I do not think that I used the same arrangement of the ponies for any of the dressage competitions during the season, and Lowther was no exception. I had come to think of any score over 40 as a disaster, but the addition of an extra 10 points for turnout instead of the separate presentation phase, inevitably increased the average scores. In spite of getting 46 for my dressage test, I was still some 30 points ahead of the other three competitors. I managed to stay ahead of John Robertson by some 10 points and won for the second time running. The weather throughout the event was hot and the ponies certainly were affected by it. They did not relish having to climb up on to the Fells twice in section A, and the sticky going meant that they had to pull the carriage downhill as well.

That brought one of my more successful seasons to an end.

RESULTS FOR 1988

EVENT	Dressage	Marathon	Cones	Pl/No
Windsor	1	2	2	2/6
Islabank	1	1	2	2/2
Holker	1	3	1=	2/5
Floors	Retired			
Sandringham	1	1	1	1/8
Lowther	1	3	1=	1/4

Ponies used: Bramble, Roy, Dawn, Ebony, Tom, Gina.

1989

The 1989 season started extremely badly. I had decided to retire Roy at the end of the previous season, and Tom, who was to become such a stalwart wheeler, was still lame and had to be turned out for the season. Luckily we had a home-bred mare, Cilla, who was just old enough to compete and I got her to Sandringham with the intention of bringing her into the team in the following year. I also had Bonnie, who I had bought at Lowther the previous year as a replacement for Tom, but practice at Sandringham convinced me that she would not be ready for competition this year. In fact she never showed any aptitude for the competitions. That meant that I only had four reliable ponies (Dawn, Ebony, Gina and Bramble) available for competition.

I was out of the country in February and again in March so that serious training could only start at Windsor in April.

Behind what is known as the Frogmore Border, there is an irregular row of chestnut trees, which used to be inside the adjoining field, and therefore had post and rail fences round them to keep the cattle away. We had moved the field fence to take these trees out of the field, and, by leaving the fences round each tree, I found they were ideally placed for practising for the obstacles. The very first time I took the ponies through this row of trees I hit one of the fence posts and pushed it down, so that, as the wheels went up the incline, the carriage turned over. The ponies bolted up the hill for home led, I suspect, by Gina. They flew up the avenue towards the castle with the carriage on its side and David Muir in hot pursuit. They reached the George IV Gate to the castle, and then turned back towards the Mews Gate, carefully keeping off the grass. As they came into the upper yard, Ebony slipped and came down on her knees and was dragged across the yard before they could be stopped. Her knees were badly scraped and she was out for the season.

During the 1983 season, I had lost patience with the inability of one of my Fells, Rosie, to keep to the right pace, and lent her to Lady Tollemache, in the faint hope of wooing her away from her passion for dressage, and taking up driving instead. In desperation I asked for Rosie back in exchange for Bonnie, and I decided to see whether Cilla could cope with competitions. I also came to the conclusion that I had to withdraw from Brighton as there was no hope of having this scratch team ready in time. Quite what 'JJ' Reep, my new girl groom, made of all this, I shudder to think, but she bravely stuck it out.

I gave the new team a trial run at the Windsor Park Equestrian Club event at the beginning of May and was agreeably surprised. Cilla did extremely well at her first outing, although she had the habit of puffing instead of breathing normally. This habit caused quite a lot of trouble at veterinary inspections during competitions, and I eventually had to get a certificate to say that this was her normal method of breathing.

Nine pony teams were entered for the Windsor event, including Mia Allo from Belgium and Karl Heinz Mulatsch from Germany. I was given a reasonable score to make fourth place in the dressage. For some inexplicable reason, we were 20 seconds within the time for the first walk in the marathon, and 17 seconds over in the second. Whether it was because we were on home ground, or whether the ponies thought that this practice session had been going on long enough, I could not get any speed out of them in the obstacles. Karen Bassett got into a muddle in obstacle 1 and then lost a wheel – yet again – in 3, while John Bennett was eliminated in 6. Pippa Bassett, now Mrs Thomas, had a fairly comfortable lead before the cones, but one of the wheels on her best carriage was a bit dodgy, and her father only got it fixed just in time. In spite of having one down, she won, beating Mia Allo and Mulatsch. I managed a clear round, but Nicholas Saphir had two refusals at the water and then knocked two cones down, which let me through to fourth place by 4 points.

Islabank followed at the end of May, sadly for the last time. This popular Scottish event moved to St Fort in Fife in 1990. There were three other entries, all new to the class. Debbie Cowdery, with the only other team of Fells, was John Cowdery's daughter and Andrew Cowdery's sister. John Cowdery had served in the Household Cavalry and had worked in the Royal Mews. He drove a team of horses in competition for a while, but then went coaching and eventually became a driving-event judge. For many years he organized the splendid event at Drumlanrig. Andrew had just taken up driving when he had a dreadful accident in a swimming pool. He sadly broke his neck and became paraplegic, but has since developed into an excellent commentator. Debbie had recently married my driver, David Key, but it did not last very long. Some years later I bought a pony, Peter, from John Cowdery, who turned out to be a brilliant wheeler and pretty good in the lead as well.

This was Philippa Gammell's first national event with a team. She lives in Glenisla, not far from Blairgowrie, and thinks nothing of driving a large horse-box and trailer to events all over the country and as far south as Brighton. After a very successful career with a pair, she promptly won the dressage phase at the first attempt with a team.

The weather was glorious throughout, and, but for a cool breeze, it might have been uncomfortably hot for the ponies. My lot did not do all that badly in the dressage, but the comments of the judges that: one of the leaders (Dawn) was hanging back; the halt was fidgety; the extensions were lacking, and so on, suggested that while the test as a whole was reasonable, the details were poor. When I first started driving in this competition, I came to the conclusion that if I could drive the test accurately, I could expect to get a reasonable score even if the horses did not do everything else expected of them. I reckoned that if I started and finished the movements in the right places, used the arena to the full and made some sort of distinction between the paces it would be difficult for the judges to mark me down too much. Results over the years seem to have confirmed that view. But, the trouble with the ponies is that their paces are not 'flashy' enough for some judges.

I had to make some changes to the team before the next event, as Gina was showing intermittent signs of lameness. She went off to the Dick Veterinary School in Edinburgh and I brought Roy out of retirement from Balmoral.

Maureen Hogg, Debbie Cowdery and Philippa Gammell turned up again at Holker at the beginning of June, where we were joined by Karen Bassett, her sister, Pippa Thomas, and Caroline Musker from Suffolk. I had left Rosie out of the dressage team and put Cilla into the lead, and I just managed to squeak ahead of Karen Bassett by 1 point. But for unnecessary penalties in sections A and C, I would have been in second place after the marathon. I do not know who made Karen Bassett's carriages, but she lost yet another wheel, this time in section A. Her sister managed a very slick round of the obstacles, with Philippa Gammell not far behind. Everyone, except Karen Bassett, had time penalties in the cones, but I did manage to close the gap on Philippa Gammell by 5 points to finish third. She told me afterwards that she owed her very much improved performance in the obstacles to my advice to buckle her reins together.

No less than ten pony teams turned up for Sandringham. This event was rather more interesting than usual. The whole layout was completely changed. The stable field was moved across the road to below the West Newton Club and the public car park was moved from the park into the School Field, with access through the gate next to Laycocks. However, this was not a total success and it was changed again for the next event.

I had at last achieved my ambition to have the obstacles close together, so that the spectators could see them all, without having to make excursions into the countryside. In the new layout, five of the obstacles were spread between the Park Pond and the water-crossing and the other three were close to Woodcock Wood. In order for the drivers to have a reasonable gap between obstacles (the rules require them to be at about 1 km intervals) the course in section E described a series of loops into the park and Woodcock Wood, between each obstacle. The system seems to have been quite successful, as this layout of the obstacles has remained the same ever since, and other events are beginning to copy it. However, I have to admit that I sometimes found it quite difficult to remember which loop I was doing.

In the hot and sticky conditions, I started badly by doing a dreadful dressage test. Dawn distinguished herself by trying to eat the grass on three occasions while walking across the diagonal.

I usually suggested the routes for sections A, B, C and E of the marathon, and I thought the competitors might enjoy driving through a field of lavender in full bloom in C. I think we all enjoyed it, but it was mostly through rather soft sand and I suspect that the ponies were not all that enthusiastic about the aesthetic qualities of the course. Pippa Thomas was the only one to make the time in C. My ponies went very well through the obstacles, although not as fast as the Bassett sisters. By rights, they should have been first and second, but it turned out that both of them had gone wrong in obstacle 1 and had been eliminated. That left me with a comfortable margin of 50 points over John Robertson. I managed a double clear round of the cones, and, to everyone's astonishment, including my own, I emerged the winner for the second year in succession.

One of the consequences of this event was a long and involved discussion about the time allowed for section E. At that time the rules specified that the maximum speed for both A and E was 15 kph, the same speed, incidentally, demanded of the horse classes. The distance through the obstacles was included in the total for section E, but the time through the obstacles was calculated for the speed of a walk, or about 8 kph. Even so, the problem was that this speed proved a bit too fast, particularly in the longer obstacles. The average time through the majority of obstacles was about 90 seconds, or the equivalent of 18 penalties (1 penalty for every five seconds, or 12 per minute). The result was that, to make up for the time lost in the obstacles, we had to do something like 18 kph between the obstacles to get home on time. This was faster than the maximum-allowed speed of 17 kph for section C – supposedly the fast section. It had to be even faster if you got held up for any reason. I suggested that the speed in C should, therefore, be increased to make it more competitive, and that in E the speed should be decreased. Unfortunately, in my opinion, the speed for C was also reduced. The result is that very few competitors get time penalties in C, which is splendid for the slower teams, but it gives no relative advantage to the faster ones.

More or less the same teams, with the addition of Philippa Gammell, gathered at Lowther at the beginning of August. Only the Bassett sisters and John Robertson managed the times in all the sections of the marathon. I made a mistake in obstacle 4, when Roy went the wrong side of a post. Dawn then got her legs over the traces and I had to do a circle, which must have added at least a minute. I also had the misfortune to incur another 10 penalties when Dawn knocked down a 'dislodgeable' element in obstacle 7 with her nose.

These dislodgeable elements were stuck to various parts of obstacles with the intention of making drivers take rather more care, instead of barging and banging through the obstacles. They are only fairly successful and there is always the chance that they will be knocked down by a pony or by the swingle trees.

I should have overtaken John Robertson in the cones, but I made a silly mistake at the end of the course and headed for the wrong pair of cones. This gave me 8 time penalties for a total of 199. John Robertson went in next and had one cone down plus 9 time penalties, which gave him a total on 193 and he retained his third place.

In spite of unexpectedly winning two events, it was not a very satisfactory season, largely because of pony problems. Losing Ebony, Tom and Gina was a real blow, although there was some compensation in the performance of Cilla, who had turned out to have a genuine talent for these competitions. Much as I liked Rosie, I was not at all unhappy about sending her back to Lady Tollemache. There is nothing quite as frustrating as a pony that simply will not walk or trot consistently when required to do so. It causes agony for the driver in the dressage phase and near apoplexy in the walk sections.

RESULTS FOR 1989

EVENT	Dressage	Marathon	Cones	Pl/No
Windsor	4	5	1=	4/8
Islabank	2	2	1	1/4
Holker	1	5	1	3/7
Sandringham	4	1	1=	1/8
Lowther	4	4	5	4/9

Ponies used: Bramble, Rosie, Dawn, Gina, Cilla, Roy.

1990

The Brighton event was the first of the 1990 season and took place in glorious early-May weather throughout the whole weekend, which is enjoyable for the drivers, but not such fun for the ponies, who, as usual, had to climb to the top of the Downs twice. As it turned out, the only pony to give the vets any anxiety was Bramble, although he recovered from sections A and C very quickly. I thought I had done quite well to win the dressage phase with 44 points, which put me 8 ahead of Pippa Thomas and 17 ahead of Karen Bassett. Just how much Pippa and Karen had improved was shown when they both caught up with, and passed, me easily in the marathon. Karen Bassett won by 12 points from Pippa Thomas, who was 19 ahead of me. At least I managed the times for all the sections, but my times through the obstacles were dreadfully slow. I did, however, beat both of them in the cones, but not by much. Cilla nearly wrecked the whole thing by giving a buck after the box. If she had come down with a leg over a trace or the pole, it could have been disastrous.

There were eleven entries for Windsor, including Mia Allo from Belgium, Franz Feichtinger from Austria and R.P.G. Verheyden from the Netherlands. Things started quite well when the ponies did a splendid dressage test with a score of 39 – their first under 40. It all fell apart after that. The marathon course was a very good one and the obstacles were designed by Tish Roberts (since renamed 'F***ing Roberts', since every one of his obstacles had 6 gates – A, B, C, D, E and F). My undoing came at the very first, when I went through B backwards instead of A. That gave me 20 penalties to start with and, with a further mistake, I collected no less than 48 in the very first obstacle. That, plus 29 time penalties in E, in spite of the speed having been set at 14 kph, put me nearly 90 points behind Karen Bassett.

There is nothing more demoralizing than to know that you have blown it so early in the course. The only redeeming feature, as far as I was concerned, was that most of the others did much worse, because I still came in third. At least I did a double clear round in the cones at nine in the morning on a very sticky course. We had a speed competition in the main ring in the afternoon, and the ponies responded brilliantly to come third behind Karen Bassett and Caroline Musker. Mia Allo won the whole event by 3 points from Karen Bassett.

The event at St Fort, at the south end of the Tay road bridge turned out to be quite an experience. The property belongs to Andrew Mylius, whose mother had married Charles Lambe, a brilliant naval officer, who became 1st Sea Lord. He had also been an Equerry to the late King when he visited Canada in 1939. Charles Lambe had been a member of my uncle's Bluejackets polo team just before the war. Much to the Army's consternation, the Bluejackets managed to get into the final of the Inter-Regimental Tournament in 1938. I had served with Charles Lambe in the British Pacific Fleet towards the end of the war, when he was in command of the aircraft carrier HMS Illustrious and I was 1st Lieutenant of the fleet destroyer HMS Whelp. When he retired from the Navy he moved to St Fort and died there. By the time Andrew Mylius, who was an enthusiastic tandem driver, decided to run an event there, the old house had been pulled down and the road to the Tay Bridge was built along what had been the main drive to the house. The whole park slopes to the south and Andrew Mylius had levelled an area to produce a splendid main arena for the dressage and cones phases. The marathon course took us through some glorious country and the weather could not have been better. From the high ground you can see across the Tay estuary and over to the east coast.

The problem had been to find some kind person in the reasonable vicinity to put me up for this event. Fortunately Ralph Anstruther, who worked in Queen Elizabeth the Queen Mother's Household, arranged for me to stay at Kilmany House with James and Diana Macnab of Macnab. The house had belonged to Diana's father, Lord Kilmany. It was rather a curious house as it had been cut in half for Lord Kilmany's two daughters. Even the garden was divided by a paling fence. This did not seem to reflect on the relationship between the two families as Diana's sister and her husband regularly came to dinner. All four were on the large size and the small dining room became quite crowded with the whole party. Later on, when the Macnabs moved away, I found accommodation with the Earl and Countess of Dundee at Birkhill. The Scrymgeours are Hereditary Standard Bearers for Scotland and I had known his father from the state occasions in Edinburgh when he had to perform his hereditary duties. The splendid old house is tucked away in deepest Fife overlooking the Firth of Tay a few miles west of the Tay Bridge. We were made very comfortable, but the whole establishment had that air of eccentricity about it, which seems to be a feature of so many old country houses in this island.

That was the best part of the St Fort event story. From then on everything to do with the driving event went wrong. In those days I did not have portable stabling attached to the carriage trailer, so I had to rely on finding local stabling. Andrew Mylius had put the ponies in an open-sided cattle court surrounded by large horizontal steel pipes. As there were not enough pens for all the ponies, he had divided one of the pens by placing metal sheep hurdles across it. We accepted this arrangement with reservations, hoping that there was not enough room between the bars for a pony to get a foot through. Little did we appreciate the ingenuity of Fell ponies. On the Friday evening, after the grooms had gone, the

Fig. 5.7 The Earl of Dundee's house, Birkhill, Cupar, Fife. (*Lord Dundee*)

shepherd looked in and found Dawn with her *hind* leg stuck between the bars of one of the hurdles. We never did establish quite how she had done it, but in struggling to get free, she had cut her off hind leg high up inside the hock and had to have two stitches, and so she was out of the event.

After a trial run, I decided to put Cilla in the lead with Lady for the dressage. It worked reasonably well, but Philippa Gammell did better by 2 points. Because I thought Cilla would do more work in the wheel than Ebony, I put the latter in the lead for the marathon. It was not a success. Ebony's reactions were much slower than I expected and in the first obstacle I shot past the gate I wanted to go through and went into gate E backwards. I went back through E the right way, but I forgot the rule at that time, which required you to go back and do the gate before the mistake. I had therefore failed to go through D, and at the end of the course I was greeted with the news that I had been eliminated.

That was not the end of this chapter of disasters. I started the cones confidently enough, but then, through a lapse of memory, which seems to hit most drivers sooner or later, I aimed for obstacle 5 after passing through 1 and succeeded in demolishing it in the process of trying to correct myself. Then, when I got to the box I must have pulled the buckle on the connecting rein to the offside leader back through the roger ring on Bramble's bridle, where it got stuck. The next thing I knew was that, as we came out of the box, Bramble's bridle had been pulled clean off his head. After a moment of confusion, the grooms got down, and at this point I thought the prudent thing to do was to retire.

If I thought that was to be the end of my problems, I was soon disillusioned at Holker. Dawn's leg seemed to be all right, so I put her back in the team, but only for the dressage and cones phases, which I managed to win by 3 points from Philippa Gammell. I then got into a dreadful muddle with the timing of the marathon sections. All went well for the first 8 km and then we were suddenly at the finish. Luckily I was able to slow down enough not to be early. In retrospect, I think the trouble was with the measurement of the course. I suspect that while the distance for section A was given as 9.51 km (i.e. 9 km plus 510 m), it was in fact 9 km plus 50 m. Similar mistakes appeared to have been made in sections C, D and E. As a result I arrived early in C and was late in D, which seemed to be 80 m too long. In fact all competitors in all classes, other than three of the pony teams, had time penalties in section D. As the speed for E was set at 13 kph and the obstacles were not all that long, I thought there was no need to hurry, only to be told to let Philippa Gammell overtake me. That held me up for two minutes. I was then held up again to let John Robertson overtake me. After all that I still arrived at the end of section E at the original time allowed.

The ponies went through the obstacles without any serious problems, although I hit a 'knock-down' in the last. Philippa Gammell hit two knock-downs, but she was still 15 points ahead of me. Meanwhile the Bassett sisters had stormed round the course at their usual breakneck speed. Karen Bassett clocked up only 39 points in the obstacles, while Pippa Thomas was not far behind with 57. Of the lesser mortals, Philippa Gammell managed 65 and I came next with 80. But for the extra 11 points that I had lost in sections C and D, the gap would have been a bit smaller. As I was some distance ahead of Debbie Cowdery in fifth place, I thought I would go for a fast round in the cones. The ponies co-operated and I did the fastest round of the day, although I hit one cone to retain fourth place.

After the cones, I noticed that Dawn was resting her bad leg, so we took her out of the team for the prize-giving and asked the vet to have a look at her. He took the stitches out and seemed to be happy, but when we got back to Windsor, the wound had opened up again. It was now questionable whether or not she would be fit for Sandringham. To add to my worries, Ebony looked to be going a bit unevenly. I could only imagine that she had hit a front leg during the marathon. If both these ponies proved to be unfit for Sandringham, I would have to withdraw.

Fortunately they both recovered, but then Cilla showed a bit of lameness and

I had to put Bramble in the wheel in her place for the dressage. He did his usual business of cantering in the extensions and pulling outwards in the rein-back. However, we were not far behind Philippa Gammell.

Tish 'F***ing' Roberts had designed the marathon obstacles and so they were rather long and complicated. However, the Bassett sisters tore into them and got miles ahead. I had almost exactly double Karen Bassett's penalties of 73 (142) and 50 points behind Pippa Thomas. Caroline Musker was eliminated when she apparently got lost on one of the loops between the obstacles. Philippa Gammell was badly caught out in obstacle 1 and eliminated, and Andy Mills and Richard Carey also joined Caroline and Philippa in the Big E Club (elimination). I thought the ponies had rather lost interest before the cones, but the moment we crossed the start line they set off and we managed a double clear. They also did well in the drive-off. Karen Bassett got a bit too enthusiastic and went out of control after the slalom.

Sandringham was followed by a new event at Drumlanrig in Dumfriesshire. The seventeenth century pink sandstone castle belonging to the Duke of Buccleuch is set in spectacular country. I had not been there since 1949 when I was invited by his father to shoot grouse. Johnny had been a near contemporary of mine in the Navy during the war. He had become a paraplegic as a result of a hunting accident. He and Jane had not used the place very much in recent years and it felt a bit neglected. However, the castle is filled with marvellous things, including a wonderful Leonardo da Vinci, which was later stolen in a daylight raid in 2002. The stable field was on the site of a Roman fort and the arena overlooked the river Nith. John Cowdery had moved to the area on retirement and the whole event was his initiative, and he organized it very well.

On recent form, Pippa Thomas was almost bound to win, however, she tipped up in obstacle 6, which gave her 60 penalties. Even at her speed, this was more than she could afford. I was going neck and neck with Philippa Gammell, but at the end I discovered that my girl groom, 'JJ' Reep, had been seen to put one foot on the ground in obstacle 3, which gave us a further 10 penalties. I also had to do an extra circle in 8, which must have added at least another 4 penalties. My double clear round in the cones and Philippa Gammell's 6 time penalties did not affect the issue.

Lowther attracted nine entries, including the dreaded Bassett and Thomas girls! I managed to beat Philippa Gammell in the dressage, but this time by an even slimmer margin of 0.3 points. Pippa Thomas was third and Karen Bassett sixth. Even though Pippa Thomas fell out in obstacle 1, she still managed to come in second, some 50 points behind her sister, and 10 points ahead of me. My ponies went really well, but Ebony delayed the first walk, and I collected an unwanted 3 penalties. Worse was to come: we were 45 seconds late in E, which added another 9 penalties. Philippa had the bad luck to turn over in obstacle 8.

Fig. 5.8 A warm day at Drumlanrig Castle, July 1990. A number of obstacles require the driver to do loops outside the structure of the obstacle. Vital seconds can be saved by getting up a good speed and turning as close to the obstacle as possible. (*Author's collection*)

Lowther was the last event of the season for me. The National Championships took place at Windsor in September, but as the ponies were based at Balmoral, it would have meant dragging them all the way down south again just for one event.

RESULTS FOR 1990

EVENT	Dressage	Marathon	Cones	Pl/No
Brighton	1	3	1	3/7
Windsor	1	3	1=	3/11
St Fort	2	R		4/4
Holker	2	4	5	4/7
Sandringham	3	3	1=	3/10
Drumlanrig	1	2	1	2/4
Lowther	1	7	5=	3/9

Ponies used: Bramble, Dawn, Ebony, Cilla, Lady.

This brought to an end the first four years with the Fell ponies, and I owe to Andrew Cowdery the information that I managed to finish in the top three of the Beneficial Bank Points League Championships for Pony Teams in each of those four years.

THE END OF THE MUIR CONNECTION

1991–1993

Despite rumours of his impending retirement from competitive carriage driving, Prince Philip has made no definite decision and certainly will not relish the prospect of relinquishing the reins.

S O WROTE ANDREW COWDERY at the start of the 1991 season in an account of an interview with me. These rumours had been voiced in the media for several years because they were convinced that I was suffering from arthritis, and various other diseases. It was confidently announced that this condition was the reason I had given up playing polo twenty years earlier. A damaged right wrist was certainly one reason why I had given up the game, although the damage was done after I had decided to give up when I reached the age of fifty. I certainly found it painful to use a polo stick, but I had no trouble with reins or a whip. Indeed, by 1991 the only sign of the original injury was a slightly limited ability to cock my right wrist. This was a definite handicap when playing squash, but none at all when driving horses.

The 1991 season started in the usual way with the ponies' fitness training at Sandringham followed by dressage, marathon obstacles and cones practice at Windsor and a Windsor Park Equestrian Club event at the beginning of April. All seemed to be shaping up well for the first national event of the season at Brighton over the first weekend in May. However, things started to go wrong when the two leaders, Lady and Dawn, took a dislike to each other and, to make matters worse, they started leaning against each other, particularly on hard or slippery surfaces. There is nothing more aggravating than the two leaders leaning against each other, except perhaps when they pull away from each other. Try as you like, they become inseparable and very difficult to steer. At one point it became so bad that when one of them got distracted for a moment and stopped leaning, (or possibly thought it might be fun to see what happened) the other one simply fell over. To make matters worse the habit seems to be catching and, before you know it, any pair of leaders starts doing it. So I had to take Lady out – she was a bit dotty anyway – and put Cilla in her place. At least she and Dawn appeared to get on together, and Cilla turned out to be a much better leader than I expected.

But that was not the end of the problems. I suddenly heard that Saturday 4th May was the ideal day for the Gulf War Thanksgiving Service in Glasgow. That was difficult enough but, for some reason, I also had to go to Evensong at Windsor on the Sunday. I thought this would make it impossible for me to compete at all. However, Joe Moore (at that time Chairman of the Driving Committee and virtual dictator of the driving world) came to the rescue, and managed to shift the dressage for the pony teams to late on Saturday and the marathon to early on Sunday. I was last into the dressage arena at ten past six, first onto the marathon course at half past eight and through the cones at a quarter to two. I was away by three. I only hope that the judges and my fellow competitors have forgiven me.

I was very doubtful about the ponies before the dressage phase, but they performed extremely well to return a score of 39, and I found myself 4 points ahead of Philippa Gammell. We were neck and neck through the obstacles, but she collected 80 time penalties in section E, while I only had 43. Caroline Musker had 34 and moved into the lead by 4 points. Pippa Thomas was also slow in E and finished third. Georgina Frith had problems in obstacle 7 and had to retire. Ursula Hirschberg, who had just transferred from the pony-tandems class and later became one of the fastest drivers through obstacles, also got into all sorts of trouble on this occasion. Caroline Musker hit two cones while I only had 0.5 time penalties, so I regained the lead.

There were two foreigners and five natives in the next event at Windsor. The same team that I used at Brighton did a splendid Dressage test for a score of 39.4. This gave me a useful lead, but I could not keep it up in the marathon, and both Pippa Thomas and the German, Diethelm Kneifel, fairly flew round the obstacles, leaving me in third place. A double clear round in the cones phase (no cones down or time penalties) ensured that I kept my place, 6 points behind Pippa Thomas (by then Karen Bassett had, thankfully, moved into the horse-teams class with a very smart team of Trakheners), and 8 points behind Kneifel. It also got me a place in a drive-off against the clock. This was a fairly new experience for the ponies, and I was not quite sure what would happen. I need not have worried, they took one look at the main arena and decided to enter into the spirit of the thing. They crossed the start line at a canter and kept it up all the way for a clear round. Pippa Thomas went in next and finished one second faster, but she had one cone down. None of the others, including the horse teams, managed the same time, so to my considerable surprise, I won that competition. To cap it all, the Committee had decided to offer a trophy for the best combined scores of teams of a single, a pair and a team. I discovered that I had drawn Jill Holah, who had won all phases with

Fig. 6.1 The marathon at the Royal Windsor Horse Show, May 1991. The first set of marathon harness we had for the ponies was made of webbing, and we soon discovered that the material was not at all horse-friendly. The ponies' shoulders got quite badly rubbed until we fitted sheepskin fleeces under their breast collars. (*Author's collection*)

Fig. 6.2 Karen Bassett's sister, Pippa Thomas, is driving her team over the bridge at the National Championships at Windsor in 1991. She was always in contention with Karen. She too eventually went over to horses and did well with them. I and, I suspect, all the remaining members of the pony-teams class, breathed a sigh of relief when the sisters moved on to horses. We thought it might give us a chance of winning every now and then. (*Alf Baker*)

her pair, and Alison Leggett, who had won the dressage and come second in the marathon with her single, so we won that trophy.

The ponies then had to make the long trek to St Fort in Fife while I was in America. I arrived back at Heathrow from Houston at half past eleven on the Thursday evening, and then flew to Leuchars at nine the following morning. Some people seem to think that driving is a leisure occupation! I just had time for a practice outing when, almost immediately, Dawn and Cilla started a barging match. I left them in the lead for the dressage, where they performed better than I expected, but I let the side down by having a 'senior moment' when I forgot to start the walk at X. Even so, we were equal second with Philippa Gammell, just 2 points behind Pippa Thomas.

I put Bramble in the lead with Cilla for the marathon and, to my intense dismay, these two started leaning on each other. The result was that I had time penalties in both walks and in the fast section. I got round the obstacles somehow, and it was only because Jane MacInnes had a groom down in obstacle 7 and Georgina Frith turned over in obstacle 4, that we managed to scrape in third, 16 points behind Philippa Gammell.

The dressage judges must have been in a very good mood at Sandringham. It is not often that pony teams get less than 40 points. This time Pippa Thomas and Philippa Gammell were given 34 points each and I followed with 36, in spite of having Cilla and Dawn in the lead again. The judges hammered poor Ursula Hirschberg with 73.

In the hope of avoiding Dawn leaning on Lady during the marathon, I put Dawn in the wheel with her hated son Tom, and Ebony up with Lady for sections A, B, C and D and then swapped Dawn and Ebony for E. It worked reasonably well, but there were rather too many incidents. The leaders jumped some straw bales in obstacle 2 and, in jumping back, Dawn got a leg over a trace, but we got it out without having to put a groom down. Then in 7, the leaders tried to be a bit too clever and I was slow in the last obstacle. I later discovered that George Bowman had turned over in 3. Pippa Thomas had the fastest round of the obstacles for 80 points, Philippa Gammell came next with 103, John Robertson had 120, I collected 125, Caroline Musker managed 127 and Dick Carey got round in 128. When the dressage scores were added, I moved up to third, Caroline Musker moved up to fourth and John Robertson dropped to fifth, but it was all very close. John Robertson hit two cones and added 16 time penalties for a grand total of 209, which eventually dropped him to sixth; Caroline Musker also hit two cones and had 13 time penalties for a total of 194, which dropped her to fifth. I went clear in the cones but had 0.5 time penalties, so I kept my third place – yet again.

Fig. 6.3 Sandringham water hazard, July 1991. We made the water obstacle at Sandringham by putting a small sluice gate in a stream running through the Park. Water is always popular with spectators, either because it is spectacular, or because they are hoping for an upset. Once horses and ponies get used to going into water, it is not a serious hazard. This is the water where Karen Bassett lost a wheel two years running. (*Peter Higby*)

Fig. 6.4 Sandringham, July 1991. Michael Muir is on the left with his cousin David Muir (Jun) on the right. David had taken over as Head Groom from his uncle David in 1987 and did an excellent job. (*Peter Higby*)

It was at this event that I first heard about, what have become known as, 'bendy poles'. The idea is said have originated in Germany, and the principle is really quite simple, although not very easy to describe. I hope the illustration will help. In all conventional four-wheeled carriages, the front axle is attached to the underside of the front end of the carriage by a single bolt through the middle of a turntable. This enables the carriage to be steered. Attached to the front of the turntable are the splinter bar, which is parallel to the axle, and the pole, which is fixed to the turntable and sticks out in front of the carriage. The traces from the two wheel horses are attached to the splinter bar, while their collars are attached to the end of the pole by pole straps (or by chains, in the case of coaches and other heavy vehicles). However, if you use a breast-collar-harness system – as opposed to a

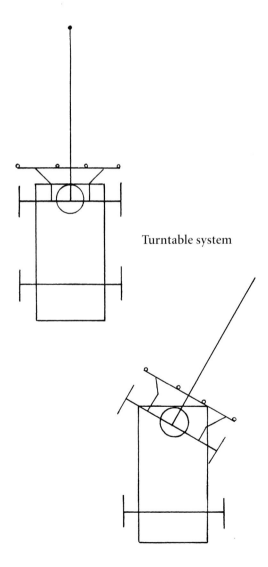

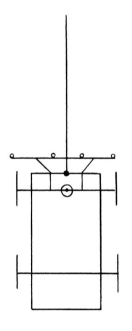

Fig. 6.5 The two diagrams on the left illustrate the conventional turntable system of connecting the pole to the front axle. The two diagrams on the right illustrate the principle of the 'bendy pole'. The effect of the bendy pole is to keep the front wheels away from a corner as the wheelers go round it. It works brilliantly in marathon obstacles, but it is no help at all in the cones, because it is impossible to make small, last-minute adjustments to the direction of the carriage as the pole has some movement from side to side without affecting the front axle.

Turntable system

'Bendy pole'

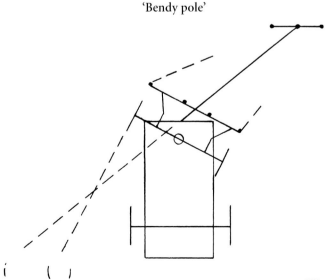

151

neck-collar system – the wheeler's traces need to be attached to movable bars (swingle bars) fixed to the front of the splinter bar. This is to enable the harness to move with the horses without rubbing their shoulders.

The traditional turntable system works perfectly well, except while going round sharp corners. The problem is that the wheel horses, in a team of four, tend to turn as soon as they see the leaders turning in front of them, or, if the leaders are in draught, they can pull the end of the pole round before the front wheels are past the corner. The result is that the inside front wheel hits the corner with more or less disastrous consequences.

Driving a team of four round a corner might be compared to driving a double-articulated vehicle from the rear. Without this articulation, the carriage would cut the corner and it would be dragged onto a gate post, or whatever obstruction marks the corner. To avoid this, the driver needs to get the leaders out of draught and then to hold off the wheelers until it is safe for them to pull the carriage round the corner. 'Holding off' means preventing both wheelers from turning too soon by shortening the rein of the outside wheeler. There are various ways you can do this, but the most usual is to slip the outside wheeler rein over either the right or left thumb, and then slipping it off when clear of the corner. All this gets quite interesting when you try to drive a carriage through a marathon obstacle at speed. Some people, like Micky Flynn, can do it, but I found it very challenging. I found that manoeuvring in confined spaces is greatly simplified by using my method of splitting the reins and buckling the two nearside reins and the two offside reins together. You can then hold both nearside reins in the left hand and both offside reins in the right hand, with the leader reins over the top of the forefingers, the wheeler reins under the little fingers and the buckles in the palms of the hands. This makes it much easier to hold off the wheelers while turning the leaders.

What the bendy-pole system does is to allow the horses to pull the pole round in the ordinary way, but the front axle and wheels do not turn as far as the pole. This means that it becomes less necessary to hold off the wheelers because the action of the bendy pole does it for you by not allowing the carriage to turn into the corner at the same time as the wheelers. It is a very crafty invention, and I suspect that the great majority of contemporary four-wheeled marathon carriages make use of such a system. The only drawback is that it makes it very difficult to keep the carriage going straight. On one occasion, George Bowman hit a post as he was going straight into an obstacle. This was very unusual for him, and he put it down to the fact that, while the wheelers and the pole were heading for the gap, the front wheels of the carriage were still slightly offset. You can see the reason if you move the pole from side to side on a stationary carriage. The outer end of the pole can be moved quite a distance from side to side without moving the wheels.

One of the effects of a bendy pole is that it requires the horse on the inside of a turn to move slightly ahead of the outside horse. However, conventional pole straps would not allow this. It is therefore necessary to fit a short swivelling cross-bar to the end of the pole, which allows the inside horse to move forward and the outside horse to drop back without breaking the pole straps or the traces. This problem was dramatically illustrated by an Irish driver, Kenneth Gracey, at Drumlanrig. He had built his own carriage and fitted a bendy system, but he had failed to fit swingle bars to the splinter bar and a crossbar at the end of the pole, with the result that he broke both outside wheeler traces during his dressage test.

I first heard about this system from George Bowman at the Sandringham event. He had had one fitted, so I contacted George Bushell, the Sandringham Estate mechanical engineer, and a one-time artificer with the Fleet Air Arm, and asked him whether he could make one for my carriage. He promptly produced a device that was a great deal simpler than the rather cumbersome arrangement fitted to George Bowman's carriage. I tried it out and it appeared to work very well, but I thought I had better do some practice with it before using it in a competition.

At the next event at Drumlanrig, I went to watch George Bowman coming down a straight gravel track on the last stretch of the fast section. It was just as well that I did, because the back end of his carriage was swaying alarmingly from side to side and Nelson, his Head Groom, was not looking at all happy as he clung to the back. I had the same experience in practice, and it turned out that the amount of differential between the movement of the pole and the turning of the axle was crucial. A little too much differential and you got a snaking problem. So I had the differential reduced before using it again in competition, and this seemed to cure the problem.

Torrents of rain had descended on Drumlanrig on the Thursday and the stable field was a real mess. It then rained all night and most of Friday, so that the dressage arena had been badly poached by the time I did my test. The ponies rose to the occasion and really put their backs into it. I think the mud encouraged them to lift their feet and make it look as if they were extending. They also managed the rein-back, which, I gathered, no other competitor had been able to achieve. I squeaked ahead of Pippa Thomas by just 4 points. Philippa Gammell's best pony had gone lame, and this was reflected in an unusually high score for her.

The weather for the marathon on Saturday was a great improvement and, although the going was quite deep in places, it was a lovely drive through the spectacular woods. Jane MacInnes went round the obstacles faster than I did, but she had a dreadful dressage score. Pippa Thomas went even faster and overtook me quite easily. She did a double clear round and I had just 2 time penalties, so I remained in second place.

Lowther always came at the end of Cowes Week, which made getting from one venue to the other with the minimum loss of time, quite a challenge. Fortunately, the Cavendishs kindly invited me to stay the night of Wednesday at Holker, so that I could drive over to Lowther on the Thursday.

The 1991 Lowther event was a chapter of disasters. It all started well enough when I cracked the 40 points barrier in the dressage, but I promptly lost the advantage when I accumulated some 8 time penalties in the two walks. I was even slower than usual through the obstacles and finished seventh out of nine. I simply made too many mistakes.

The Lowther marathon was my first with the bendy pole, and it had its problems, which we discovered by trial and error.

The cones produced an unusual drama. When I got to the third pair of cones, it was quite obvious that they were much too close together, and I hit one. Then, when the second pair were also much too close together, I drove over to the judges and asked them to have the measurements checked. It turned out that the arena party of Sea Cadets had managed to break 30 cm off the end of one of the measuring sticks. They had not only failed to report it, they went on measuring the cones as if it was still the right length. I went back and started again, but I got in a tangle in the slalom and had two cones down. As luck would have it, Georgina Frith hit four, so I just retained my third place. The best six went down to the main ring for a drive-off, where I had no luck at all. I hit three cones and came in last.

It was all rather a sad ending to the season, particularly as it was the last for Michael Muir and 'JJ' Reep. Michael was going off to marry Katrina Long, the daughter of a chap who used to work for me at Buckingham Palace, and 'JJ' was going to take up driving herself. These two, and David Muir, made a very good team. They were always willing and cheerful, and they were very fond of the ponies. Michael eventually succeeded his father as Head Ponyman at Balmoral.

RESULTS FOR 1991

EVENT	Dressage	Marathon	Cones	P/N
Brighton	1	2	2	1/9
Windsor	1	3	1=	3/11
St Fort	2=	3	3	3/5
Sandringham	3	3	3	3/10
Drumlanrig	1	3	3	2/7
Lowther	1	7	5=	3/9

Ponies used: Dawn, Ebony, Tom, Cilla, Lady.

The departure of Michael Muir and 'JJ' Reep caused a bit of a problem, but we managed to find two girl grooms to take their places. As they were both called Elizabeth, Milan was known as Lisa and Halcombe as Liz. They were both tall and good looking, which inevitably drew comments from some reporters.

1992

The 1992 season got off to a somewhat challenging start. I had travelled back from Adelaide in Australia, east-about, in a BAe 146 of the Queen's Flight, and arrived with only the Friday morning to practise before the first Windsor Park Equestrian Club event. I had, rather unwisely, agreed to judge the dressage on the Saturday morning. After three hours of judging singles and pairs of ponies, I found it quite difficult to stay awake, and I can only imagine what my writer thought of my frequent and copious yawns.

When it came to my turn, the ponies behaved very well. They fairly flew round the cones, although I just caught two. It was the first time I had used a bendy pole

Fig. 6.6 The Windsor Park Equestrian Club event, 1992. For several years I used webbing harness for the marathon, but it was inclined to rub the ponies (see Fig. 6.1). I later started to use the New Zealand-made Zilco harness worn by the ponies in this photograph. This is a sort of reconstituted leather, which not only looks much better than webbing, but also does not rub. The other great advantage is that it does not need to be treated with saddle soap like ordinary leather. It just has to be washed down with a hose and wiped dry. (*Srdja Djukanovic*)

for the cones, and I was obviously suspicious because I noted at the time 'I am not yet sure whether it needs a slightly different driving technique for the cones'. It was only towards the end of the season that I discovered the problem with making a fine adjustment to the steering just as you are getting to the next pair of cones. It was this feature that made a bendy pole wholly unsuitable for driving the cones.

The next WPEC event in April is better forgotten, and things did not augur well for Brighton. When I looked round the course in Stanmer Park on the Friday, it was hard and dry, but the wind and rain set in on the Saturday. The ponies went well in the dressage test, although they jumped a bit when the marker for P was blown across the arena. In the end I was just 2 points ahead of Philippa Gammell. As usual, I failed to keep it up and had a disastrous marathon. I thought the obstacles were much too difficult for the beginning of a season, largely because the designer had failed to include any escape routes, and also because of the very slippery muddy surface. Obstacle 3 had to be taken out altogether, as so many horse teams had come to grief in it. In obstacle 6, my whole outfit, leaders, wheelers and carriage slid past a vital gate in the mud, and the net result was that I dropped to fifth. Fortunately I managed a clear round of the cones with just 1.5 time faults. Philippa Gammell was not so fortunate. As the leader, she went in last and, after going really well, she had a major lapse, and instead of going to 15 after 14, she went through 1 backwards. This let the two Germans into first and second places and I moved up to fourth behind Georgina Frith.

Windsor came next on the calendar, and the weather could not have been a greater contrast. We had brilliant sun throughout and the going was perfect. I was equal first with Pippa Thomas in the dressage. This was in spite of the fact that Cynthia Haydon gave me 4 for one movement, for which another judge gave me 8!

Apart from the usual business of getting stuck and going wrong in the marathon obstacles, which was my fault, Dawn managed to break the bolt attaching her leader bar to the main bar and I had to finish the course using a piece of elastic rope. This had to be retied after every obstacle. At least I managed one of the only two clear rounds in the cones so that I finished sixth overall, behind Philippa Gammell. It was won by Pippa Thomas with a team of Dartmoor ponies, ahead of Kneifel from Germany, and Edwin Flerackers from Belgium.

The following weekend, the ponies made the long trip to St Fort in Fife. Weather reports indicated that, while the whole of the rest of the country was bathed in sunshine, St Fort enjoyed a persistent diet of low cloud and drizzle. My dressage was obviously not up to standard as I found myself lying third, 10 points behind Philippa Gammell and 2 points behind Pippa Thomas. This time I decided to ask Sydney Smith what she thought I was doing wrong. She ventured the opinion that the ponies were 'not sufficiently rounded', and added 'beat them and hold them', an expression picked up, no doubt, from Cynthia Haydon. This was not very helpful advice, particularly when Fell ponies are concerned. In any case, it has always seemed to me that what really matters in driving – particularly a four-in-hand – is to have a team that is light in hand and responds willingly and quickly to voice, rein and whip.

For once the marathon obstacles were a pleasure to drive and everyone had much lower scores than usual. Pippa Thomas raced away with a score of 77.4, to be followed by Georgina Frith on 92, and even I managed to get round in under 100, on 95.6, just ahead of Philippa Gammell on 96.4.

Pippa Thomas won fairly easily followed by Philippa Gammell, who had one cone down for 5 penalties, while I had 5.5 time penalties. So she beat me by more or less the difference in the dressage scores. Georgina Frith was let down by her dreadful dressage score and came fourth.

There were nine entries for Sandringham, including Ursula Hirschberg, who had not been at St Fort. Although I was equal first with Pippa Thomas in the dressage, she flew ahead of me in the marathon by some 50 points. Carrick gave me problems in section C by breaking into a canter all the time, which earned me 8 time penalties. I managed most of the obstacles – if a bit slowly – but for a near disaster in obstacle 4. We hit a post, and I was convinced the carriage was going to roll over. Fortunately, Dawn got the wrong side of another post, and in wriggling clear, the carriage hit a post on the other side and righted itself. I then had a dreadful round of the cones, largely because Dawn decided to be cranky and leant against Carrick. It was bound to end in tears and it happened in the zig-zag, when I hit two cones in succession and then a third further on. Even so, I came in fourth behind Georgina Frith, and managed to stay ahead of Ursula Hirschberg. Philippa Gammell did well in all phases, ending with a clear round of the cones. I slightly redeemed myself in the speed competition, when I did the only clear round, but it was not quite fast enough to win. It was altogether a very successful show and the weather was glorious throughout the weekend.

We made another excursion to Scotland in mid-July for the event at Drumlanrig. It started badly when I discovered that I had been given 56 penalties in the dressage, nearly 20 more than the first three competitors. It turned out that a Dutch judge had been a bit fierce and given me 20 more penalties than one of the judges, and nearly 30 more than the other judge. However, I made up for it a bit by doing – unusually for me – the second fastest round of the marathon.

As usual, it was a tough marathon course, but the weather could not have been better. The only snag was that the horse teams had done their marathon on the

Saturday in torrents of rain, which left the obstacles in a muddy mess. I was very impressed by my ponies, who were still full of energy at the end. I then rather spoilt it by hitting a cone and getting 0.5 time penalties. Fortunately, it did not make any difference as Emily Brookes had a double clear round and would have kept her third place anyway. Pippa Thomas won by some 10 points from Philippa Gammell.

Lowther followed in August and Philippa Gammell did a very good dressage test to come 6 points ahead of Pippa Thomas, and 10 ahead of everyone else. Saturday started cloudy and gradually gave way to drizzle and then to steady rain. I got through the first obstacle without trouble, but in obstacle 2, Liz tried to move a low branch out of my way, but only succeeded in nearly blinding me and knocking my hat off. Things were not made any easier by very slippery reins. In obstacle 3 the reins got twisted round the handle of the whip, which resulted in my getting a front wheel behind a stake holding a straw bale. The obstacle was on a slope, and I thought we were stuck for the day, but David got down and persuaded Tom to move over and we were free, but with 10 extra penalties for putting a groom down in an obstacle. It was a slight consolation when I heard that George Bowman had done exactly the same thing, but he got out without having to get a groom down. At least I beat Philippa Gammell through the last two obstacles!

In the cones Georgina Frith and Ken Gracey each had two down, while the rest of us had double clear rounds. I was fairly lucky to finish in fifth place. It must have been one of Philippa Gammell's best performances. Not only did she win the dressage, she went on to do the fastest marathon and rounded it off with a double clear in the cones.

One of the great features of the weekend at Lowther is the barbecue organized by the Lonsdales on the edge of the escarpment looking over the Lowther valley, with Askham Fell in the background. It is usually attended by everyone staying at Askham Hall plus any members of the family living in the vicinity, and some of the people involved in the organization of the Country Fair and Driving Event; a total of some twenty people in all. A tent is provided in case it should rain and, oddly enough, considering the average rainfall in the Lake District, I do not remember a single occasion when the party had to be abandoned.

Having done quite a lot of charcoal grilling, I took a keen interest in the equipment. I thought the charcoal grill was a fairly primitive affair, but it managed to produce sausages, chicken legs and steaks in large quantities. While the cooking was going on, all hands were employed preparing a massive bonfire. By the time everyone had filled themselves with food – and drink – the light was beginning to go and the bonfire was well under away. The only trouble with bonfires is that they can only keep one side of you warm at a time, but there was never any shortage of the stuff to keep the inner man glowing, and to stimulate the occasional song.

One year, although I am not quite sure which year it was, I noticed that the bottom of the grill had rusted through and a big hole had appeared to let the coals drop out. It so happened that the mechanical engineer at Balmoral had just completed a grill to my design, so I asked him to make another one for the Lonsdales. It had been delivered by the following year, when I had to demonstrate how the thing worked. I am glad to say that it was pronounced a success.

Fig. 6.7 This is an illustration of the charcoal grill which I gave to the Lonsdales at Lowther after their barbecue disintegrated. It has three independent racks so designed that the three interchangeable grills can be slotted-in at three different levels above the fire. The black space under the fire box is a shelf for keeping things hot. (*Balmoral Estate*)

That brought the 1992 season to an end, as far as I was concerned. The National Championships were usually at Windsor in September, by which time I had gone to Balmoral and, if I were to compete, it meant keeping the ponies up for another month without any chance of practising.

I had been rather doubtful about the ponies at the beginning of the season. Lady and Dawn had taken to leaning against each other and it was Carrick's first season. However, after a bad start they improved a great deal. Carrick turned out to be a star and went on to complete another seven seasons. I then lent him to Naomi Ferranti to get her started in driving. He lived the life of Reilly at Henbury, and Naomi once said 'If I could teach that pony to go up stairs, I'd take him to bed with me'. Tom's strength got us out of some difficult situations, and Dawn showed a remarkable agility for getting out of awkward situations.

EVENT	Dressage	Marathon	Cones	Pl/No
Brighton	1	5	3	4/9
Windsor	1=	7	1=	6/12
St Fort	3	3	1	3/6
Sandringham	2=	5	6	4/9
Drumlanrig	4	5	5	4/7
Lowther	3	7	1=	5/10

Ponies used: Dawn, Ebony, Tom, Lady, Carrick.

1993

If I had hoped that I would have fewer problems with the ponies in the 1993 season, I was sadly disappointed; in fact, it was notable for the difficulties I had with them.

I started out with both Dawn and Lady, but Dawn had taken to shying at everything, and nothing, and caused endless trouble by leaning against her neighbour. When we were returning to the stables after a practice outing in April, she leant so heavily on Sacha, a new pony, that when Sacha stopped pushing back, Dawn fell over. Lady's problem was that she had taken to going along bent like a banana. There was nothing for it but to drop both of them from the team.

I had planned to start the new pony, Sacha – Gina's daughter – anyway, but dropping two ponies meant that I also had to bring in another young pony, Myrtle, who I had intended to bring in the following year. She had to do a crash course, but she took to the job without a qualm.

It was, however, now quite evident that Tom was no good in the lead and that Carrick's inclination to break into a canter when in the lead, meant that I had no option but to put them together in the wheel, where they did extremely well in the marathon. In addition, Carrick could not be trusted to maintain the right paces in the dressage, and he was also inclined to start cantering the moment he saw a pair of cones; and Tom hated any noise behind him and had a nasty habit of jumping forward whenever I hit a cone! In fact, on one occasion, when I was practising down by the Thames, I got a cone stuck under the carriage and he took off. Having prevented them from plunging into the Thames, I let them go along the bank and then galloped them round the tan track until they had had enough.

Fortunately, Ebony, who had been in the team since 1984, was still up to going in the wheel for the dressage and cones, which left me with Sacha and Myrtle to go in the lead. Unfortunately there was obviously something chronically wrong with Sacha's metabolism. On the whole, Fell pony mares do not react very strongly to being in season, but while Sacha behaved perfectly normally in the stables and on exercise, the moment she was put under pressure in the obstacles, and sometimes in the cones, she behaved exactly as if she had come violently into season. It did not noticeably affect Sacha's own performance, but it certainly distracted the others, particularly the two male wheelers!

All these anxieties about the ponies, made me set off for Brighton with considerable trepidation, but my dressage went rather better than I had dared hope. I was 0.7 points behind Philippa Gammell and just 3 in front of Georgina Frith. John Robertson was fourth, with two newcomers, Carl Barnard and Alison Leggett, fifth and sixth. I was consistently slow through the obstacles, although, this time, I did get round a bit faster than Philippa Gammell. Georgina Frith raced away, and Carl Barnard did very well to keep within 20 points of her. I very nearly caught him in the cones, but he had a double clear while I got 8 time penalties, which meant that he beat me into second place by 0.8 points. Philippa Gammell made a mistake in obstacle 4 and then, unusually for her, accumulated 11 time penalties in the cones, which dropped her to fourth place.

Fig. 6.8 Accidents do happen occasionally, but modern cross-country carriages are so robust that they seldom get damaged. Inexperienced horses can take off for some distance, but in most cases they calm down fairly quickly and are not often hurt in any way. This carriage overturned at Brighton in 1993. (*Alf Baker*)

Six of the eleven entries for Windsor were foreigners. The five natives were Ursula Hirschberg, Philippa Gammell, Carl Barnard, Georgina Frith and me. In spite of my anxieties about the ponies, they went reasonably well in the dressage, but our 51.3 did not look good against Philippa Gammell's 37, although it did get me into third place. Two Germans were eliminated in the marathon and Carl Barnard had to retire, so I was fortunate to end up sixth in the marathon.

I collected 1.5 time penalties in the cones, but that did not alter my final placing. Poor Philippa Gammell had a real disaster in the cones. She was comfortably in the lead with 15 points or three cones in hand when she hit three cones and collected a further 10.5 time penalties and dropped her to second behind Edwin Flerackers. Needless to say, she was desperately disappointed to miss the chance of winning the only international event in this country. Georgina Frith had a good marathon, but failed to make third place after she hit no less than four cones.

Only Philippa Gammell and I turned up at St Fort for the pony-teams class. By now, I was resigned to the maddening behaviour of the ponies and not all that surprised to find myself some 10 points behind her after the dressage. We both had dramas in the marathon, and, in spite of having to get both grooms down in obstacle 2, she beat me by just 6 points. In the cones phase, she had one cone down

Fig. 6.9 Ursula Hirschberg had done brilliantly with a tandem before moving to a team. She had a particular talent for driving the marathon obstacles, but she was rather too frequently let down by her dressage. Growing children and other distractions persuaded her to move to the pairs class, but I suspect her heart lies with the team. Here, she is driving through an obstacle at the National Championships at Windsor in 1993. (*Alf Baker*)

and 12 time penalties, while I collected 7.5 time penalties, which made Philippa the winner by 6.6 points. It shows just how much it pays to do well in the dressage.

The usual 'hardy annuals' such as the Derby, the Birthday Parade, Garter Weekend and Ascot Week stop me attending any events in June until the end of the month, and so Sandringham was my next event. I had yet another change of team: I risked Carrick and Myrtle together in the lead and Tom and Ebony in the wheel for the dressage. It was not a huge success, made worse by my making a silly mistake, although, according to the marks, it went unnoticed by one of the judges. The test was, however, just good enough to put me in second place behind Philippa Gammell and just ahead of Ursula Hirschberg.

I put Sacha and Myrtle in the lead for the marathon. All went well to start with, and only Philippa Gammell and I managed all the sections without penalties but, when it came to the obstacles, the ponies had one of their obstinate days, or I was too slow with the reins. At any rate I went very wrong in obstacle 1 and had quite a problem finding the best way to get back on course. However, real disaster struck at the water. Myrtle tried to refuse to go in, and then Sacha kicked over a trace on the way out, so David had to get down to sort it out. This was just as well as I made a hash of getting to gate C and got wrapped round a post. As David was already down, he was able to push the leaders into the right gap without incurring further penalties. But that was not the end of our misfortunes. A leader rein slipped from my hand as we went through the water for the third time and we came out through the wrong slot. I had to do an extra circle to put things right. All that notched up some 33 penalties, which I could ill afford. Apart from shying at the bridge over the ditch in obstacle 4, we managed to get through that and obstacle 5 without trouble, but in obstacles 6 and 8 the leaders went their own way again, which cost me further penalties. In spite of all that, I only slipped to third place, but 33 points behind Philippa Gammell and 29 behind Ursula Hirschberg.

We all had clear rounds with a few time penalties, so the order was not changed. There were four with clear rounds and we were invited to take part in a drive-off. The ponies went really well and cantered virtually the whole way round as if they had done it every day of their lives, whereas this was the first time they had ever done it as a team. I went faster than Ursula Hirschberg while poor Philippa Gammell overshot in the slalom, so at least I won that.

There are strict rules about designing courses and then competing over them, but I did not think that this applied to making suggestions where sections A, B, C and D might go at Sandringham. As I always spent January there, I had time to look around and suggest a different route for these sections each year. Most other courses tend to be repeated, with minor variations, or in the reverse direction. Finding a new course of the correct length, and so that the sections follow on from each other and end up fairly close to the start of E is rather more complicated that it might appear. The important thing is to avoid, if possible, any section crossing a public road, which the police would not care to close on a Saturday. If there are any busy roads in the way, the art is to arrange for one section to end on one side of the road and the next to begin on the other. Competitors can then cross the road during a lull in the traffic. In addition the two compulsory halts need to be accessible to timekeepers and back-up crews without using the course itself. I have always thought that it would be nice to arrange for the halts to be near a pub, but that is seldom possible. It is even more difficult since the distance for section A has been reduced by the FEI.

I remember trying to find the route for the 1993 event, because I wanted to take it through a field of lavender and then along the Babingley River. I find it is better to start measuring at the point where I want the section to finish and work backwards, because it is often easier to adjust the starting point. Even so, I had to put in all sorts of kinks and loops to make it come out at the right point. The required speed for section C is not particularly demanding, but it can be made rather more interesting by including as many turns and loops as possible. The walk sections, on the other hand, can be rather tight for time, and most competitors only get in with seconds to spare. On the whole, competitors do not appreciate rough going, hills or tight turns in the walk sections. They are also averse to other distractions. I remember a walk at Streatlam later in 1993, which went through a field full of sheep. Fell ponies are nothing if not inquisitive, and mine are not accustomed to sheep; cattle they know and tolerate, but not sheep, and they all hate pigs. On this occasion I had the greatest difficulty in preventing them from investigating every one of these intriguing woolly things as I tried to keep them on the course. I only just made the time and, by the end, I was in a state of nervous exhaustion.

Having suggested the course, I leave it to the course designer to make the detailed measurements, and to mark it so that competitors cannot cut corners. This has been a problem ever since the competition started and was the main reason why competitors were originally required to take a referee with them to ensure that they followed the intended track. Even so, some course designers are a bit lax when it comes to marking the course. When I was with the FEI I had the greatest difficulty trying to prevent the Driving Committee from introducing rules which said that competitors had to keep to within so many metres of the track shown on the map. I thought this was unrealistic and maintained that it was up to the course designer to place the compulsory turning flags so that competitors could not materially reduce the distance they were required to travel, while giving them a little discretion in choosing a route.

I had an opportunity to make this point at the European Championships in Switzerland in 1981, where one of the walk sections had been measured along a farm track with only the start and finish marked with flags. The track had a kink in it and I noticed that, if I went across an adjoining field, I could cut the corner. I took the precaution of pointing this out to the President of the jury and asked whether I would be breaking the rules if I took the direct route. He could not object, but I told him that I was only going to take this short cut to make the point that it was up to the course designer to mark the course properly. I was not very popular at the time, but course marking thereafter improved considerably.

Streatlam in County Durham was the venue for the next event and I stayed with the owners, Nigel and Ailsa Pease at Sledwich. Streatlam is a glorious estate with views across the Tees valley. The house was built by John Bowes (the Bowes of the Bowes Lyon family and Earls of Strathmore) in the late eighteenth century. Queen Elizabeth, my mother-in-law, spent some of her childhood there, but in 1926 her father, the Earl of Strathmore, sold the property to Mrs Marshall Field, the wife of a wealthy American and a relation of the local Pease family, to whom it eventually passed. The house had been allowed to fall into ruin after the First World War and was subsequently pulled down with only the orangery left standing. Mr Bowes had owned the Triple Crown Winner, West Australian, and when the horse died he had him buried at Streatlam. I noticed the grave as we were walking the obstacles.

There were only three entries and I trailed Philippa Gammell all the way, although I was slightly faster through two of the obstacles, and ended up 14 points behind her. Carl Barnard was the only other entry and he had to retire in the second obstacle. In obstacle 3 there was an option to go down a short, but quite steep, bank to get to gate A by the shortest route. It looked a bit daunting, but I knew that the two wheelers happened to be very good at holding the carriage back while going downhill and I thought I would give it a go. I had invited Brian McGrath to come with me round the marathon course. He knew about this option and urged me to take it, but I had not told him which route I intended to take. As we approached the obstacle, he said 'I dare you to take the direct route'. Down we went, and I have a photograph of the wheelers sliding down almost on their back-sides and it shows Brian clutching his straw hat with one hand and clinging to the carriage with the other. The look on his face suggests that he wished he had kept his mouth shut. All went well and I managed to make the best time through this obstacle of any of the teams.

It was great fun doing an event in a new place, and it was made all the better by considerate hosts and a spell of good weather. Unfortunately, the Streatlam event only lasted for three years, although it has to be said that it was not an ideal

Fig 6.10 a and b I invited Brian McGrath to come with me on the marathon course at Streatlam in July 1993. In obstacle 3 there was an option to go down a fairly steep slope and gain a few metres. Brian McGrath had dared me to take this short cut. I said I would think about it, but I did not let him know that I had decided to go that way. Photograph a) shows the moment when he realized that I was going down the slope and b) illustrates how the wheelers tucked their hind legs under them and simply slid down the slope, almost on their bottoms. (*Nick Morris*)

location for such an event. The only access for competitors and spectators to the area with the obstacles was down the main drive. The fields on either side are used for grazing sheep, and the fences are so close to the road that two-way traffic was not at all easy.

Drumlanrig came the following weekend. The seventeenth-century pink sandstone castle is set in an amphitheatre surrounded by formal gardens and wooded hills. I had stayed there in the early 1950s with Johnny Buccleuch's father and mother, the glamorous Mollie. Johnny and Jane made us wonderfully comfortable and the weather was perfect.

This would make it three events on successive weekends, but the ponies seemed as lively as ever and the two girls were getting really good as leaders. I was only 1.7 behind Philippa Gammell in the dressage, but just 1 point ahead of Georgina Frith, who was beginning to show her true form. The obstacles were nice and open, but this meant that speed counted almost more than skill. However, I made a bad guess in obstacle 1 and took the long route only to find that Philippa Gammell, Georgina Frith and Ursula Hirschberg had taken the short route and got away with it. I did at least beat Philippa Gammell in obstacle 4. Georgina Frith had to put a groom down in 4, but even so she was breathing down my neck only 1.8 points behind by the end. Philippa Gammell did a clear round of the cones, but with Georgina Frith so close behind me I was quite relieved when she hit one. It was just as well she did as I went in and managed to knock over one of the very

Fig. 6.11 The start of the marathon at the Drumlanrig event in July 1993 was right in front of the dramatic seventeenth-century castle. This photograph was taken by the Dowager Duchess of Northumberland, the Duke of Buccleuch's sister. The course then went up into the magnificent woods before coming down again to the obstacles in the park below the castle. (*Elizabeth, Duchess of Northumberland*)

first pair. Things went better after that, but Brian McGrath and the castle spectators were in a perfect frenzy of anxiety during the rest of my performance. Fortunately for their nerves, I just managed to keep my second place.

I had noticed for some time that all was not well with the grooms. David was having trouble with the Elizabeths, who were becoming inclined to do their own thing, so much so that I had to read the riot act to them. Furthermore, I had heard rumours that David had been offered a very good job in Saudi Arabia. I was anxious that he would not be encouraged to accept simply to get away from the girls.

Fig. 6.12 I came second out of five at the 1993 event at Drumlanrig. David Muir (Jun) is sitting next to me and the two glamorous Elizabeths are holding the ponies. The event was abandoned in 1999 when the organizer, John Cowdery, decided to retire. It was a very popular event and its demise was much regretted by all competitors. As I was fortunate enough to be invited to stay in the castle, I had a particular reason to feel sad when it came to an end. (*Author's collection*)

Lowther was in the first week in August but, while I was at Cowes, the news came through that King Baudouin of the Belgians had died in Spain, and that the funeral was to be on the following Saturday – marathon day – in Brussels and I had been deputed to attend. I managed to do the dressage on the Friday, and was second, yet again, to Philippa Gammell. I flew to Brussels on the Saturday morning and, as there was no hope of my getting back in time to do the marathon, I asked Jim Corbett, the President of the jury, whether David Muir could drive the ponies in that phase. He managed to get the other competitors to agree, but, having done well in obstacles 1 and 2, David got in a muddle in 3 and broke the pole, so he had to retire.

I went in first to drive the cones and got round without hitting anything, but I accumulated 4 time penalties. Only Ursula Hirschberg managed a double clear round, so I came in second in that phase. Georgina Frith won, but only 5 points ahead of Ursula Hirschberg with Philippa Gammell in third place.

This was the end of an odd season. It started badly with both Dawn and Lady having to be retired, and Myrtle dropped in the deep end at short notice. After a shaky start, things got better and by the end the two leaders were doing really well.

In October, I was invited by Finn Caspersen to watch the World Championships for Pairs of Horses at Gladstone in New Jersey. I stayed with Finn and his wife Barbara at their very comfortable house at Hamilton Farm. The event was brilliantly organized in ideal country, and the standard of driving was impressive. Having seen the way they got round the obstacles, I was quite glad that I was not in their class!

RESULTS FOR 1993

EVENT	Dressage	Marathon	Cones	Pl/No
Brighton	2	2	3	3/6
Windsor	2	8	2	6/11
St Fort	2	2	1	2/2
Sandringham	3	3	2	3/8
Streatlam	2	2	2	2/3
Drumlanrig	2	2	2=	2/5
Lowther	3	R	2	7/7

Ponies used: Dawn, Ebony, Tom, Lady, Carrick, Sacha, Myrtle.

These accounts of competitions make it look as if nothing else goes on in the driving world. This is a false impression. Every so often the FEI Bulletin appears with changes to the rules, and it is quite certain that many competitors do not read them. I have frequently attended British Horse Driving Trials Association Judges Clinics, where everyone tries to improve their judging abilities. I cannot do any judging of the marathon or cones phases while competing at the same event, so I have been principally concerned with judging the dressage phase at Windsor Park Equestrian Club events, as I can judge classes other than my own, while competing myself.

I have always been deeply impressed by the ability of riders to train horses for the ridden dressage competitions. As the President of the FEI has his own box beside the arena at the Olympic Games, I was able to watch the world's best dressage riders. If anything, I am even more impressed by the dressage horses. They are made to do what appear to be highly unnatural movements with patience and grace. I know that some of the very best horse-team drivers train their horses to a high standard of ridden dressage, but I have always remained somewhat sceptical about making too close a comparison between ridden and driven dressage. For one thing, everyone accepts that it takes years to train a dressage horse, and probably even longer to train dressage riders. The trouble about driving is that it is a combined event based on the ridden three-day event. Dressage is only one of the three phases, and I think most drivers would agree that coping with the marathon obstacles and the cones demands as much, if not more, training and practice than the dressage. It is worth repeating that the relative value of the three phases is intended to be 3:12:1. That translates into scores of 30 for the dressage, 120 for the marathon and the equivalent of two cones down (under current rules, one cone down incurs 5 penalties).

Therefore, many of the more erudite dressage expressions mean little or nothing to the ordinary driver. The challenge for them is to get their pony/horse or ponies/horses to follow the sequence of movements demanded by the test as accurately as possible and at the correct paces. For beginners, or even for quite experienced competitors, the following description of the collected trot in the rule book cannot mean very much:

> The pace is slower than the working trot. The neck is raised enabling the shoulders to move with more ease, the hocks being engaged. Impulsion is maintained notwithstanding the slower movement. The steps are shorter and lighter and more mobile.

I have to admit that, when I was editing the original *FEI Rules for Driving Events*, I lifted that piece directly from the FEI Rules for the dressage competition in three-day events. I did not have a clue what most of it meant, but I thought it sounded impressive.

An accomplished dressage rider may know how to 'engage the hocks' while sitting on a horse, but I must confess that I have never had the slightest idea quite how to persuade my ponies to arrive at this apparently desirable physical contortion while pulling a carriage; least of all while driving a 20 m circle at a collected trot with the reins in one hand. Nor have I ever been able to recognize this in any of the novice dressage tests I have ever judged.

The trouble, I suspect, started when the word 'dressage' was chosen for the driven competition; I think a better term would have been 'compulsory figures'. As a result of calling it 'dressage', I suspect that the judges of driven dressage are rather too inclined to equate it with ridden dressage, and a number of very competent ridden dressage judges have been invited to give their opinions at conferences for driven dressage judges. I have not been entirely unsuccessful in driven dressage, but I would never dream of telling a dressage rider how to ride a test. I will be quite prepared to listen to any dressage rider or judge, who can get up on a box seat, and demonstrate to me how to drive a dressage test with a four-in-hand.

Only recently, I was judging some single-pony novice drivers, and I had to stop one for going wrong, which happens to everyone sooner or later. I got out of my car to explain what had happened and what I wanted her to do next. At the end of the test, I got out again to have a word with her and suggest how she might improve her test. She apologized – quite unnecessarily – for going wrong, and then said 'You will hardly believe it, but I used to do ridden dressage', so I said 'I expect you find this a bit different' and her emphatic reply was 'This is completely different'. It was music to my ears!

Apart from the judging of dressage, there are endless arguments about every other driving topic. When 'knock-down' – or what the FEI describes as 'dislodgeable' – elements were introduced to marathon obstacles, there was a fierce argument about what form they should take. They have varied from quite substantial poles fixed into small holes in the ground by breakable pegs, to strips of wood stuck onto the sides of gates by Velcro, and golf balls placed in bottle tops nailed to the tops of gate posts. The snag with the poles is that, when they are broken off, they are quite capable of getting between the spokes of a carriage wheel, or between horses' legs or other dangerous places.

Then there are problems with bizarre decisions by judges. Some took the view that if the penalty for knocking a ball off a cone was 5 penalties, then knocking off the other ball in the same pair of cones incurred a further 5 penalties. When to ring the bell to stop a competitor after they have got into trouble in a 'multiple' obstacle, is also frequently a problem for judges of cones competitions. There was almost an international incident when a competitor at an international championship, inadvertently hit a pair of cones, which were not on his route, while driving from one pair to the next in sequence. The quite reasonable decision of the judge was to eliminate the competitor for taking the wrong course, but the outcry was such that the rule was subsequently changed.

Among the most difficult people to contend with are the legally-minded, who work on the principle that anything that is not specifically forbidden is allowed. The inevitable consequence is that every time this happens, a new rule has to be introduced. New rules are splendid, as far as rules committees, and the legally-minded competitors are concerned, but the problem is to ensure that all competitors take the trouble to read the new rules. In my experience, many competitors are loath to read the rules until they have been caught infringing one of them. From then on these competitors are inclined to see all rules and all judges as pointless, unreasonable and bureaucratic.

This is hardly fair. Judging is no easy matter. Watching an endless procession of dressage tests on a warm day can be soporific – until you suddenly suspect that someone has gone wrong, and you have to decide within seconds to sound the hooter. In a recent case, I was a spectator when a judge in a cones competition thought that a driver had missed the number 14 pair of cones, but only rang the bell after the driver had passed 16. There was then a long discussion as the driver was adamant that he had gone through 14. After some delay the announcer explained that the driver had indeed gone through 14 and would be allowed to drive the course again, and that any penalties incurred in the second round up to and including 16 would not count. I am sure it was the right decision, but there is nothing in the rule book about such a case.

Having spent quite a lot of time and thought in writing rules, I have come to the conclusion that it is quite impossible to anticipate every conceivable situation. The most unlikely things can, and do, happen, and it is the business of the judges to make common-sense decisions.

CHAPTER SEVEN

MICKY TO THE RESCUE

1994–1996

MY ANXIETIES ABOUT DAVID MUIR proved right and he went off to his new job in Saudi Arabia at the end of the 1993 season. The two Elizabeths told me that they were perfectly capable of managing the team, but I was a bit doubtful about keeping them on. They were certainly capable enough, but their behaviour towards David during the previous season did not fill me with confidence. I therefore found myself at the end of the season with six ponies and no grooms at all.

This was a fairly desperate situation, but I had heard through the driving grapevine that Micky Flynn had returned from a job in America. I had always greatly admired the way he trained and produced – and also drove – Alan Bristow's team of Hungarian horses, and I just wondered whether he might be interested in looking after the Fell ponies. I managed to get in touch with him, and discovered that he was presently at a loose end, but he protested that he had never had anything to do with ponies in his life. I think he was a little unsure about the idea of coping with ponies after a lifetime spent with heavy horses and carriage horses. Anyway, in September 1993 I invited him to come to Balmoral to talk about taking them – and me – on. I was delighted when Micky agreed and he now admits that Fell ponies are great characters and that he really rather enjoys working with them. I am quite certain that without him I would have given up competing long ago.

By one of those strange coincidences, Norton Romsey (grandson of Lord Mountbatten), Penny, his wife, and Micky were on the same flight to Aberdeen and they came out to Balmoral in the same transport. Penny had not thought of starting to drive at that time and had no idea that Micky would soon be teaching her and getting her started in competition carriage driving.

It was only later that year, while I was staying at Broadlands, that Penny Romsey referred to my interest in this 'driving thing', and asked me whether it might be possible to teach her daughter's pony Campion to pull a trap. She had found an old two-wheeler in a loft and a set of harness, and she thought it might be fun to drive the pony round the estate while her daughter was away at boarding school. I told her that I was sure it would be possible, and that Micky Flynn would be just the chap to train the pony and teach her to drive him. However, I also told her that on no account should she use the old trap and harness. There was no knowing what condition they might be in, and that more accidents occurred as a result of broken harness or a defective carriage than for any other reason. If she wanted to pursue the idea, I said I would lend her a modern four-wheeler and a set of New Zealand Zilco harness. I also said that there was really no point in just driving round the estate; what she needed was an incentive to drive. I suggested that she had the option of going in for 'pleasure driving', which comes under the British Driving Society, or she could try 'combined driving', which comes under the auspices of the British Horse Driving Trials Association. She had not the slightest idea what she might be letting herself in for, but she agreed to have a go at the latter and, in the spring of 1994, she started serious driving lessons with Micky Flynn.

Meanwhile, the 1994 season started badly and got steadily worse. Micky brought the ponies to Sandringham in January for his first experience of driving Fell ponies in a Norfolk winter, and we began the cold process of getting them fit. We started by taking them out in two pairs. One memorable morning in early January, I took the old hands, Tom and Carrick, while he took the two girls, Myrtle and Sacha. I cannot remember exactly what set them off, but quite suddenly Myrtle and Sacha took off down the hill past Appleton Farm. They shot close past a bramble bush, which took off Micky's cap, and on down the road until he managed to drive them into a thicket, and stop them. Fortunately, no serious harm was done (although Micky hit his knee against a tree) and we went on.

When I had problems with pulling horses at Sandringham, I used to drive them into the nearest ploughed field until they settled down. I mentioned this to Micky and suggested that he might try this treatment if they ever attempted to run away again. It so happened that they were silly enough to have another go just as we were passing a particularly soft ploughed field. Micky put them into it and within a few strides they had given it up as a bad idea. I do not think they ever tried running away again. That was the first of a series of misadventures in 1994.

Later in the spring, I thought I would invite Penny Romsey to come for a drive with me in Windsor Great Park, just to give her an idea of what the combined driving competitions were all about. I took her out with the team while Micky took her daughter with the two spare ponies. After a pleasant and uneventful drive, I took the team to the Cannon Ground, near Cumberland Lodge, where the Windsor Park Equestrian Club driving events are held. At the top end of the ground there is a large dewpond, which is used by the club as a water obstacle. I was driving an experienced team and I had just pottered slowly through a couple of the other club obstacles, so I thought I would end up by taking the team through the water.

Unfortunately, and for some inexplicable reason, the shackle, which holds the swingle trees to the end of the pole, chose that precise moment to come off. The swingle trees fell onto the leaders' hind legs and they were off. I had buckled the reins together, so I was able to hold onto them for a short time, but my arms were getting longer and longer and I was halfway over the dashboard. The next thing I knew, we were heading straight for a fence. Luckily, the leaders decided against jumping it and turned sharp right instead. When drivers have to hold the reins with both hands, they cannot hold onto any part of the carriage in moments of crisis. The result in this case was that this sudden turn caused me to leave the carriage describing a graceful parabola through the air, and into the long grass.

The leaders then set off on their own, while Penny Romsey and the girl groom were left with the galloping wheelers, unable to do anything to stop them. The groom suggested baling out, but Penny Romsey was against the idea, and tried to stop them by grabbing one of the cruppers (the loop that goes under the tail). Fortunately, they turned towards Micky, who was watching all this with the pair standing quietly under a tree, and the wheelers decided they had no reason to be exerting themselves to such an extent and stopped. Meanwhile I picked myself up from the grass and started off in search of the leaders. I was relieved to see that they had only got as far as the gate in the fence where they had just stopped and were standing there looking, I thought, faintly embarrassed.

To say that the leaders might have been embarrassed is nothing to what I felt. I had spent years trying, so far unsuccessfully, to get various friends and relations to take up this sport and now, just as I thought I had one about to take the hook, this had to happen. I need not have worried, the new recruit turned out to be made of sterner stuff, and went on to survive several rather more unpleasant accidents without losing interest or having a nervous breakdown.

Micky Flynn had no difficulty in training Campion, and teaching Penny Romsey to drive him, but it soon turned out that, whenever her daughter came home from school, she wanted to ride her pony or take him hunting. This was all right until the hunting clashed with a WPEC weekend. Fortunately, my old pony, Ebony, was available as she had just been retired after ten years with the team, and so I offered to lend her to Penny. She turned out to be a brilliant 'teacher' and I think it was largely owing to Ebony that Penny Romsey continued her foray into this new sport. That episode in the Cannon Ground dewpond was the second in the series of disasters in that memorable season.

The first WPEC event in March did not go well. Sacha's metabolic affliction seemed to be worse, and I collected a lot of penalties in the dressage. Carrick was too exuberant in the cones, but at least the team went reasonably well through the obstacles.

When I had the horses, I used to practise dressage on the East Slopes of Windsor Castle, but the arena took up part of the golf course, and I was not very popular with the Household Golf Club. I was aware of a small triangular field down by the Thames, which I was sure the Farm Manager would be delighted to give up, and he agreed to take it out of cultivation and put it down to grass. I was then able to use it for both dressage and cones practice. However, the field happens to be right next to the water obstacle used for the Royal Windsor Horse Show driving event, and it did not take long for the Chairman of the Driving Committee, Joe Moore, to notice that it had been put down to grass, and he thought it would be just the place for the dressage and cones competitions for that event.

Incidentally, the water feature is reputed to have been made as a swimming pool for King Charles II. The pool is fed by a stream, the Broadwater, which comes off the Thames, and passes under the Riverside Station and Datchet Road into the Home Park. It widens out into a pool just before rejoining the Thames. At the castle end of the avenue, beside the Broadwater, there is a sluice gate, which used to feed what are now the remains of a Victorian skating rink. You can still see the depression with an island in the middle. The old rink has been used as the site for a driving obstacle for several of the Windsor events.

I could hardly refuse Joe Moore's idea, but it meant that I had to find somewhere else to practise. I then got hold of a part of the immense and unused walled kitchen garden on the south-eastern edge of the Home Park. The difficulty with any pre-season practice area is that heavy use of it early on, while the ground is still wet, cuts it up badly for the rest of the year. Spring 1994 was wet and this meant that preparation for Brighton was severely hampered.

Rachel, my second girl groom, had gone off for a weekend in Cornwall from which she failed to return. We only discovered later that she had had an accident in her car, but had not told us anything about it. Fortunately, Griselda, one of the Queen's riding grooms, volunteered to help us over the crisis. She might well have thought better of it had she known that when the party arrived at Stanmer Park for the Brighton event, they had to put up the portable stabling for the first time that year in pouring rain.

In what could only have been a desperate measure, we put Tom in the lead with Myrtle, and Sacha in the wheel with a new pony, Storm. I had tried out this arrangement at Windsor, and although Sacha's affliction was not so evident, she was obviously not very happy in the wheel. In the event, it was not an unqualified success. Tom was never a natural leader. I suspected he was short-sighted, because he shied at virtually anything remotely unusual. He started by shying at a puddle on the way into the arena and then thought that the mark at X was something seriously dangerous. Both leaders were fascinated by the spectators, and went down the sides of the arena with their heads cocked sideways. At the rein-back, Tom tripped over his own feet, and everything went sideways. I thought I was very lucky to be only 6 points behind the leaders, Georgina Frith and Philippa Gammell, who were tied on 38.7. Alison Leggett and John Robertson were not far behind.

As it rained all day on Saturday, the marathon course had been shortened, and obstacle 8 was taken out altogether. There is nothing more awkward than trying to steer a team through the marathon obstacles in pouring rain. Gloves get sodden, the reins get slippery or stiff and sticky, water gets down your neck and, as likely as not, you get an eyeful, or a mouthful, of mud. Furthermore, waterproof over-trousers usually have a slit in the front. This is perfectly acceptable under a long jacket and when standing up but it is not quite such a good idea when sitting on a box seat, as the water runs down the front of the coat and straight into the slit. You soon know about it when the rain is heavy and persistent.

Alison Leggett gave me a slight breathing space when she clocked up 8 time penalties in the cones. However, I made a mess of 12 and then nudged the very last pair, to which another 3 time penalties had to be added, making 13 penalties to Alison's 8, and I therefore dropped to fourth.

The dressage at the Windsor event took place in what had been my practice field and, in spite of heavy rain on the Thursday morning, it stood up to the eight classes in two days very well. Nine pony teams were entered, including Peter Schenk from Austria, Tobias Bucker and Diethelm Kneifel, both from Germany, and our old friend, Edwin Flerackers, from Belgium.

I reverted to Sacha and Myrtle in the lead with Tom and Storm in the wheel for the dressage. I did not think much of my performance, but the judges thought it was good enough to put me in second place, 1 point behind Georgina Frith and the same ahead of Philippa Gammell.

Saturday started fine and sunny, and the pony teams got through the marathon in the dry. It then started to rain and the whole horse-teams class had to go round in very unpleasant conditions. All of them got soaked and several turned over on the slippery surface.

I was delighted with the way the ponies were going in the early sections of the marathon, and set off to do the obstacles full of confidence. All went well in the first three, but then disaster struck in a big way in obstacle 4, the water. Apart from having to go through the water several times, it also involved crossing and then recrossing a wooden bridge. I had a bit of a struggle getting the ponies back onto the bridge, and I must have got a bit too close to the rails on the way off it. The next thing I knew I was out of my seat and flying through the air to the left. I landed on my back beside Tom's hind legs, with my right foot trapped over the splinter bar and under the turntable. Very luckily for me, the ponies only went a few yards down the slope before they came against a rail and stopped. Tom was dancing about a bit and trod on my arm and then pinned me to the ground by standing on the sleeve of my jersey.

I am not quite sure what my referee thought of all this, but as an experienced tandem driver (later to become a very successful team driver), Emily Brookes remained cool and collected throughout this minor drama. Micky very quickly freed my foot and I was back on the box, and we were away again in a very short time.

Fig. 7.1 Emily Brookes was unfortunate enough to be my referee at the 1994 Windsor event. She was not to know that it was to be my *annus horribilis*, with no less than eight disasters. At this event I was pitched off the box seat after crossing the bridge at the water obstacle – fortunately not into the water.
(*Alf Baker*)

I reckoned that we had only been in the obstacle for an extra minute, but the problem, of course, was that I had accumulated an extra 50 penalties for having the driver (30) and both grooms (10 each) down in an obstacle. I managed to finish section E in the time, but I was naturally last on points. This was the third of the series of mishaps in this year.

When I went back to the scene of the problem, I discovered that there was a small stump, just on the course side of the post and rails as you came off the bridge. I could only conclude that, when I got so close to the rails, I must have driven over this stump and, at the speed we were going, it was enough to pitch me out. I made sure that the offending stump was removed before the next event.

The rain continued well into Saturday night, and by the morning it was obvious that all the events in the main show grounds would have to be cancelled. However, there is a cinder arena, now a car park, on the south side of the castle, which had been built as a practice arena for the King's Troop when its barracks at St John's Wood were being modernized. It was decided that the cones could be run on that arena, even though it was a bit cramped.

The competition only produced one double clear round by Germany's Tobias Bucker, but Philippa Gammell had enough points in hand, after a very good dressage test, to be able to afford to have one cone down and 8 time penalties and still win by the slender margin of 4 points from Flerackers. This made up for her missing the previous chance to win this international event. I did a clear round with just 3.5 time penalties and managed to beat Ursula Hirschberg by 0.6 points to end up in eighth place.

There was one bright spot in all this. *Horse & Hound* reported as follows, and my comments are in italic:

Britain's pony drivers were awarded The Duke of Edinburgh's Trophy for the third year running and this time the trophy was won by a team led by The Duke of Edinburgh, driving The Queen's team of Fell ponies, along with pairs driver Mike Dingwall *[also Fells]* and Anne Gilbert with her single Hackney pony. Although Prince Philip was tipped out when his carriage hit a bump in the Knightsbridge obstacle, his second place in the dressage helped the team to overall victory.

In the pairs Section, the position was reversed with the top three places being filled by Germany's Andreas Pues-Tillkamp and Detlef Randzio and Holland's Jaap Verboom. John Pickford, who was third after the dressage, lost a wheel in obstacle six and had to retire. National champion, Ian Barlow, was the highest placed British driver in fifth place overall.

British drivers shone in the singles Section with Sally Moreton winning the competition driving her husband Ivor's Section D gelding Thorneyside Echo.

Scottish driver Anne Gilbert *[later to become a successful tandem driver]* was sixth after the dressage but won the marathon and went on to take second place overall.

John Pickford was later to compete with a team of ponies with considerable success. Mike Dingwall was doing very well with his pair of Fells, but he lost several of his ponies when his farm in Aberdeenshire was attacked by grass sickness. He eventually sold his farm and moved elsewhere and gave up driving.

The 'Hampshire Remembers D-Day' event on the Friday prevented me from getting to St Fort until late that day. As I had assumed that this was to be another two-day event, I was not unduly bothered, until I discovered that it had become a three-day event, and I was due to drive the dressage on the Friday. However, Philippa Gammell was the only other competitor, so we arranged to do our dressage on the Saturday morning and the marathon in the afternoon.

I just managed to get ahead of her by 0.6 points in the dressage, and things in the marathon were just as close until the very last obstacle. I heard snatches of the commentary as we went through the obstacles and I got the impression that we were just keeping ahead of her. I later discovered that I beat her in obstacles 1, 4, 6 and 7, and we had the same time in 5. It all fell apart in the last obstacle when I allowed a little too much room round a post and hit the post on the outside of the turn. Things got a bit confused after that and I went through gate D backwards, collecting 20 penalties, and had to go round and go through C again. I did not improve matters in the cones as I hit two and added 6.5 time penalties, so Philippa Gammell won fairly easily.

After a very encouraging performance at St Fort – apart from the last obstacle – I was rather hoping for a good result at Sandringham. Sadly it was not to be. I did a diabolical dressage test, or at least one of the judges thought so, and I could only manage third place. That evening I took all the pony-teams drivers, with their husbands/fathers/wives to the Anmer log cabin for a barbecue. The country was bone dry and it was a beautiful evening until a series of the biggest thunderstorms I had ever seen boiled up over Hillington. We were all so intent on watching the dramatic display of lightning that we never noticed another storm creeping up behind us, until a sudden explosion unleashed a torrent of rain, and those standing outside got quite wet before reaching shelter only a few yards away. After that everyone left fairly smartly to see to their ponies. A thunderstorm did hit the stable field, but luckily no harm was done. We got back to Wood Farm to find the electricity had failed, but we managed to get to bed quite easily by the light of the almost continuous lightning.

I am not sure what got into the ponies when we started section E of the marathon. They were completely sluggish and would only meander round the obstacles in a daze. They may have been unable to sleep during the thunderstorms, although none of the other teams appeared to have been affected. The ponies' lethargy was certainly nothing to do with the obstacles, which, if anything, were bigger and more open than usual. A new course builder had just been appointed to replace Tish Roberts, not because of his designs, but purely because Tish tended to ruin the nerves of the organizing committee by leaving things to the very last moment.

Georgina Frith did the only double clear round and beat Philippa Gammell by 14.6 points overall. I ended up 4th, 7 points behind Ursula Hirschberg.

At Drumlanrig I achieved yet another dreadful dressage score. This was wholly deserved as Sacha had another dose of her affliction, and Tom seemed to take a day off. Philippa Gammell won it from Georgina Frith by 6 points. We were the only three entries.

Sections A and C of the marathon were particularly challenging and B was very tight for time. The going on the course was quite good in places, but parts were through deep mud and up and down steep hills. I was doing quite well in C when, about three quarters of the way round, the 1994 jinx struck again. I heard a loud crack behind me, and investigation showed that the arm of the trailing link suspension on the offside rear wheel had broken. Luckily the wheel did not come off, and as it had happened on a narrow bit of track through a wood, I decided to drive on and get clear of the course. On closer inspection at the end of the section, it was quite obvious that I would have to retire. This was mishap number four.

Things did not get any better for me when I drove the cones phase. In spite of having nothing to lose, I managed to knock down three cones and had time penalties. Unusually for Georgina Frith, she had no less than four cones down, which left her in second place and me in third place overall.

In a desperate attempt to improve my dressage at Streatlam, we put Storm back in the lead with Myrtle, and Sacha went with Tom in the wheel. Storm was completely out of practice and seemed to be mystified by the whole proceedings, and nearly took me out of the arena twice. The result was that I was 11 points behind Philippa Gammell. Ursula Hirschberg collected 60.3, while John Robertson and Elizabeth Cartwright-Hignett were in the 70s.

Ursula Hirschberg did her usual high-speed circuit in the marathon with Philippa Gammell some 25 points slower. I continued to have pony trouble in the obstacles when the leaders, Myrtle and Sacha, decided that they were going to do all the work. Accurate steering with pulling leaders is virtually impossible, and it was a case of an accident waiting to happen. I struggled through the first six obstacles, but then the jinx struck for the fifth time in obstacle 7. On the way out of gate

C, the leaders saw a gap and made for it at speed before the wheelers could get round the last post. We hit it hard – hard enough to throw Barbara off the back step – but we got clear. However, before we could get to gate D, it was quite obvious that something was seriously wrong. The full extent of the damage only became evident when we got stuck in D. The offside front wheel was sticking out at an angle of twenty degrees, the pole was badly bent, and the tyres of both front wheels had come off almost completely. There was nothing for it but to take the ponies out and manhandle the carriage out of the obstacle. Mishap number five.

As I had been the first to go, I was able to watch the others through that obstacle from the back step of my derelict carriage. They all had problems, and quite how Ursula Hirschberg got through it is a mystery. She seemed to bounce from one post to another. Philippa Gammell managed quite well, but even she overshot one gate and hit several posts. John Robertson and Elizabeth Cartwright-Hignett took the long route, but they also got into difficulties.

I went back to the dressage team of ponies for the cones, and by some miracle I managed to get round without hitting anything, and only collected 3 time penalties. I was followed by Elizabeth Cartwright-Hignett, who suddenly veered off course, left out a pair of cones and was eliminated, which moved me up a place. John Robertson had a torrid time, and hit six cones, but he stayed in third place, 100 points behind Philippa Gammell, who did a very tidy double clear round. Poor Ursula Hirschberg had a dreadful time. She hit cones-obstacles 7 and 8 and then had two refusals at the box, and for a moment it looked as if I was about to move up another place. She got through at the third attempt, but with 51 penalties. Even that was good enough to move her into second place ahead of John Robertson.

At the beginning of August I went to sail at Cowes, and in the early stages of the last race, I became so intent in getting to windward that I failed to notice that I was perching with one buttock on the edge of the cockpit combing. By the end of the race the buttock had swollen to the size of a large melon and was very painful. My poor backside was the sixth victim of the 1994 jinx.

This did not augur well for the driving event at Lowther. I managed the dressage without too much discomfort, but it was not a distinguished performance, and I ended up fourth after Philippa Gammell, Ursula Hirschberg and Georgina Frith, some 10 points ahead of John Robertson.

I was a bit anxious about my backside before the marathon, but I used a foam-rubber cushion to ease the bumps and to equalize the swelling in my left buttock. It worked brilliantly. I felt no discomfort on the circuit, and all went much better than I had dared hope. After such a good start, I was just beginning to wonder what was going to go wrong this time. I did not have long to wait. I must have gone over a hump just as I turned into the gate on the way to the first obstacle in front of the castle. At any rate, we slowly rolled over just as we were going between a pair of gateposts, and we were all deposited in a bed of virulent stinging nettles. The 1994 jinx had struck for the seventh time. I was all right, as I was wearing gloves, but my referee suffered agonies for the rest of the course. Micky caught his foot against a gatepost, and it later transpired that he had broken a bone in his foot.

All this took place within a short distance of the castle terrace and the first obstacle, but the roll was out of sight of the spectators. The first they knew about it was when the ponies came galloping round the corner dragging the carriage on its side. The ponies were stopped without difficulty and, by the time we caught up, everyone had got busy helpfully unbuckling every buckle they could find.

As the turnover had happened outside an obstacle and no serious harm had been done, other than Sacha losing a front shoe, I was able to continue, and we started to put all the harness together again. I drove the next four obstacles without any great difficulties, and it was only as we went down to the second group of obstacles by the river, that I noticed that Tom was holding his head rather awkwardly to one side. I traced the problem to the buckle on the coupling rein from the other wheeler. Some enthusiast must have unbuckled it before we arrived

Fig. 7.2 Galloping out of the sandpit obstacle at Lowther in 1994. Barbara Duncan has already lost her hat and she is clinging on for dear life. As it costs the competitor 10 penalties every time a groom puts a foot on the ground inside an obstacle, grooms who fall off the carriage are not very popular. Even Micky is looking a bit apprehensive. (*Nick Morris*)

on the terrace after the mishap. It says a lot for the ponies that they behaved so normally in the obstacles after such an unnerving experience. But for a wheeler to respond so well without a coupling rein, I thought was quite remarkable.

When we decided to continue, I had rather assumed that the delay would have made it very unlikely that we could finish within the time. It was only as we came out of the last obstacle that I looked at the clock and the schedule, and noticed that we still had ten minutes to finish. With a little encouragement, and keeping Sacha on soft going as much as possible, the ponies did wonders and we were only 11 seconds late. We then heard that Georgina Frith had turned over in obstacle 6 and that I had moved up into third place.

Georgina Frith went into the cones first and had one down. She was followed by John Robertson, who went clear but had 23 time penalties. I went in next with some 40 points in hand. I hit one and had 10.5 time penalties and kept my third place. Philippa Gammell went in last with some 10 points in hand. She managed a clear round with 3.5 time penalties, and so retained her lead.

Altogether 1994 was a very remarkable year. Any one of those disasters would have been enough for one season, but I thought that eight was really overdoing it. On top of that, I was beginning to feel that I would never get a good team of ponies together. I simply had to get rid of Sacha (although I did drive her once in 1995), and we had also come to the conclusion that Myrtle was not likely to get any better.

RESULTS FOR 1994

EVENT	Dressage	Marathon	Cones	Pl/No
Brighton	3	4	3=	4/5
Windsor	2	9	4	8/9
St Fort	1	2	2	2/2
Sandringham	3	4	4	4/6
Drumlanrig	3	R	2	3/3
Streatlam	2	R	2	4/5
Lowther	4	3	5	3/5

Ponies used: Tom, Carrick, Sacha, Myrtle, Storm.

1995

After the dramas of 1994, anything in 1995 would have been an improvement, and I had the greatest faith in Micky's ability to get the ponies going properly. It was disappointing that Tom had developed a cough during March and had to be turned out for a time, but we had a new pony, Jane, to fall back on, and the first Windsor Park Equestrian Club event provided an opportunity to give her some competition experience. She was on the small side, but there was no doubt about her intelligence and willingness. Her one fault was that she was inclined to bother her neighbour, and she was definitely not keen on going in the wheel. To add to the difficulties, Sacha had started to show ominous signs of her metabolic problems again. I was hopeful that she might improve, but Micky was not so sanguine.

Meanwhile, Penny Romsey was making encouraging progress. A complete dress rehearsal of the three phases of a driving event with Ebony produced a very competent dressage test and a creditable performance over a five-section marathon course, including both walks without time penalties, and satisfactory times through six obstacles. All this was achieved in filthy weather at Sandringham in January. Wet and partly frozen, she then managed a slightly truncated cones course with just one cone down. Micky was delighted with his student and, after such a promising start, even the rather diffident student was beginning to feel more confident. However, starting any new sport can produce difficulties, and I thought the following account of her first two qualifying club events might just illustrate the fickleness of fate, and the hazards facing a beginner.

The first Windsor Park Equestrian Club event was at the end of March and the day of Penny's first qualifying competition dawned clear and bright – the sort of weather we may want at the end of March but seldom get for a WPEC event. The dressage test seemed to be going reasonably well until her anxious trainer saw her wandering somewhat vaguely about the arena. Her mind had obviously gone completely blank – which is not unknown to happen to experienced drivers – but, with a little help from the judge, she recovered consciousness and just managed to complete the rest of the test, although her mental state on completion was anything but cool and calm.

The cones were next. Having been a little demoralized by her experience in the dressage arena, our novice took infinite pains to learn the course. Her time came; the hooter sounded for her to start, and she set off in great style. She counted off the pairs of cones as she sailed confidently through them: 8, 9, 10…then suddenly, a complete blank again – where was 11? She had, in fact, already been through 11, but had failed to count it. Fortunately, her groom was able to hiss '12' through clenched teeth, but it was too late to prevent her crossing her tracks on the way to 12. This sort of thing would have unnerved anyone, and she hit the next two pairs of cones, before pulling herself together sufficiently to get through the final pair. Not perhaps the most encouraging start, but many experienced drivers have done worse – although perhaps not twice on the same day. Anyway, there was the marathon to come on the next day, and no-one could have been more diligent about walking the obstacles – over and over again – working out the best lines, and making notes and sketches.

Apart from getting through the obstacles as quickly as possible, the most important thing about the marathon is to follow the correct routes through the five sections and to arrive at the end of each section at the correct times. Needless to say, it helps to have a map, a stopwatch and a time sheet. It did nothing for her peace of mind, therefore, to be told by her groom soon after starting that the stopwatch was not working. This could be rectified by starting it properly at the next kilometre marker, but her groom then made a further confession that she had dropped both the time sheet and the map. There they were, out in the wilds of Windsor Great Park with only the tracks of their predecessors to follow.

Morale at this point must have been at a pretty low ebb, but the marker signs kept appearing, and so on they went. The course took them to a gate into the Deer Park. In order to allow riders to open the electrically operated gates, there is a button at the top of a post at a convenient level for riders, but a bit too high for Penny's rather short groom. Mounting despair turned to helpless laughter as she watched her groom vainly leaping into the air in her frantic efforts to reach the magic button. She eventually managed it by scrambling up the wire fence.

Thinking she was bound to be late, Penny urged on Ebony, until she noticed that she was catching up with the competitor in front of her. By slowing down and doing some judicious circling, she arrived at the end of section A at the right time. Ebony strode out to complete the walk section with time to spare. Not knowing the rules all that well, our novice slowed down so as to arrive at exactly the right time. It was only later that she discovered that there is no minimum time and that drivers go through agonies in their efforts not to be late in the walk sections.

The ten minute halt must have been a great relief, but all too soon it was time to start off on the final section, and tackle the obstacles. No problems with the first two, but then came the more complicated third obstacle. She went in through gate A and across the middle to gate B; but then she turned left instead of right, and suddenly realized that something was seriously wrong. Memories came flooding back and she shot off to the other side of the obstacle but, as she got round the corner, she made to go into gate D from the wrong direction. Fortunately her groom realized the mistake and shouted 'not that one', to which Penny, still going forward, responded – reasonably in her view – 'why not?'… 'because it's D back-wards' came a strangled squawk. After that she managed the rest of the course without any further dramas and she had completed her first qualifying club competition.

A month later, and after further intensive instruction and practice, she was as ready as she could be for her second club event. Everything went well in the dressage this time, followed by a really good double clear round of the cones and our novice was understandably over the moon.

The next day, after thorough and diligent walking of the obstacles, checking and rechecking time sheets, map and stop watch, she set off on section A. All seemed to be going well until she had the feeling that something was not quite right. It later transpired that she had missed a compulsory turning flag, but then, by sheer bad luck, she had come across another marker sign and continued happily on her way. What she had not appreciated was that she had inadvertently stumbled into section B, the walk section. Unaware of the fact that she had missed the end of section A, she trotted past the sign announcing the end of section B and past the timekeeper at the end of that section and on through the deer gate – open this time – in search of the end of section A. It was some hundred metres further on that she began to appreciate that she was on the wrong course. So back she went, through the deer gate and past the timekeeper at the end of section B again, who must have wondered quite what this competitor was doing trotting to and fro without any obvious intent. Back she went to where she remembered seeing the last turn flag and managed to get back on the course. However, by the time she had completed section A, she had amassed a total of no less than 230 time penalties.

I think many people would have been so discouraged at this point that they would have been sorely tempted to give up and have a quiet cry behind the nearest tree, but not so in this case. Our beginner was obviously made of sterner stuff and after completing the walk section, she set off fairly confidently for the obstacles. All went reasonably well, although she did have another of those dreaded blanks, but this time it was in the first obstacle. There is little more disconcerting for a driver than to go wrong in the first obstacle. It does dreadful things to a fragile peace of mind at that crucial stage of the course, and a novice could well be forgiven for being badly rattled. She got into such a muddle that she appealed to the obstacle judge for help, but his lips had to be sealed. The only thing for it was to go back and start all over again. After that, there was only one further incident in obstacle 4 when her groom tried to stop her from going the right way into gate C. After that, all was plain sailing.

But the fates were not quite satisfied yet. No sooner had she finished than she was informed that she had been eliminated from the competition. There were two classes for single ponies: one was described as 'Novice Qualifier for Single Ponies' and the other simply as a 'Club Class for Single Ponies'. By sheer chance she had been entered in the former, without anyone appreciating that there was a difference between the two classes. The difference, however, was crucial. Close examination of the conditions revealed that, in 'novice' classes, there had to be a presentation phase, where the whole turnout is judged for cleanliness, correct harness and general suitability. She should have reported for this examination an hour before the dressage on the previous day. Since all the other entries in the class had been through this ordeal, our novice obviously had to be eliminated, but it would have meant having to do another qualifying event. Fortunately, the understanding officials decreed that, though she had been eliminated from the novice qualifier class, her scores could still count if she was transferred to the club class, so at least her efforts and anxieties had not been completely in vain. Indeed, when all the scores had been calculated, it turned out that, in spite of her high number of time penalties, she ended up sixth out of nine.

While all this was going on, I was using the club event as a further chance to give the new pony, Jane, some much needed experience. Tom had recovered by then, so we put him in the wheel with Carrick for the cones phase, and all seemed to bode well for the coming season. As I could only get back from South Africa on the Sunday morning, Micky drove the team in the dressage and cones phases. He won the dressage easily with Jane and Sacha in the lead and Storm and Carrick in the wheel. He then swapped Jane with Myrtle for the cones round, but he was mortally embarrassed when he discovered that he had failed to go through the start flags. However, the judges let him go round for the practice and, needless to say, he did a double clear round.

I did the marathon on the Sunday evening with Jane and Sacha back in the lead and all went reasonably well. I was particularly impressed by the wheelers. They were still a bit green, but they went very well together. The only snag was that Carrick was still inclined to break into a trot when he should be walking and into a canter when he should be trotting. At least I had reason to hope that things would go better this year.

The season started in earnest with the Brighton event in early May. We decided to try Storm and Jane in the lead. They were not very well matched, but we hoped that Storm's potentially impressive paces might go down well with the judges. Unfortunately, he was maddeningly idle, which spoilt the whole effect. Nevertheless, I was placed second, less than 1 point behind Georgina Frith and 3 points ahead of Philippa Gammell in a class of six.

The ponies went exceptionally well in the marathon, in spite of it being a hot day, and having to climb to the top of the Downs twice. They made both walks with ease – thanks to Micky's training – and flew through most of the obstacles. I even managed to beat Georgina Frith in obstacles 1 and 5, and Philippa Gammell in 6 and 7. Oddly enough, I had exactly the same marathon score as Carl Barnard.

I had to return to London after the marathon for the VE-Day Banquet in the Guildhall that evening, and the service in St Paul's on the Sunday. Micky was allowed to drive in the cones phase, but it put us *hors concours*. He did the only clear round of the cones, with a few penalties for time. So we would have finished in second place overall, although only 1.3 points ahead of Beverly Mellstrom.

There were eleven entries for the Windsor event, including Edwin Flerackers from Belgium, yet again, Hansueli Klay from Switzerland, Tobias Bucker and Josef Riediger from Germany, Aart van de Kamp from Holland driving a team of Shetlands (the eventual winner) and Peter Schenk from Austria.

I put Jane and Myrtle together in the lead with Tom and Carrick in the wheel for all three phases. They must have gone quite well in the dressage, because I came second, despite the fact that the leaders were still reluctant to go forward and, try as I might to ease him into it, Carrick persisted in breaking pace at the start of each extension. Klay won the dressage, and I was 2 points behind him with Georgina Frith only 1 point behind me.

The ponies did very well in the marathon and, once again, Micky's training for the walk sections paid off handsomely, as we had 25 seconds to spare in the first obstacle and 50 seconds in the second. They flew round section C, and set off at a great pace in E. Thereafter it was a sad story of driver error. I was in fairly high-class company, but I was the slowest through obstacles 5 and 7 and could only manage seventh place at the end of that phase. At least I got round, but poor Ursula Hirschberg had a dreadful time in obstacles 1 and 2 and eventually had to retire.

The timing of the marathon sections must have been very tight as no one got through all five without penalties for time. I was 14 seconds slow in section E, but Flerackers, who had won the previous year, was three minutes late. There were only two double clear rounds in the cones. I had one down, thanks to Myrtle shying at an advertising board, plus 10 penalties for time. Georgina Frith was the best of the locals in fourth place overall, while Philippa Gammell came in sixth with me in seventh place, 7 points behind her. I thought that was the end of it, but I discovered at the last moment that I was included in a 'Topscore' competition in the main ring in the afternoon. This turned out to be a pick-your-own-course competition through cones set at various widths with different values and a box in the middle as a 'joker', worth 200 points, but which counted against you if you knocked it over. The ponies went brilliantly and we ended up in third place.

Only Philippa Gammell, Georgina Frith and I turned up at St Fort. We tried Storm in the lead again with Jane, but it was not a successful pairing, and I was 5 points behind Georgina Frith. Philippa Gammell put in a new pony who gave her endless trouble in both the dressage and the marathon.

I am quite sure that designers and manufacturers are only trying to be helpful, but there are moments when I find their efforts deeply frustrating. It rained all Saturday morning, and my wet-weather gear got soaked while I was watching the other classes go through the obstacles. I went back to my car, which was parked next to the caravan containing lunch. In the hope of preventing it from locking me out, I took the ignition key out, but left it inside the car. When I shut the door, I heard an ominous click and, sure enough, it had locked itself. Meanwhile, the key to the caravan could not be found and there I was in the pouring rain with all my kit in my car, including everything else I needed for the marathon. Fortunately, I had a spare car key in my briefcase, but that was back at Birkhill. Brian McGrath just had time to make a frantic dash back to the house to get it.

I thought we were going really well through the obstacles, so it was rather disconcerting to hear the commentator say that Georgina Frith was beating me by some 10 seconds in each one. That put me 20 points behind her in the marathon, although 5 of those points were picked up in obstacle 2.

Fig. 7.3 For many years Andrew Mylius organized a splendid event on his estate at St Fort in Fife. He levelled an area for an arena and he built a special water obstacle, which my ponies seemed to enjoy. They are obviously not wasting any time in this picture taken in 1995. (*Peter D. Bulman – Expo Life*)

Having walked the cones course and seen where there might be problems, I took a few measurements and laid out the trickiest part of the course with my own cones and then practised it with the ponies. All seemed to be going well on the course itself, when Tom suddenly gave a skip sideways just as we got to the awkward bit and, naturally, we hit it. We each had one down, but I collected an extra 0.5 penalties for time, although it made no difference to the final result. Georgina Frith won fairly easily, I came second and Philippa Gammell took third place.

Sandringham followed at the end of June, but it turned out to be quite a complicated weekend. King Constantine's son, Pavlos, was due to be married on the Saturday in London, and there was to be a great evening party at Wrotham Park (near Potters Bar) on the Thursday. For some reason, which I cannot recall, I only got back to this country from Rome on the Thursday morning, and I was already committed to an Army visit at Wilton on that day. When I got back to Windsor, I just had time to change before going on to the party. It was a spectacular event, but it meant that I could not get to Sandringham until the early hours of the Friday morning. I had to drive my dressage test in the afternoon, so that only left me the morning and evening to study the obstacles.

I put Storm and Carrick in the wheel again for the dressage, and it seemed to work quite well. At any rate there were less than 2 points between the first four competitors. I think this was the first event for Emily Brookes with a team. She later married Peter Bennett, a successful horse-team driver. It was not an auspicious start for someone who had already been national champion in the single-pony and the pony-tandem classes and was to become national champion of the pony-teams class a few years later. She amassed a large number of penalties in the dressage phase, and then got into a muddle in the first obstacle and had to retire after the second.

On Saturday morning I hired a helicopter to get me to London in time for the wedding at eleven o'clock. Fortunately the Russian Church is no distance from the landing site at Kensington Palace. Unusually for such events, everything went as planned, and I just got back to Sandringham in time to start the marathon at half past three. The ponies went exceptionally well, in spite of the heat and hard going, and we had the third fastest time round the course, although only 1.4 points better than Beverly Mellstrom. Ursula Hirschberg had the misfortune of one of her ponies getting a leg over a trace in the water and had to put a groom down, but then she overturned and had to retire.

Beverly Mellstrom was the only one to do a double clear round in the cones and it was entirely due to my better dressage score that I managed to stay ahead of her in the overall results and keep my third place.

Every now and then the dates for regular annual events have to shift by a week.

In 1995, Sandringham, Drumlanrig and Streatlam followed each other on consecutive weekends. This had the effect of discouraging some of the England-based drivers from going to Drumlanrig. In the event, only Philippa Gammell and a new competitor from Aberdeenshire, Anneke Wallace, turned up at Drumlanrig. Anneke Wallace had been a successful tandem driver and this was her first outing with a team. My dressage was nothing to boast about, but at least it was considerably better than the other two. Philippa Gammell had again put a new pony in the lead and it gave her a really difficult time throughout the competition.

For once I made no significant mistakes in the marathon, and achieved the rare distinction of completing it with fewer than 100 penalties. This put me some 30 points ahead before the cones (equivalent to six cones) and I then did a double clear, which clinched it. The last time I had won an event was at Brighton in 1991!

Seven of us started at Streatlam the following weekend. I thought I had done a reasonably good dressage test, but I reckoned without Philippa Gammell putting her old leader back in, and she beat me by 10 points. I thought I could probably hold my own against the others in the marathon, but I had no realistic chance against Philippa Gammell and Ursula Hirschberg, both of whom, barring accidents, had a well-deserved reputation for speed through the obstacles. My ponies went brilliantly until I made a silly mistake in obstacle 6. However, worse was to befall Philippa Gammell. She managed to go through a wrong slot in 6, failed to correct the mistake and was eliminated. Without that mishap, she might have got to within 0.3 points of Ursula Hirschberg in the overall results. As it was, I moved into second place. They both did double clear rounds in the cones while I had just 3 time penalties which were not enough to alter the final order.

Streatlam was to be Penny Romsey's first national novice event with Ebony. She got herself into a high state of anxiety about the dressage, which never became her favourite activity, and spent hours walking the obstacles. In the event she did a reasonable dressage test without going wrong; this was a triumph in itself. Ebony (as befitted an old campaigner) was rather too laid-back and not at her most lively. Micky and Marina Flynn, Barbara and Sarah (the two grooms), Brian McGrath and I spent an anguished time as we followed her round the marathon, and had the greatest difficulty in restraining our comments when she arrived 10 seconds *early* at the end of section A. She frightened us all when she came to the end of obstacle 2 shouting 'Where's out?' After that all went well, and she moved up a place to fifth. None of us dared breathe during the cones phase, but she did a clear round with only 4 time penalties. Then the next competitor went in, hit a cone and had time penalties, so she moved up another place to finish fourth overall. Penny was naturally delighted; we were greatly relieved, and as she then went off with Micky to look at a couple of Fell ponies for sale – which she eventually bought and named Hamble and Medina – I was fairly confident that she was finally landed.

A gang of eight contested the Lowther event at the beginning of August. They were Carl Barnard, Anneke Wallace, Beverly Mellstrom, John Robertson (he and his daughter, Helen Cruickshank, took it in turns to drive and groom), Georgina Frith, Philippa Gammell, Ursula Hirschberg and me. There was a moment of considerable concern when it was announced that Georgina Frith had managed the remarkable dressage score of 31. Philippa Gammell had a respectable 42 and thought that she was trailing by 10 points. It later transpired that Georgina Frith's score should have been 41. Ursula Hirschberg had an unusual lapse, and only managed 54.4. As she always had trouble making her ponies walk consistently, I suspect this may have been the reason for such a disappointing score. My lot were certainly not on their best form and I was relieved to see that I had scored 49.8.

As the weather had been very hot and sultry, the technical delegate had added two minutes to section A and one minute to C, and extended both halts by an extra five minutes. I remember thinking at the time that a fifteen minute halt before E would be a very good idea for all events. I think the walk sections must have been

Fig. 7.4 Penny Romsey took part in her first national novice event at Streatlam in 1995. She was driving Ebony, one of my older and very experienced ponies. The nerves of her supporters club were severely stretched, but she did well to finish fourth. From left to right: Sir Brian McGrath, me, Inspector Paul Fuller, Marina and Micky Flynn, and David Key with the video camera. (*Nick Morris*)

rather generously measured as I came in with over a minute to spare in section B and 50 seconds in D. As it happened, the sun shone, but the air was cool, and even in C the ponies barely worked up a sweat. In fact they stormed round C so fast that I had to lose nearly a minute in the last kilometre.

I thought we were flying through the obstacles but I could not keep up with Ursula Hirschberg who got round in 69.8, which included 2 penalties for hitting a knock-down. All the obstacles must have been fairly short and easy as all but two of the class managed to get round in under 100.

Oddly enough, the people in fifth, sixth and eighth places had double clear rounds in the cones, while the winner, Georgina Frith and I each had two cones down, and Philippa Gammell and Ursula Hirschberg each had one down. The first three (the 'flying fillies') were very close together on 125.8, 126.8 and 129.2. I was some way down on 145.6 in fourth place.

Fig. 7.5 The sandpit at Lowther, usually the last of the eight obstacles, has become quite notorious. You come down quite a steep slope and then you are expected to wiggle to and fro in the bottom before galloping out (see Fig. 7.6). The main problem for drivers is the need to handle the reins very quickly. (*Nick Morris*)

Fig. 7.6 The sandpit at Lowther 1997. The exit is up the slot in the right foreground. This picture shows the layout of the main obstacle. (*Author's collection*)

So ended the 1995 season, which had been a vast improvement on the previous year. There were some hiccups, but thankfully no accidents and no dramas. I was still having problems with the leaders in the dressage, but it is asking a lot of Fell ponies to expect them to prance around the ring pretending to be Hackneys, particularly when one of them has an unfortunate affliction. I am afraid we decided that this was going to be the last season for Sacha, who went up to Balmoral to become an excellent stalking pony. She was sent to a stallion but, sadly, she died of grass sickness just after foaling. Her orphan was named Hope and everyone rallied round to look after her and feed her from a bottle. As she lived near the Head Ponyman's kennels, she began to think she was a dog and eventually David Muir got hold of a Shetland pony to keep her company and to persuade her that she really was a pony.

Micky Flynn and his wife Marina were doing a marvellous job. At the time when I asked him to look after the ponies, I did not realize that I was getting an extra very accomplished and hard-working groom in his wife. On top of that, she produces sumptuous breakfasts and generally looks after everyone. The two girls, Barbara and Sarah, also worked hard and ensured the ponies were always turned out shiny and fit.

RESULTS FOR 1995

EVENT	Dressage	Marathon	Cones	Pl/No
Brighton	2	3=	HC5*	(7/7)
Windsor	2	7	6	7/11
St Fort	2	2	3	2/3
Sandringham	3	3	2	3/11
Drumlanrig	1	1	1=	1/3
Streatlam	3	2	3	2/7
Lowther	3	4	5	4/9

Ponies used: Tom, Carrick, Sacha, Myrtle, Storm, Jane.

* hors concours

1996

After the usual cold, but generally dry, training session at Sandringham in January, the 1996 season began with a Windsor Park Equestrian Club event in mid-April. The planned event for the end of March had had to be abandoned because of heavy rain. I was quite pleased with the way the ponies performed, although Myrtle is always a problem in the dressage as she will stick her nose out and fidget during the halts.

This was the first event for Penny Romsey with her new ponies, who Micky persuaded her to drive as singles for the first year. Things did not start brilliantly, as she had expected to do a different dressage test, but the judge kindly allowed her groom to 'talk' her through the right test. Much to everyone's surprise, she came first and then drove her second pony *hors concours* and would have been third. There were no dramas in the cones and she drove the ponies very accurately and calmly through the obstacles. As Micky had trained the driver and both ponies, he was highly chuffed by the performance of his three pupils.

As I was booked to visit Hereford on the Friday morning, I had to hire a helicopter to get to the Brighton event in time to do my dressage test. When I heard that Georgina Frith had been given 30.7 I rather imagined that the judges must be in a generous mood. No such luck, they gave Philippa Gammell 42.7 and I collected no less than 49. I was gradually getting used to the comments from judges, that the ponies 'lacked impulsion' and had 'poor extension'. I only wish I knew how to get Fell ponies to demonstrate the sort of 'impulsion' the judges were looking for. As far as the ponies are concerned, they do the paces and the movements accurately, so what are they expected to do to show impulsion as well?

The next day I had to get up very early to be able to study the marathon obstacles before the competition started. The first to go were the novice single ponies, and so I had the chance to watch Penny Romsey through the obstacles. Unfortunately, disaster struck in the first when she, rather ambitiously, tried to take the shortest route only to get stuck. In order to get out, she had to go through gate E backwards. 'Outside assistance' is strictly against the rules, but I managed to convey to her that she had to go back and start again. Unfortunately, she took this to mean starting the whole obstacle again and drove through the start flags for a second time. She managed the rest of the obstacles quite well and only discovered that she had been eliminated when she finished the course.

My obstacles round went really well, apart from a nasty moment in obstacle 2, when the ponies helped me to correct a mistake by backing dead straight out of the wrong gate! I was pleased to be only 11 points behind Georgina Frith and even more delighted to have beaten Philippa Gammell by 3 points.

Georgina Frith finished with a double clear, but Philippa Gammell had two down, while I only had 3 time penalties, which meant that I beat her by just 4 points overall. Beverly Mellstrom had a disappointing dressage round and was unusually slow in the marathon to finish fourth.

The weather was bitterly cold on the Friday and Saturday of the Windsor event, although it got a bit warmer on the Sunday, but at least it was dry and mostly sunny. I tried Storm with Jane in the lead again for the dressage, and I thought the ponies did quite well – but the judges thought otherwise. They gave me 59.7, the worst score I had ever had in my entire driving career. I would like to think that it was only because the two continental judges, Mrs T.J. Velstra and Mr E. Georg, did not like the Fells, but Diana Brownlie did not think much of them either. It has to be said that they were just as unkind to six other competitors and, to my considerable surprise, I found myself in third place despite my dreadful score. However it meant that I started the marathon 17 points behind Georgina Frith and 9.7 behind Philippa Gammell.

I had trouble with the timing in section C, when Barbara's stopwatch gave up the ghost, and instead of arriving 30 seconds inside maximum time, I arrived 30 seconds early and collected an unwelcome 3.1 penalties. I managed to get through obstacle 1 without difficulty, but there was obviously something wrong as we left obstacle 2. Micky then noticed that the snap shackle holding Tom's collar to the crossbar at the end of the pole had come undone. We had to make a short stop to put it back again. We then went through obstacles 3 and 4 before Micky saw that he had inadvertently replaced the shackle over, instead of under, Tom's connecting rein, so we had to make another short stop. I had a moment of panic in obstacle 7 when I saw that the knock-down poles for the singles and pairs had not, as I

Fig. 7.7 Beverly Mellstrom driving at Brighton in May 1996. The Brighton event in Stanmer Park started in May 1981 and has been the first national event of the season ever since. After a reasonably dry winter and in fine weather with the spring blossom out, it is a real pleasure; in rain with water-logged tracks it can be a real trial. (*Alf Baker*)

had expected, been removed, and I nearly lost my way. I had further timing problems in this section and was 24 seconds late, although all but three of the others were even later.

I had a really bad round of the cones, with two down and 4.5 time penalties, not that it would have made any difference, as I was too far behind to catch the German ahead of me. However, it is never over until the end and, sadly for him, he took the wrong course so that I moved up to an undeserved fifth place in a class of nine.

Philippa Gammell and Anneke Wallace were the only other entries for St Fort. I was led to expect awful weather and heavy going after unusually persistent rain. Although it was still cold, it remained fine and dry until the Sunday afternoon when a typical east-coast drizzle set in.

The pony-teams class was the last to start the dressage, and my ponies looked really good with their coats gleaming in the bright afternoon sun. I thought my test was nothing like as good as the one I did at Windsor, however I was delighted to find that the judges were quite pleased with it and the upshot was that I finished 6.3 points ahead of Anneke Wallace and 7.4 points ahead of Philippa Gammell.

Section E of the marathon course winds its way down the hill in the old park, and it is quite easy for the spectators to see a competitor through all the obstacles. Andrew Mylius, the owner of St Fort, always built very good and imposing obstacles, each of which is distinctive and therefore more easily remembered. I thought the ponies went brilliantly, but I could hear from the commentary that Philippa Gammell was catching up, and only had to make up 8 seconds in the last two obstacles. She equalled my time in obstacle 7 and then caught up 7 seconds in obstacle 8. That left me 0.6 points ahead of her, until I heard that she had hit a knock-down in obstacle 1, which added 2 points to her score.

With such a slender margin, everything depended on the cones. You can imagine how I felt when Philippa Gammell hit a cone in the zig-zag and also collected 0.5 time penalties. I now had a margin of 8.1. I nearly frittered some of that away when I saw Jane kick the very cone that both Philippa Gammell and Anneke Wallace had knocked over. It definitely wobbled, but stayed in place. However, I had to concede 3.5 time penalties and therefore won by just 4.6 points.

Six pony teams turned up at Sandringham: Georgina Frith, Beverly Mellstrom, Alison Leggett, Anna Grayson, Helen Cruickshank and me. Georgina Frith started rather too well for my liking with a dressage score of 37.3, while I could only manage 46.7, but it put me in second place.

Georgina Frith raced away in the marathon for a score of 92. I pursued as best I could, but I started badly by making a hash of obstacle 1. I thought I had been through gate E, but Micky insisted that I had missed it. I rather reluctantly believed him, which was just as well as I had indeed missed it and would have been eliminated. As it was, it cost me a lot of time penalties to put right. Altogether, my round was very scrappy, and I only kept ahead of the others because they were all much slower through section E.

In the cones, Georgina Frith had one down, and, although I did not hit anything, I collected 11 time penalties and finished some 40 points behind her. The next to finish was Beverly Mellstrom nearly 50 points behind. The whole event was brought to a conclusion with an accumulator competition, which, much to my surprise and everyone else's astonishment, I won with 260 points of a possible 280. It was altogether a very successful and enjoyable event. The weather was glorious, the course and obstacles were excellent, there were lots of competitors and, from the sponsorship and trade stands points of view, an encouraging number of spectators.

Four competitors turned up at Drumlanrig, including the now unbeatable Georgina Frith. None of the dressage scores were very impressive, but she still managed to get 10 points ahead of me, while I only just got ahead of Anneke Wallace by 3 points. The fourth competitor was Debbie Wicks, who was 12 points further back.

Saturday started dull and grey with occasional drizzle, but it improved during the day and turned into a glorious evening. The marathon course was as demanding as ever through woods, over hills and into patches of deep mud. I rather expected all this to take some of the exuberance out of the ponies, but I could not have been more mistaken. They fairly shot off into section E, which made me slightly apprehensive about getting through the obstacles. The first obstacle demanded a lot of galloping, which only seemed to stir them up even more. Myrtle was thoroughly enjoying herself and saw no particular reason why she should have to turn. Twice she just kept going when I wanted to make a sharp turn and I was forced to take remedial action. The only consolation was that Georgina Frith had gone through a gate backwards in one of the obstacles and collected 20 penalties. Things improved after obstacle 3, but it was a little discouraging to find that Georgina Frith was still 7.6 points ahead even with the 20 penalties for going wrong and a further 3.8 time penalties in section C.

Sunday was clear and bright with a cold north wind. I put Storm in the wheel with Tom (his ears stuffed with cotton wool, as he was very sensitive to the noise behind him) instead of Carrick for the cones and it made all the difference. The trouble with Carrick is that he anticipates, and gets wound up as soon as he sees a cone. This makes accurate driving rather difficult. I managed a double clear round for the first time that season, and the only one, except for George Bowman, in the pony-teams and horse-teams classes. Georgina Frith had two down so that I ended up only 5.9 points behind her and 15 points ahead of Anneke Wallace.

At Lowther the dressage scores were a bit closer. I just managed to sneak into the lead from Georgina Frith by 0.6 points and from Philippa Gammell by 1.3 points. Ursula Hirschberg, Anneke Wallace and Helen Cruickshank were about 10 behind.

The rain absolutely sluiced down on the Saturday morning, but it had cleared up by the time I started in the afternoon. The course took us over Askham Fell with spectacular views over Ullswater and the hills of the Lake District, but the going seemed even rougher than usual. The Fell had changed very considerably since the first time I took the horses over it in 1973. The heather had almost disappeared, due, I suspect, to overgrazing by sheep and keeping the sheep on the Fell for much longer into the autumn. This was made possible by the use of tractors to take feed up on to the Fell for much of the winter. In the old days, the sheep had to be brought 'inby' (near the house) and fed root crops during the winters.

The first time I drove over the Fell in the 1970s it was quite soft and boggy in places. During the 1980s the climate was much drier and the Fell tracks became hard and even dusty in some years, then in the 1990s the rainfall must have increased as the soft conditions returned. The use of tractors in wet conditions was very evident to the carriage drivers, as we had to negotiate the deep ruts in the tracks. These ruts are just the wrong width for all carriages, and it is a problem keeping pairs and teams of horses and ponies out of them. It is not so bad for singles and tandems as they can go between the ruts.

Delighted as I was with my dressage score, I had no illusions that 0.6 was enough to keep me ahead of Georgina Frith in the marathon. I was only too right. She flew round the obstacles in 68. Ursula Hirschberg did it in 77.6, which included 4 penalties for hitting knock-downs. Anneke Wallace got round in 82 and I came panting up behind in 93.4. Poor Philippa Gammell failed to go through gate B in obstacle 2 and was eliminated. I might have done better had not Myrtle got a bit above herself, and decided that she knew the way through the obstacles better than I did. I remember watching a singles driver go wrong, and then heard her shouting at the pony 'Can't you read? B comes after A'. I was tempted to say this to Myrtle after she tried to go her own way in all but the first and last obstacles. I had watched a single and a tandem turn over as they galloped out of obstacle 8 and very nearly did the same myself. I had warned Micky and Barbara of the possible problem and they were leaning well out but, even so, we were on two wheels for a moment.

The scores in the marathon, excluding Georgina Frith, were very close. Ursula Hirschberg was lying second, just 3.5 points ahead of me in third place, with Anneke Wallace breathing down my neck only 0.6 points behind. The tension was slightly relieved for me when Anneke Wallace hit two cones and had 3.5 time penalties. I managed a clear round in the cones phase, but I was 3.4 seconds over the time allowed. That gave me 2 time penalties, which meant that the 0.4 seconds gave Ursula Hirschberg one cone in hand by that fraction of a point. Otherwise, had she hit a cone, we would have tied. I was a bit disappointed not to end the season with a clear round, but it would not have made any difference to the result of that competition.

Fig. 7.8 Coming out of the gateway to the old castle at Lowther in August 1996. The burnt-out ruin can be glimpsed behind the carriage. Sir John Miller is standing in the gateway on the left. It was between the gateway and the castle that the ponies and the upturned carriage came to a halt after we had tipped up while turning into a farm gate on the way to the first obstacle in 1994. As no harm or damage was done, we put everything together and went on to finish third overall. (*Author's collection*)

Fig. 7.9 (*below*) Philippa Gammell going strong at Brighton in 1995. One of her grey leaders was still competing at twenty years old. As her home is in Glenisla in the Highlands not far from Balmoral, it is obviously a major challenge to get her whole outfit right down to Brighton at the start of her season. We have had a number of close finishes over the years. (*Alf Baker*)

I have no doubt that the generally more consistent performance of both ponies and driver was due, in large measure, to Micky Flynn. His almost uncanny understanding of the ponies and his guidance through the obstacles, made all the difference.

RESULTS FOR 1996

EVENT	Dressage	Marathon	Cones	Pl/No
Brighton	3	2	2	3/5
Windsor	3	6	8	5/9
St Fort	1	2	1	1/3
Sandringham	2	2	2	2/6
Drumlanrig	2	2	1	2/4
Lowther	1	3	2	3/6

Ponies used: Tom, Carrick, Myrtle, Storm, Jane.

CHAPTER EIGHT

TOM RETIRES

1997–1999

I HAD A SAD START TO 1997 because I had to say goodbye to Tom. He seemed to be in good order while he was at Sandringham in January, but then we noticed that, after working for a time, his head started to 'nod' a little. This usually indicates lameness and an examination showed that there was something wrong with the tendon in one of his front legs. As he was bound to be off work for some time, whatever treatment was prescribed, we reluctantly decided to retire him. He had laboured stoutly for eight years as a wheeler; he was immensely strong and had frequently got me out of all sorts of trouble. His one great weakness was his horror of unfamiliar noises behind him and he carted me twice as a result of this problem. In the end we resorted to putting cotton wool in his ears before doing the cones because of the noise made when a cone got knocked or caught under the carriage.

Fortunately, we had a delightful filly called Polly in reserve and, although she was only four years old, she had already shown great promise in early training. I drove her in the lead, with Jane as instructor, and they seemed to manage quite well. The only problem with this team was that I had to use Carrick and Storm in the wheel and they had developed some bad habits. Carrick was all too inclined to break into a canter while he should have been doing a fast trot and although Micky Flynn cured him of the habit in the marathon, the excitement of the cones was usually too much for him. Not that cantering in the cones is a bad thing, it is just that when one wheeler canters and the others are trotting it seems to unbalance the whole team. Storm, on the other hand, trotted when he was supposed to walk, which made life frustrating in the dressage and in the walk sections of the marathon.

Fig. 8.1 Red deer, here crossing the Long Walk in Windsor Great Park, are quite wary of walkers, but they take very little notice of the ponies, and I have often passed very close to them. The ponies are quite unmoved, even when the deer stare at them and then suddenly bound off. Tom's large rump can be seen in the nearside wheeler's position. (*Author's collection*)

Having competed with her new ponies in the single-pony class in 1996, Penny Romsey had to decide which class to join this year. The pony-pairs class would have been the obvious choice, but Medina and Hamble were not all that well matched in size or in temperament, besides which, I thought the national pony-pairs class was about the hottest one of all. I therefore suggested that a tandem might be the answer and pointed out that tandem driving required great skill and attention, and that the class was composed of mildly eccentric masochists and amiable lunatics, which, I was sure, would suit her temperament. Micky was of the same mind, and, as Penny Romsey had no idea what we were talking about, she agreed to have a go in the tandem class. Practising for and doing the dressage test nearly drove her to distraction, but she soon mastered the marathon obstacles and the cones surprisingly well, and without disasters.

Brighton was the first national event, but I had to reorganize my accommodation arrangements. I was unable to stay with Lady Rupert (Micky) Nevill, whose husband had been my Private Secretary and Treasurer for some years until he died. Micky Nevill had a small cottage on the Glyndebourne estate, just over the hill from the opera house, with dramatic views over the Downs. It was very convenient for the event as it is just east of Lewes, not far from the main A27, while Stanmer Park is north-east of Brighton on the same road. Owing to rearrangements in the Christie family, Micky's lease of the cottage came to an end, and I had to find somewhere else. Micky very kindly persuaded one of her neighbours, Lord Gage, to put me up at Firle Park, a spectacularly beautiful – originally Tudor – house, below Firle Beacon on the South Downs. His ancestor, General Gage, was one of the leading military leaders during the American War of Independence.

There was a full turnout of nine pony teams for the Brighton event. I could only get there on the Friday afternoon as I had been in Bristol to see off the replica of John Cabot's ship 'Matthew' on her way to Newfoundland on the 400th anniversary of his epic journey across the North Atlantic and the discovery of Newfoundland. He also discovered the vastly rich cod fishing grounds on the Grand Banks.

Friday was a lovely day, but I was somewhat unnerved to hear that the ponies had given Micky Flynn all sorts of trouble that morning, and they were no better when I tried to get them ready for the dressage. At one stage I wondered whether I was going to be able to get them into the arena at all. I noted at the time: '…it felt like trying to play four large salmon at the same time'. However, when I got them into the arena, they had apparently decided on grudging co-operation. That is until Jane flatly refused to turn to her side when I started a one-handed circle. For the first time ever in my dressage-driving career, I had to put my other hand on the reins to get her to come round. Imagine my surprise when I found myself in second place, 6 points behind Philippa Gammell, 3 ahead of Beverly Mellstrom and 5 ahead of Georgina Frith.

I was a bit anxious about the marathon obstacles. Having arrived late on the Friday, I had thought that I would have plenty of time to look at them on the Saturday morning, only to discover that they were 'closed' as soon as the first competitor started section E. I explained my dilemma to Joe Moore, who kindly gave me permission to walk the obstacles between competitors. I was somewhat embarrassed by being the only competitor allowed to do this, so I just went in to look at the really awkward corners, and decided to rely on Micky to give me instructions in each obstacle when we got to it. This is not an ideal arrangement, but it was all I could do.

The ponies really did their stuff and Georgina Frith and I were the only ones to make the times in all the sections, but she went very much faster through the obstacles, and got ahead of Philippa Gammell. I was third fastest, but only a neck ahead of Anneke Wallace.

Sunday started in pouring rain, but, thankfully, it had cleared up and the sun had come out by the time we started the cones. Anneke Wallace was in fourth place and did a double clear round. I followed and hit one cone and had 1 time penalty, but I managed to stay ahead of her, and kept my third place. Philippa Gammell went next and had 2.5 time penalties. Georgina Frith went in last and did a double clear round to clinch her first place by 14 points. In the end it turned out to be an encouraging start with my virtually new team.

There was a Windsor Park Equestrian Club event over the weekend between Brighton and Windsor and the ponies went really well. Unfortunately, Polly had taken to shaking her head violently and I suspect that this caused her to bruise the bars of her mouth, so we had to leave her out. The weather on the Sunday was dreadful, and I had to dress up in full wet-weather gear. In the event, it did not rain during my round of the marathon, but there was a gale-force wind. The first part of section C was in the direction of the castle and the ponies sailed along thinking, no doubt, that they were on their way home. My concern was what would happen when I had to turn them back and into the wind. Fortunately they took it very well, and I got in with time to spare. They swept confidently through the obstacles, and I thought they were in very good form for the Windsor event.

There were eleven entries for the international event at Windsor. Georgina Frith, Philippa Gammell, Anna Grayston, Ursula Hirschberg, Anneke Wallace and I represented Great Britain against Gerrie Herfst and Eyk Backer from Holland, Josef Schoftner from Austria, Louis Droemont from Germany and the ever-faithful Edwin Flerackers from Belgium.

Sadly, I had to leave Polly out of this event altogether, as the bars of her mouth had not healed properly, and Jane has never, and never will, enjoy – or even tolerate – dressage; she simply loses interest, but becomes a different pony in her best event, the marathon.

I did not think my dressage was very inspiring, but the others must have been worse as I found myself in second place, just 0.5 points behind Flerackers.

The marathon obstacles were, I thought, the best I had ever seen, with plenty of options, and sharp, but manageable, turns and good flowing sections. Georgina Frith went like the wind, but could not quite equal Flerackers' times, and Ursula Hirschberg was close behind. I managed to get through the first five without trouble, but in obstacle 6, the leaders got themselves either side of a post and, although they got out of it quickly, it cost me some valuable seconds. The same thing happened again in obstacle 8 and I ended up in seventh place in the marathon and sixth overall.

The Dutchman, Herfst, was only 11 points behind me before the cones, but he had one down and 18.5 time penalties, which gave me a welcome margin. I hit one cone and had 9 time penalties, so I retained my sixth place. Philippa Gammell was fourth, Ursula Hirschberg third and Georgina Frith second to Flerackers by 8 points. I was quite encouraged to see that I was only 30 points behind the winner.

Philippa Gammell, Anneke Wallace, Anna Grayston and I turned up for the event at St Fort. Polly's mouth seemed to have recovered, and I decided against

Fig. 8.2 Anneke Wallace (seen here at the Royal Windsor Horse Show, May 1997) comes from Scotland and has been successful as a tandem and as a team driver. She had a very successful spell as Chairman of the Rules Committee of the British Horse Driving Trials Association. It is not an easy task to reconcile some of the more contentious changes proposed by the FEI. One of the more difficult challenges has been to devise a system of qualification for novice drivers to enable them to compete in open national classes. (*Alf Baker*)

Micky's – and Brian McGrath's – advice to put her in the lead for the dressage. Unfortunately, they were proved right and I had a dismal score: 7 points behind Philippa Gammell and 0.2 behind Anneke Wallace. It seems that Anna Grayston could not do anything right that day as she ended up 20 points further back.

Saturday started out misty and cold with a biting east wind, but the sun had come out by the time we started on the marathon course, and it turned into a lovely afternoon. From the top of the course, you look south-east towards the airfield at Leuchars and out over the North Sea. I was the first to go and the ponies were in great form. I thought we were doing rather well through the obstacles, but I heard the commentator announce that Philippa Gammell had beaten me in the first obstacle by 8 seconds. However, by the end, she had only gained 4 points, putting her 11 points ahead, while Anneke Wallace had increased her lead over me by 0.5 points.

Things were a bit tense as we started the cones. Anna Grayston went in first and hit three cones. I went in next, and started badly by hitting the fourth, and then all went well till the very last, which I hit with a back wheel. I also added 2 penalties for time. That took the pressure off Anneke Wallace, who went in and sailed to a double clear round. As Philippa Gammell had two cones in hand, we thought it was all over, but she hit one, and then another and, amazingly, she then hit a third, which let Anneke Wallace through to win.

It was quite an exciting competition, but more of the same was yet to come in the horse-teams class. Richard Margrave, in second place, did a clear round with a couple of time penalties. Then George Bowman came in with just over three cones in hand. We could hardly believe our eyes when he copied Philippa Gammell, and also had three down. He just scraped home to win by 1 point.

This exciting and enjoyable event ended with the sad announcement by Andrew Mylius, the owner of St Fort, and instigator, manager and course builder (also a Fell pony tandem driver), that he was giving up the chairmanship of the organizing committee. It was, however, intended that the event should continue the following year.

Things most certainly did not go right for me at Sandringham. Having done some more practice with Polly, I tried her in the lead again with Myrtle, but there was not much improvement in my dressage score – just 2 points better than St Fort – which put me equal fourth with Anna Grayston.

I had no problems with any of the early sections of the marathon, and I even managed to do quite well in the first three obstacles (fourth fastest in obstacle 1, sixth fastest in 2, and third fastest in 3 – the water), but then things went seriously wrong in obstacle 4. I failed to anticipate a turn to the left after gate D, and sailed through F backwards. I then had to go back and do D again. This time Myrtle just turned her head to the left, and cruised through F for the second time. I made it at the third attempt, but with a serious burden of penalties. I think we were all rather unnerved by that experience, and I did the rest of the obstacles in hopelessly slow times. Furthermore, after the delay in obstacle 4, the ponies were unable to make up the lost time, and the extra two minutes netted me another 25.4 penalties, which dropped me from equal fourth to seventh. The time for section E must have been very tight anyway as only three made it. Ursula Hirschberg did the fastest round and pulled up to fourth place.

I slightly redeemed myself by doing a double clear round of the cones, but then so did four others, and it made no difference to my seventh place in any case as

Beverly Mellstrom was some 60 points behind me and Anna Grayston 20 points ahead of me. Poor John Pickford had a much worse time: he had a massive dressage score, was eliminated in obstacle 4, and then knocked two cones down. The score sheet says that his eliminated score was 1258, which I am sure was a mistake, but I am equally sure that if it was correct, it would have been a record. Georgina Frith won fairly easily with Philippa Gammell second and Anneke Wallace in third place. It all ended with an accumulator competition in the main ring. I just failed to get through the last two pairs of cones and tied with Philippa Gammell and Ursula Hirschberg, but they beat me on time.

Drumlanrig came round again in mid-July. John Robertson and Beverly Mellstrom were the only other pony teams there. My dressage went rather better than I had dared hope, and I clocked up 47.5 points. Not brilliant, but it was my best score for the 1997 season so far. However, it was only 3 points better than Beverly Mellstrom.

The marathon course was, as usual, quite demanding but the ponies coped with it very well. They did both walks with 50 seconds to spare in each, and we fairly shot through the first five obstacles in great style, doing the fastest times in each of them. My undoing was the fifth obstacle, where I attempted a turn that I should have known was much too tight. I jackknifed the carriage and it then hit a post, which turned it over. Luckily we were going quite slowly at the time and none of us was hurt, however the ponies took off with the carriage on its side. First they went up the hill towards the castle, but when they came to the security fence of iron hurdles, they turned down the hill making for the stable field. As they turned, the carriage swung out and banged against the fence, which set the ponies off again, and they very nearly upset an elderly obstacle judge who was sitting on a chair beside the fence. By then, they were going so fast down the hill that they were quite unable to avoid yet another metal fence just by the finish of section E. The leaders jumped it, and the wheelers tried to do the same, but the pole knocked it over and they had to scramble over the fallen hurdles somehow. Quite how the wheelers managed without doing themselves serious damage was a miracle. They then made their way towards their stables, but one of the front tyres had come off and was thrashing about. It hit Carrick on the rump, which set him off again, but they only went another fifty metres or so before stopping under a tree.

Needless to say, the carriage was a write-off. Fortunately there was only superficial damage to Carrick and Jane. Myrtle was untouched, but Storm had a minor cut on a leg, all of which left me with only three fully fit ponies, so there was nothing for it but to withdraw from the cones phase. It was a disappointing end to what looked like being a successful event.

Lowther was the next event. I had ordered a new carriage from Michael Mart who was as good as his word, and delivered it just in time for me to try it out on the Thursday afternoon. It felt a bit strange as it was fitted with conventional axles and leaf springs – as opposed to the trailing link, torsion box, four-wheel independent suspension of the old carriage – and it had smaller wheels, which gave it a much harder ride, and made me feel as if I was sitting higher and slightly further back. In addition, it was much noisier; but the most noticeable difference was the extremely sensitive brakes, which gave me a lot of trouble in section A of the marathon. The going on the Fell was dry and very bumpy, and every time I tried to use the front brakes on the way down, the bumping made me stamp on the brake pedal and this caused the brakes to snatch and throw the back of the carriage up. Every time this happened I expected to see Micky and Liz Elwick come flying over my head.

Micky had somehow managed to persuade Jane to keep up with Myrtle, so we decided to leave Polly out and put those two in the lead for the dressage. The weather was glorious, and I managed a reasonable test finishing just 6 points behind Georgina Frith, who had recently returned from winning the European Championships for the second time. (She went on to win it a third consecutive

Fig. 8.3 Georgina Frith rose rapidly through the ranks of pony-team drivers to capture the European Championships three times over a period of four years. She sold her team in 2001, so was unable to defend her title at Sandringham in 2002. Here she is driving the cones to win the 1997 Championships at Meissenheim in Germany. (*Alf Baker*)

time two years later.) Ursula Hirschberg came next, followed by Emily Brookes and Anneke Wallace.

The sky clouded over on the Saturday, making it a bit cooler for the ponies. After some quite hard going in sections A and C (I was nearly a minute early when the end of C, the fast section, loomed up), I rather hoped that the ponies would be a little less enthusiastic in the obstacles. I decided to take no chances and entered the first obstacle (the sandpit) with caution. It was just as well as the ponies were quite a handful. Typically, when I wanted them to get on with the job in the water, they decided to paddle round at a sedate trot. It was only because Anneke Wallace had 6 time penalties in section E that I managed to tie with her in the marathon. Georgina Frith and Ursula Hirschberg whizzed round the obstacles nearly 30 points faster than the rest of us.

Sunday was another scorcher and our cones phase was in the afternoon. I managed a clear round with just 1.5 time penalties to win that phase and retain my third place overall.

In the pony-tandems class, Penny Romsey drove her tandem into second place in the dressage, after thinking that she had made a mess of it. She then drove a faultless round of the marathon, but hit three cones to end up third overall. Michael Onslow was well in the lead of the tandems until he turned over in obstacle 5.

The 1997 season was rather disappointing and I was particularly sad to smash the carriage at Drumlanrig. Fortunately the incident did not have any serious effect on the ponies, as they proved by their subsequent performance at Lowther.

The insurance paid for the new carriage, but I asked Danny Harvey (the new mechanical engineer at Sandringham) whether he thought he could repair it – rebuild it, might be more accurate. If so, I thought it might be an opportunity to make some improvements to it. He was fairly confident that he could manage, so I bought it back – or what was left of it – from the insurance company.

All four-wheel carriages for pairs and teams suffer from too much weight in front. This is due to the weight of the pole and turntable over the front wheels. There is not much that can be done about it, but I reckoned that it might be possible to save some weight in front and get a better balance between the front and rear. He eventually made a very good job of restoration and the old carriage was back in service in 1998 and going better than ever.

It was unfortunate that I could not foresee that the FEI would introduce a rule to set the minimum track width for cross-country vehicles. This rule was based on the thinking that there was a greater chance of vehicles turning over if the track width was too narrow. I found the whole idea particularly irritating, because it seemed to me that it was none of the FEI's concern anyway. If drivers want to risk turning over, it is their business. There was another case of this 'nanny attitude' when the FEI forbade the use of patterned treads on the tyres. It argued that treads might prevent sliding and therefore increase the risk of turning over, but it seems to me that treaded tyres increase the braking action, which can help to avoid much worse accidents.

I had chosen 120 cm for the track width because that just about covered the width of the two wheelers. I then discovered that the new standard width was to be 125 cm. Since my wheels were attached to the body by stub axles fitted into torsion boxes, adding those extra 5 cm was quite a complicated, and expensive, business.

RESULTS FOR 1997

EVENT	Dressage	Marathon	Cones	Pl/No
Brighton	2	3	6	3/9
Windsor CAI	2	7	8	6/10
St Fort	3	3	2	3/4
Sandringham	3=	8	1	7/10
Drumlanrig	1	R		3/3
Lowther	2	3=	1	3/5

Ponies used: Carrick, Myrtle, Storm, Jane, Polly.

1998

After Myrtle's performance in 1997, when she had taken to sticking her head out in dressage, and become very difficult at the marathon obstacles, there was really nothing for it but to send her back to Balmoral to carry stags. That left an awkward gap in the team for 1998. I suppose I could have managed with just four ponies, but not having a spare pony means that, if anything goes wrong with any of them, the whole team is out. Micky, therefore got busy on the grapevine and he was lucky to hear from John Cowdery who was prepared to let me have a Fell pony on loan.

Some years previously, John Cowdery's daughter Debbie had driven a team of Fells, and I think he had just kept this one in a field after she had given up. Peter duly turned up at Sandringham looking a bit lean and hairy and obviously not at competition-level fitness. However, he thrived on ample rations, tender loving care, lots of exercise and the Norfolk air. By the end of January he had become a valued member of the team and Micky persuaded John Cowdery to sell him. It was one of the best buys he ever made.

We were still not quite out of the woods with the team because Polly persisted with her head shaking, particularly when she was in the lead, and we simply could not cure Carrick of the habit of breaking into a canter instead of extending at the trot. In spite of all this, I was moderately pleased with their performances at the Windsor Park Equestrian Club competitions at the start of the season.

For once I managed to get to Brighton on the Thursday, and I used the opportunity to take the dressage team out for some practice. With the exception of the new pony, Peter, replacing Myrtle, it was the same team that I had driven in the previous year – Storm and Peter in the lead with Polly and Carrick in the wheel – and they behaved just as badly. This was a bit discouraging, although when Micky had them out on the Friday morning they went marginally better. Imagine my amazement and relief when they behaved perfectly as soon as I got into the arena. There were several mistakes in my dressage test, but at least I got within 10 points of Georgina Frith (having the reigning European Champion in your class can be a bit discouraging at times) but I could only get 3 points ahead of Anna Grayston and 4 points ahead of Beverly Mellstrom.

I put Polly and Jane in the lead for the marathon with Storm and Carrick in the wheel, and they went brilliantly. I was particularly pleased with Polly in her first competition in the lead. I should have stayed ahead of Anna Grayston in the marathon, but I made a couple of silly and rather expensive mistakes, and she just moved ahead of me.

Alison Leggett had to retire after obstacle 4, so she went in first to do the cones. She had one cone down and 1 time penalty. Beverly Mellstrom went in next and had just one cone down. I managed a clear round, but collected 2 time penalties. Anna Grayston did a double clear round, so she beat me by 5 points. Georgina Frith also managed a double clear round – not that it mattered very much as she won by some 40 points.

When the Brighton event and the Windsor CAI are a fortnight apart, there is usually a WPEC event on the intervening weekend. I was really pleased with the way the ponies went at this club event, and I had high hopes of doing well at Windsor. The four foreign entries at Windsor were Franz Feichtinger from Austria, Mia Allo from Belgium, Dirk Sonntag from Germany and Aart van de Kamp from the Netherlands with his usual team of piebald Shetlands. They were rather on the large size for purebred Shetlands and I would imagine that they were crossed with another breed. Even so, quite how he managed the times for the walks and the fast section with the ponies' short legs remains a mystery. At any rate, they flew round all the obstacles at a hand gallop.

It all started well enough when I found myself in second place to Georgina Frith in the dressage phase out of eleven entries and, the ponies went very well through all the early sections of the marathon, although I had trouble with both Carrick and Polly breaking pace in section C. We set off in section E full of hope and got through obstacle 1 without touching a thing in what I thought was a respectable time. I later discovered that only three of the others had been slower than me. I had a hesitation in obstacle 2, and then obstacle 3 turned out to be rather tighter than I had expected. I thought I got through it rather well, and it was only when I had finished the course that I discovered I had failed to go through gate B. As I did not appreciate that I had been eliminated at the time, I continued and got through the remainder without any further dramas, but it was all in vain. Beverly Mellstrom was also eliminated, and we both ended up with the eliminated score of 172. That gave me a combined total, before the cones, of 222.9 and Beverly Mellstrom had 224.3. Alison Leggett's combined score was 203.1.

Beverly Mellstrom went in first to do the cones and amassed a total of 39.5. I went in next and managed a clear round with just 1 time penalty for a total of 223.9. Alison Leggett then went in and hit two cones plus getting 11 time penalties, which put her total up to 224.1. So, much to my surprise, I moved up to ninth place. Georgina Frith won, with Aart van de Kamp in second place after doing the fastest marathon.

John Pickford, Anna Grayston and Emily Bennett were the only other competitors at St Fort. The Friday dawned with a bitterly cold east wind, but at least it was not raining. I thought the ponies did quite a good dressage test but, again, the judges did not share this opinion, nevertheless, my score was enough to put me in the lead, but with a very inadequate margin.

The marathon course followed much the same route as in the previous years. Recent heavy rains had made the going soft and muddy, and it was made considerably worse by the eleven horse teams doing their rounds. This did nothing to deter the ponies, who went through it all as if they were just out for the exercise, except, that is, for section E, where we, and everyone else, had time penalties. I had obviously started to suffer from advancing senility as I made a silly mistake in the very first obstacle. I simply failed to go through gate C after B and had to go all the way round to correct the omission, but then I succeeded in missing it again. Round I had to go for the second time with the seconds ticking away – to me almost audibly – giving 10 points to Anna Grayston. I managed a reasonable time in obstacle 2, in spite of a small hiccup, but then in 3, Carrick let me down badly. He had become progressively more difficult in the obstacles, and I suspect that he was counting the gates and when it came to six, he concluded that that was the end of the obstacle, and the moment had come for him to gallop out. On this occasion he shot forward after a gate and ran straight into a post. The result was that we missed gate B and had to go round again – another 10 points to Anna Grayston.

Things went rather better after that, and I beat Alison Leggett's times through obstacles 7 and 8. Having started some 10 points ahead of John Pickford, I was somewhat alarmed to find that he had caught up to within 2 points after the marathon.

The weather on the Sunday was simply appalling. It sluiced with rain all day and by the time we got to do the cones phase the collecting ring was a sea of mud. It was almost impossible to go wrong on the course as the previous drivers had created a set of deep tramlines. Emily Bennett had made a serious mistake in obstacle 1 and had to go in first to do the cones; she completed the only double clear round. John Pickford added 21.5 to his score, which helped me to breathe a bit more easily. I added 9.5 to my score to finish some 40 points behind Anna Grayston.

I was very disappointed with Carrick's performance. He had started so well in 1992, and had become one of my stalwarts. He was now virtually unmanageable in the obstacles, and he also caused problems both in the dressage and the cones. At a WPEC event in mid-June I took the opportunity to try Peter in the wheel with Storm for the marathon, and it worked very well. It was his first effort in this position, and he took to it like a veteran. I now felt a bit happier about the coming Sandringham event, for which nine competitors turned up.

With the new arrangement for the dressage with Peter and Polly in the lead and the two old boys in the wheel, I managed what I thought was quite a respectable score of 41.9. That put me 5 points ahead of Philippa Gammell, 7 ahead of Anna Grayston and 8 in front of Emily Bennett.

All went reasonably well in the marathon, although senility reared its head yet again in obstacle 2 when I lost my way, but I was not fast enough anyway. Philippa Gammell failed to go through gate B in obstacle 1 and was eliminated, so I was a little lucky only to drop to third, just ahead of Emily Bennett and John Pickford.

Five of us managed double clear rounds in the cones phase, so there was no change in the order. I was particularly pleased as it must have been the first time for several years that I had managed to get round the cones without any time penalties. The show ended with the usual accumulator competition. This time there were seven pairs of cones, each pair slightly narrower than the previous pair. I drew first to go and got through the first five before hitting pair six (10 cm over track width), but just succeeded in squeezing through the last pair (5 cm over track width) to score 250. Ursula Hirschberg got through the lot, although she hit one of the last pair, but the ball stayed in place and she scored the maximum of 300 points.

Drumlanrig attracted nine teams in mid-July. I was rather better pleased with my dressage than the judges, and I suspect this was due to the foreign judge, who gave me 10 more penalty points than the other two, so that my total was no less than 50.7. Georgina Frith won that phase fairly easily with 45.6 from the Australian driver Boyd Exell, who was on 50.1. He had been lent a team of Georgina Frith's spare ponies for this event.

These two competitors chased each other round the obstacles, with Georgina Frith finishing just 0.8 ahead of Boyd Exell. For once everything seemed to go right for me and I was third fastest round the course and it was one of the few occasions when I got round in under 100. Even so I was 20 points slower than the leaders.

It poured with rain all day Sunday, and by the time the pony teams started the cones, the other classes had gouged deep ruts through the course. Anna Grayston managed to hit two cones, while Philippa Gammell had an off day and hit three. Poor Emily Bennett was taken out of the slalom by her ponies, and, as she failed to start again from the beginning, she was eliminated. Disasters did not end there. John Pickford had to retire when he lost control. It later transpired that two of his ponies had been stung by horse flies at the girth. Georgina Frith did the only double clear round and Boyd Exell was just over time by 1.5. As I had only 1 time penalty, I was second in that phase and third overall, which was a very satisfactory result – at least for me.

Fig. 8.4 Galloping out of an obstacle at Drumlanrig in 1998. Unfortunately, this did not help me catch the two leaders, Georgina Frith and the Australian, Boyd Exell, who was driving a team lent to him by Georgina. Thanks to a series of disasters suffered by the other competitors in the cones, I managed to squeeze into third place. (*Nick Morris*)

I had seen from the schedule of events that there was to be a competition at Normanhurst in Sussex. As Normanhurst is not far from Glyndebourne, and I was able to persuade Micky Nevill to put me up, I entered for it. It did not get off to a very auspicious start. When we got close to the turning off the A271, it was completely blocked in both directions by stationary queues of horseboxes, trailers and caravans. It turned out that the trouble had been caused by the owner of a house on the track leading to the stable field parking her car on the track, and no-one could get past it. When she was eventually persuaded to move the car to let us in, Micky Flynn discovered that he could not get the box through the narrow entrance gate to the estate, and had to divert down a lane where the branches scratched the sides of the box and trailer. There had been a lot of rain recently and the single gateway into the stable field became so badly poached that boxes, trailers and caravans had to be towed in by tractors.

After that, the event went quite well, although Julia Liles was the only other entry in the pony-teams class. She amassed a score of 88 in the dressage to my 38. As it was a two-day event, we did the cones after the dressage and I just managed to squeak through with a double clear round.

We went round the marathon course on a beautiful Sunday afternoon, and I thought the ponies went really well again through heavy going and some quite challenging obstacles. Micky and I were nearly victims of the health and safety craze when we were threatened with elimination by a steward because we had undone the chinstraps of our hard hats as we crossed the finishing line.

Having solved the problem of getting the box and trailer out again through even softer mud in the entrance gate, I set off on the A23 for the M25 and Windsor. No sooner did I get on to the M25 than I hit a tailback from a crash at the intersection with the M23. Luckily, Micky saw the jam before he reached the M25 and diverted onto the A25. Three hours later I caught up with the box at Runnymede.

After this event, Micky and I came to the conclusion that Medina had become a real handicap for Penny Romsey and we persuaded her to swap him for Jane for the next event. I suggested Jane because I noticed that she was a bit of a loner and never seemed to get on with her neighbour. Even when the ponies were turned out in a field together, Jane was always on her own. A bit of practice with Jane in front of Hamble showed Penny that this was a considerable improvement.

Lowther came round again in August. It had rained heavily during the previous week, and there were intermittent showers on the Friday and Saturday. Sunday turned into a warm, sunny and muggy day. The dressage arena was soggy, which made the going heavy, and many competitors found the marathon seriously hard work.

Nine pony teams were entered, and Georgina Frith not only won the dressage, she raced through the obstacles and finished it off with a double clear round in the cones. Philippa Gammell came second in the dressage and I followed in third place, 8 points behind Georgina Frith.

Section A of the marathon was soft going over the Fell and section C was tight for time, but the ponies seemed to revel in it, perhaps because it was their ancestral home. I made errors in obstacles 1 and 4, but the rest went really well, and Medina, in his first event in the lead of a team, did his job next to Polly without any problems. At the end, I calculated that I had kept a slim lead over Ursula Hirschberg by 0.1 of a point to finish fifth. I then discovered that both Penny Romsey and I had been given an extra 10 penalties for 'deviating from the course' between the last obstacle and the finish. This was one of the provisions in another FEI gimmick to try to stop people, who were late, from galloping to the finish line, and arriving with panting and sweating horses. Equally, if they were early, it was intended to prevent them wasting time by going round in circles.

We had simply failed to notice a course marker on a kink going up the hill from the last obstacle. Instead, we had gone straight to a gate in the fence on the track. That dropped Penny Romsey to third place and I went down from fourth to fifth place. Ursula Hirschberg completed a double clear round to retain her third position, and, although Anna Grayston had 7 penalties to my 1, my extra 10 penalties for 'deviating' meant that I just retained my fourth place overall.

Fig. 8.5 A very sharp turn and sudden acceleration on the way out of the famous sandpit at Lowther in August 1998 very nearly got rid of Micky Flynn. (*Nick Morris*)

After a rather sticky start, it turned out to be an excellent season. I was surprised to discover that I had finished second to Anna Grayston in the points league championship. I have to admit that it was partly due to the fact that I had competed in rather more events than some of the others. I was delighted with the ponies and, considering that Lowther was his first experience in the lead of a team, Medina did very well indeed.

Results for 1998

EVENT	Dressage	Marathon	Cones	Pl/No
Brighton	2	3	3	3/5
Windsor	2	E	2	9E/11
St Fort	1	3	3	2/4
Sandringham	1	3	1=	3/9
Drumlanrig	3	3	2	3/9
Normanhurst	1	1	1	1/2
Lowther	2	5	3	4/9

Ponies used: Carrick, Storm, Polly, Peter, Jane (swapped with Medina for Lowther).

1999

From time to time I am asked to judge dressage, mostly the novice single pony class at Windsor Park Equestrian Club events, and sometimes at Sandringham, if I can get there in time. In order to qualify as a national judge, you need to attend a British Horse Driving Trials Association Judges Clinic at least once every two years. These usually take place at the splendid facility of the Unicorn Trust at Stow-in-the-Wold. The trust was set up by Sydney Smith, and its facilities are much used and appreciated by all the equestrian disciplines.

I began the 1999 season by judging the Open Single Horse Class at the first WPEC event of the season at half past nine in the morning. It was a particularly challenging experience since the selected test was the new FEI No. 7 Advanced. As luck would have it, this test had been discussed at the Judges Clinic in March, so that I had some idea what it was all about. It soon transpired that this was more than could be said for the competitors. It was just as well that I knew the test and was paying attention, because the very first competitor went wrong while doing the two circles at X. I rang the bell and showed him the sketch of how the movement was intended to be done, and sent him on his way to try again. Off he went and got it wrong again. I did not have the heart to stop him so I let it go and gave him a score of 2. After his final salute, I made another attempt to explain what he should have done, but I suspect he was too traumatized to take it in. The next competitor came in and, believe it or not, he made exactly the same mistake. I was beginning to think that it was going to take a very long time to get through the class, but fortunately things improved after that.

When it came to my turn, the ponies behaved as if they had never done such a thing as a dressage test in their lives. They either wandered around in a daze or jumped about and broke into a canter. Peter Munt was judging and I cannot imagine what he thought of it all. I was quite embarrassed, but he was very forgiving. At least they pulled themselves together for the cones and we managed a double clear round, which is always encouraging at the start of a season.

The ponies always have a good day out on the Sunday at a WPEC event as they have to go the six miles from their stables in the Castle Mews up to Cumberland Lodge before the three-section marathon, and then back again afterwards. On this occasion they did rather better than I expected, which was also encouraging. The only incident was when Medina slipped and nearly came down in obstacle 2, but he recovered very quickly. No such luck for Penny Romsey. Jane decided that she had not been in the square obstacle for long enough, and suddenly turned back into it just as she was expected to gallop out. This took her driver completely by surprise, and in trying to stop Jane, she simply rolled off the carriage, much to Micky's considerable and obvious amusement.

I had returned from a State Visit to Korea on the Thursday, and after the time change, I was not entirely confident that I would be in a fit state to judge anything on the Saturday morning of the second WPEC event at the end of April. I discovered that I had been allocated the classes for the novice single ponies and novice pairs of ponies – all twenty of them. It took three hours, and there was never a dull moment. Drivers went wrong in the most unexpected places, ponies spooked at imaginary dangers, or simply stopped and refused to move. I was reminded of a conversation with a lady competitor at Lowther. When I asked her how she had managed in the dressage, she said that all had been going well until her pony stopped at X and decided to have a pee, which was about the only thing that did not happen on that Saturday morning.

This event was also notable for the first appearance of two new recruits to the sport. I had been working on Naomi and Sebastian Ferranti for some years to get them to give up hunting at their advanced ages, and to take up carriage driving. To get Naomi Ferranti started, I lent her Carrick. After years in a team, I think he was quite happy to go on his own and proved to be a brilliant teacher. He went off to Henbury where he lived in the lap of luxury.

Sebastian Ferranti had also taken up the sport, but he bought what he described as a 'job lot' consisting of a pair of grey Welsh ponies, a carriage and a set of harness. For a polo player and a hunting man, driven dressage was an unfathomable mystery, and it took him a bit of time to get the hang of it. After he had been going for a time, I asked Naomi how he was getting on with his dressage. 'Splendidly' she replied, 'he can now drive to X and halt, then asks "what comes next?"'. He improved by using diagrams of the movements and driving them on a quad-bike in his practice arena.

After they had been driving for a while, I persuaded them to join the WPEC so that they could take part in some club events, and qualify for national events, and I found myself judging their first dressage tests at the end-of-April event. I later found out that I had placed Sebastian third with his pair of ponies, and Naomi twelfth, although that was largely owing to the fact that she made a major mistake.

Joe Moore was judging the pony tandems and placed Penny Romsey first in her new, and very smart, two-wheeled carriage.

I just had time on the Sunday to whiz round the marathon – and make a thorough mess of the water obstacle – before setting off for Saudi Arabia in the afternoon.

We arrived at Stanmer Park for the Brighton event in glorious spring weather, and it remained cloudless with a cool breeze for the rest of the weekend. The weather must have affected the ponies because they decided to co-operate, and did a really good test, spoiled only by Polly, who, when not waving her head about, felt an overwhelming urge to sniff her neighbour, the long-suffering Peter. At any rate the score of 43.2 was good enough to put me second to Georgina Frith by 1.1 points. Most of the other seven entries were in the early 50s.

The marathon was unusual, to say the least. The FEI – in its infinite wisdom – had thought up a new formula, and the British Horse Driving Trials Association wanted to try it out at the Brighton event. Apparently there had been criticism on the Continent about some of the horses sweating and panting at the end of the marathon – even human runners have been known to pant a bit after running a marathon. The object of the new formula was to ensure that horses were given a period to recover from the rigours of section E before arriving at the finish. In order to achieve this, the second walk (section D) was moved to follow section E, and the speed reduced to the equivalent of a leisurely stroll. This reduced the section to a farce, made even more farcical by having ground judges on this section, but not for section B (the first walk) which was at the usual speed. The consequence of this rearrangement was that section C (the fast section) followed immediately after A, which made the first part of the course much harder than before, particularly in the hilly country of the South Downs. It also meant that there was now only one ten minute halt. I gathered that the general, and not wholly

Fig. 8.6 and (*below*) 8.7 I had been working on Naomi and Sebastian de Ferranti for some time to get them to give up hunting and take up carriage driving. Naomi eventually succumbed and persuaded Sebastian to have a go as well. I lent Carrick to Naomi to get her started, and she then got her own pony. Sebastian started with the smart pair pictured, but they did not suit him, and he bought two of Georgina Frith's grey ponies. I suggested he try them as a tandem and got Micky Flynn to show him how to drive them. I am not sure that he appreciated quite what he was letting himself in for, but, much to his credit, he persisted and made considerable progress. (*8.6 Author's collection, 8.7 Alf Baker*)

unexpected, opinion was unfavourable, and I am glad to say, nothing further has been heard of it.

After inspecting the obstacles for longer and more often than ever before, I still thought they were hideously complicated, even though there were no really tricky bits. Come the day, all went reasonably well, except that Medina (who had been given the stable name Dina) would do an occasional jig-jog in the walk section. Fortunately, he seemed to know the walk rule, which allowed him five seconds of non-walking, and he nearly always started walking again just in time.

I began the obstacles badly by having a serious 'senior moment' in the very first. I had it firmly in my head that I had to go past two tractor tyres after passing through gate A and, deaf to Micky's urgent entreaties, I headed straight for gate C and went through it. That meant an immediate 20 penalties plus, and I had to go back and start again. Things did not improve in obstacle 2, when I misjudged gate C and destroyed a lattice panel. The resulting jerk to the carriage took it straight against a knock-down – another 2 unwanted penalties. After that there was not much I could do to recover, and I ended up last, although adding my dressage score moved me up two places.

Julia Liles went in first to do the cones and collected some time penalties. Beverly Mellstrom also acquired some penalties before I went in and did a clear round but added 4 penalties for time. Emily Bennett only had 5 points in hand, so she went rather carefully, rather too carefully as it turned out, as she collected 26.5 time penalties, and so I moved up a place. Emily was followed by Helen Cruickshank with 9 points in hand, but she hit four cones, which moved me up another place to fourth. The other three made no serious mistakes, but the out-come for me was rather better than I might have expected, although I was still a long way behind the leaders.

There were eight entries for Windsor. Mia Allo from Belgium and Cees van Opstal from the Netherlands were the only foreign competitors. I was delighted to see van Opstal again. We had competed against each other at several international events in the horse-teams class and his vivacious Italian wife always added a bit of spice to the social events. Otherwise the usual gang of locals were invited: Emily Bennett, Ursula Hirschberg, Anna Grayston, Beverly Mellstrom, Georgina Frith and me.

I do not know what it is about Windsor, but I never seem to be able to get my act together for these events. At least this one started fairly well as I won the dres-sage by 2 points from Mia Allo, but the marathon was the usual disaster. I worked it out later that it had taken me 3½ minutes longer to get through the obstacles than Georgina Frith. I was also somewhat mortified to discover that Penny Romsey had beaten me through them by 14 points. I grinned and bore it as best I could, but Micky was, I thought, offensively delighted with his pupil. Nothing was changed by the cones and I was saved from being last by Cees van Opstal.

St Fort would have been next in the calendar, but the National Championships were due to be held there in September, and Andrew Mylius thought that it would not be possible to organize two events in the same year. To fill the gap left in the calendar, the Lothians Driving Club persuaded the Earl of Rosebery to allow it to run an event on his property at Dalmeny. This lies along the south coast of the Firth of Forth between Edinburgh and the Forth Railway Bridge. Years ago, I had spent the night at Dalmeny when Neil Rosebery's father was the Lord Lieutenant of East Lothian and I had almost forgotten how brilliantly the house is set, looking out over the Forth across to Burntisland. It is difficult to believe that this rural estate is wedged into this built-up area so close to Edinburgh. It is a lovely place, but sadly not very convenient for a driving event. The only flat area in the park is part of the golf course, and this was considered to be too sacred for a driving arena. While the stable field and the arena were fairly close together, the latter had a distinct hump in it. I remember coming into the arena for my dressage and was surprised to find that the judge at A was almost out of sight over the horizon.

The weather on the Friday and Saturday was simply awful, although I was lucky enough to do both the dressage and the marathon between showers. The ponies were not at their best for the dressage, but at least they were good enough to win by a meagre 6 points from Philippa Gammell and Jane MacInnes. The other two competitors were Anneke Wallace and Ann Robarts in what I think was Ann's first national event.

I thought the ponies had gone really well in the obstacles and, for once, I made no serious mistakes. I did have a problem in obstacle 5 when Dina took great exception to some flapping flags on top of straw bales and we overshot gate F. I chose to circle round, instead of trying to back out, and that must have cost me a couple of extra penalties. Even so I was a bit disappointed to find that both Philippa Gammell and Anneke Wallace had beaten me by 17 and 8 points respectively. That left me 12 points behind Philippa Gammell and only 3 points ahead of Anneke Wallace before the cones.

Ann Robarts went in first and had what can only be described as a difficult round. She was followed by Jane MacInnes, who had just 3 time penalties. The heat was on me when Anneke Wallace did a double clear round and I could not afford to hit a single cone. Luck was with me and I added nothing to my score to retain second place. Philippa Gammell also did a faultless round, and emerged the winner.

I managed to get to Wood Farm for the Sandringham event on the Wednesday evening so that I could drive the ponies on the Thursday morning and walk the obstacles in the afternoon. I then had to take a helicopter back to Windsor for the 'return banquet' by the President of Hungary at the conclusion of his State Visit. The Hungarians had chosen to hold their banquet in the The Compleat Angler in Marlow. This rather odd choice was made because the designer of the suspension bridge over the Thames next to The Compleat Angler was the same man who had designed the famous suspension bridge over the Danube in Budapest. I was driven back to Wood Farm after the dinner.

The 'cats', in the shapes of Georgina Frith, Philippa Gammell, and Anna Grayston, were away at the European Championships, so without them the 'mice' could play by having a great time at Sandringham and a very close competition.

The Friday was a glorious day with not a cloud in the sky, but apparently this was not good enough for the ponies who showed little interest in, or enthusiasm for, the dressage. However, when I looked at the score sheets, I saw that I had been given 145 – out of 160 – by one judge, 135 from another and 117 by the third, which turned into a total of 53.1 penalties. Later that day I saw Penny Romsey coming out of the arena swearing to shoot her ponies and then herself – a sentiment not infrequently expressed by many drivers. It turned out that she was seventh with a score of 55.

Saturday was another brilliant day with a cool breeze. I was delighted with the ponies as they were really lively and willing. All mistakes were entirely due to driver error: I forgot where I was going in obstacle 4; then I very nearly went through the wrong gate in obstacle 5, which wasted time; and I was again delayed in obstacle 8 by getting stuck against a post. I got ahead of Jane MacInnes, but Emily Bennett squeezed ahead of me.

Sunday started cloudy but dry. There was a short shower at lunch time and I thought it was going to clear up, so I took off my wet-weather gear. However, no sooner had I reached the collecting ring than it started to rain in earnest, and by the end of the prize-giving I was soaked to the skin. In fact, it was raining so heavily that it had been decided to end the show there and then. I was in the middle of doing my cones round when I heard Marcus O'Lone, the Land Agent, making the announcement in the main ring. I then heard the National Anthem being played while I was still negotiating the cones. The thought crossed my mind that I should stop and take my hat off, but I decided to continue and hope that I might be forgiven for completing my round.

The position before the cones phase was that Emily Bennett was in front, I followed in second place, with Jane MacInnes and Anneke Wallace in third and fourth places respectively, all within about 10 points of each other, and so there was all to play for. Anneke Wallace had one cone down for 5 penalties and 8 time penalties, and then Jane MacInnes went in and hit one cone. That gave me a little more breathing space, which was just as well because, although I went clear in the cones, I added 4.5 time penalties. That gave Emily Bennett a slightly bigger safety margin of 6.4 points, or one cone and a few time penalties, a margin she did not actually need as she did a faultless round to win.

For once, the weather was glorious for Drumlanrig and the hot sun had dried up the arenas to make the going perfect. The ponies were a bit ragged in the dressage, so I was quite surprised to find that I had done better than the other competitors. However, my lead over Emily Bennett of 1.1 was never going to be enough to keep her at bay in the marathon. Although the weather was ideal for the marathon, it had been raining for the last three months and the tracks through the woods were quite soft. By the time I went round, as the last competitor of all, they were badly poached I heard later that nearly a quarter of all the competitors had been sent home before starting section E because of the distressed condition of their horses and ponies. My ponies seemed to be quite unmoved by the conditions, and I thought we were doing really quite well through the obstacles, but Emily Bennett must have stormed round as she was 12 points ahead of me – she also knocked down several rails in the process. I managed to increase my lead over Jane MacInnes by 3 points. Both Emily Bennett and I did double clear rounds in the cones, so the final order was not changed.

There was rather a sad end to the event as the main sponsors, British Nuclear Fuels Limited, had decided to pull out, and John Cowdery announced that he could not continue to organize it. There were vague rumours that some other local enthusiast might take it on, but they were not given much weight. It is a great pity, as it was a wonderful site for a driving event and I always thoroughly enjoyed staying at the castle.

Early in the year, Joe Moore had told me that, in the previous year, he had organized a club event at Barons Court in Northern Ireland, and that it had been a great success. This year he had managed to fit it in between Drumlanrig and Lowther in the hope that some competitors from the mainland might enter. I thought this was a splendid idea, as I had known the owners of Barons Court, the Duke and Duchess of Abercorn, for a very long time and I had always wanted to visit the place. Needless to say there was a certain amount of anxiety about going to Northern Ireland just after the collapse of the so-called 'peace initiative', but all was well in the end, and it turned out to be a very enjoyable event in glorious country. There were rather fewer entries than would be expected at a national event: fifty rather than the more usual 100, and quite a number came from south of the border. I was interested to see that the Irish had introduced classes for what were described as 'roadcarts'. These are two-wheeled carts on pneumatic tyres and most of them looked as if they had been home-made. They were driven with all the passion you would expect from the Irish equestrian community.

The dressage took place on the lawn in front of the very handsome house, but the going was a bit soft, which made things difficult for the horses and ponies. There were five pony teams: Helen Cruickshank, Ann Robarts, Emily Bennett, a local entry, Jeffrey Lyons, and me. My ponies were not brilliant but at least they went better than the others and I found myself just 1.2 points ahead of Emily Bennett.

The marathon course was set out over a variety of country from open fields to woods, and along better-than-average forestry tracks. The ponies did all the sections without difficulty, and the open, flowing obstacles, many of original design, gave them a chance to move on. Having had the unusual experience of getting round the marathon without any problems, I was, however, still 5.4 points slower than Emily Bennett.

The cones phase was also set up on the front lawn. As Helen Cruickshank had gone wrong in obstacle 8 and incurred 20 extra penalties, she drove first and had one cone down and a few time penalties. Ann Robarts was unlucky to hit two cones and to pick up some time penalties. She was followed by Jeffrey Lyons, who had just one cone down and a couple of penalties for time. I was 4 points behind Emily Bennett, but I made a proper mess of the course and hit two cones (the first of the season), probably from overconfidence, but it made no difference as Emily Bennett added nothing to her score to win by some 16 points.

The hospitality of the organizing committee was more than generous, and there was great enthusiasm at the prize-giving on the Sunday evening. I suspect that the ensuing party went on well into the night.

This event at Barons Court was from the 16th to the 18th of July and the next event was over the weekend of the 6th to the 8th of August at Lowther. As it would have made a very long round trip to return to Windsor from Ireland and then go back up to Cumbria, Sebastian Ferranti very kindly offered to put up the ponies at his place at Henbury in Cheshire, and found comfortable accommodation for the grooms in a local pub.

Sebastian Ferranti had been chairman of his very successful family electrical and electronics company when it won a contract from the Ministry of Defence to design and manufacture a ground-to-air guided missile system. The 'Bloodhound' system proved to be highly successful, and, as a result of winning many export orders, it made the company a lot of money, so much so that MPs complained that it had made too much profit on the contract and persuaded the government to impose what was virtually a fine for being too successful. He was also ordered to float the company on the Stock Exchange and employ a Chief Executive Officer. The man, who was virtually forced upon the company, turned out to be a serious disaster, and through injudicious acquisitions succeeded in ruining the company.

It was then acquired by Lord Weinstock's GEC. When part of that merged with a French company, and the rest turned into Marconi, which in turn suffered an almost complete collapse through mismanagement, one of Britain's most successful electrical, electronics and computer companies virtually disappeared.

The house at Henbury is Sebastian Ferranti's pride and joy. He has had a long and abiding interest in classical architecture and interior design, particularly in the Italian sixteenth century Palladian school. He set about building a house in that style on the site of the old house on his estate near Macclesfield. The result is a most delightful building in the surroundings of a typical English country-house park.

After a brief period of rest and refreshment, the whole party moved on to Lowther where there were a number of occurrences over which I would prefer to draw a veil. Storm and Peter had not been going all that well together in the lead for the dressage, and I suggested to Micky that it might be an idea to swap Peter for Carrick, but Micky did not greet this idea with enthusiasm. The team remained the same, therefore, and the result was a disaster. Polly leant against the pole with her head turned out most of the time, while Storm decided to pull away from Peter, so that his head was bent inwards. I had quite a struggle keeping them going fairly straight, and when I got to X to start the two circles, I completely lost track of what I should have been doing and set off to do the left circle first. I realized my mistake at once, but the judge sounded the hooter before I could correct

Fig. 8.8 Sebastian Ferranti's father pulled down the old Henbury Hall, near Macclesfield in Cheshire, and Sebastian decided to replace it with this charming Palladian Villa. The dome sits above a large hallway, with the result that there is not much space left for the upstairs bedrooms. However, it is extremely comfortable, and full of delightful things and his idiosyncratic collection of pictures. The park and surrounding countryside lend themselves well to driving events. Unlike most of the other events on the circuit, no provision has been made for paying spectators, so that it becomes a very happy 'family' event. (*Sebastian de Ferranti*)

it. This earned me an extra 5 penalties, and I ended up last in eighth place with a score of 51.5, but not all that far behind Georgina Frith's 39.5.

The only marginally bright spot was that I was sixth in the marathon, although some 30 points slower than Georgina Frith, and in seventh place before the cones. Just to rub salt into the wound, seven competitors managed double clear rounds. Only John Robertson, with four cones down, and me, with one cone down, had any penalties at all. That pushed me back to eighth place again, although only 0.3 points behind Anneke Wallace. This was a very discouraging performance.

The week after Lowther, I joined seven other competitors for the second event to be held at Alnwick Castle. Having reached the age when I seem to have known everyone's father, or even grandfather, I was reminded that I had once stayed at the castle with the father and mother of the present Duke of Northumberland. I had also known his mother, Elizabeth, during the war, when she was a WRNS officer. When her husband, Hughie, died, she reconstructed an unoccupied farmhouse near the old priory in Hulne Park, and very kindly invited me to stay there for the event. Friar's Well is at the top of the park with glorious views over the Northumbrian countryside. The grooms and ponies were nearly as lucky because the stable field is on the other side of the Aln river from the castle, and when it is floodlit at night it is a spectacular sight for everyone in the stable field.

Things went a great deal better than at Lowther. After much discussion, we decided to try Carrick in the lead with Storm, and to bring Peter back to partner

Fig. 8.9 The first obstacle at Lowther under the terrace below the old castle in August 1999. Everything was going all right here, but it was a disastrous event in every other respect. I was last in the dressage, and even though I came fifth in the marathon, I ended up eighth out of nine competitors overall. (*Nick Morris*)

Fig. 8.10 The water obstacle across the Lowther River in August 1999. Spectators love watching competitors at this obstacle, it always looks dramatic but, once the horses or ponies get used to the idea of paddling through the shallow water, they seem to enjoy it. (*Nick Morris*)

Polly. To my great relief, it worked. They were much easier to drive and Polly seemed more relaxed. At any rate, this time I got to within 1 point of Philippa Gammell and Jane MacInnes, who were tied in the lead.

I am not sure what inspired the ponies, or me, in the marathon, but I heard the commentator announce that I had been through the first four obstacles faster than Philippa Gammell. I finished the Marathon on 99 – one of the very few occasions that I managed to achieve a score under 100 – and just under 4 points faster than her. Anneke Wallace was only 0.6 points behind Philippa Gammell.

There was a very unfortunate incident just before the cones phase started. Anna Grayston's ponies spooked at something in the collecting ring, spun round, throwing her off the box, and took off towards the stable field. They were caught fairly quickly, but it was an unnerving experience for Anna Grayston and she withdrew from the competition.

The top three places were very close together before the cones: I was on 142.7, Anneke Wallace was on 144.9 and Philippa Gammell was on 145.9. There was very little in it, but at least I stood a chance of winning the event. However, I had not reckoned with the FEI. It turned out that it had asked the British Horse Driving Trials Association to try out a new formula for the cones phase.

Under the existing system every cone knocked down costs 5 penalties. There is then a 'time allowed' for the course, before time penalties are given on the scale of half a point for every second over the time allowed. Under the system proposed by the FEI, each competitor was to be timed over the course and the seconds then converted into penalties at the rate of 0.2 penalties per second, then 10 seconds, or 2.5 penalties, were to be added for every cone knocked down.

I had not worked it out at the time, but it transpired that I had 10 seconds (2.2 points) in hand over Anneke Wallace and 16 seconds (3.2 points) over Philippa Gammell. They both went round in exactly the same fast time of 151 seconds. I drove as fast as I dared, but it took me 162 seconds, or 11 seconds slower than Anneke Wallace, which meant that she beat me by one second! The irony is that I would have beaten her under the old rules, as my slower time was still within the time allowed, and I would have had a double clear round. The new system was not popular with either the competitors or with the judges and scorers. It was also difficult for the spectators to follow what was going on. I am glad to say that nothing more has been heard of the idea. Whatever the result of the event, it was a wonderful way to end the season.

I was particularly interested in this latest FEI proposal because, in May of 1999, I was asked by Anneke Wallace, Chairman of the British Horse Driving Trials Association's Rules Committee, whether I would be prepared to serve as a co-opted member of the Committee. I think this was in response to the announcement by the FEI that the International Driving Rules were to be revised in 2000 (all the FEI publications are revised every four years). When I heard this, I got in touch with the Chairman of the FEI Driving Committee, Jack Pemberton of Canada, and offered to rewrite the rules from beginning to end. I argued that so many amendments had been added over the years that they had become quite confused and included many contradictions, and that the system for arranging the articles, paragraphs and sub-paragraphs had become inconsistent. Furthermore, the sport had developed since the first edition of the rules was published in the early 1970s so that a more logical sequence of subjects had become desirable.

Jack Pemberton accepted the offer, and I made it my holiday task for the autumn of that year. Oddly enough, the fact that I have a laptop and a printer at all is entirely due to the FEI. The various FEI discipline committees revised their own rules for their particular disciplines, but I found that it worked better if I, as Chairman of the Bureau (Executive Committee) and of the Annual General

Assembly of Affiliated National Federations, co-ordinated the revision of the Statutes and General Regulations. The first time I attempted this task in 1980, I had to do it with scissors, paste and a photocopier, and very laborious it was too. Suggestions were invited, and then debated in committee before deciding whether to incorporate the suggestions in a new draft. The drafts then had to be circulated to all members of the Bureau, and further changes incorporated. Finally, they had to be accepted by the General Assembly.

When I undertook the same task four years later, in 1984, I thought that a computer would eliminate the laborious process of cutting, pasting and photocopying, so I acquired a large Apricot desktop computer and a huge IBM printer. Having a particular use for the relatively simple machine, I found it fairly easy to get the BOSWriter software to do, roughly, what I wanted. When I had completed the work, I put it all on a disk and sent it to the FEI Head Office. I was about to return all this equipment to my office, when it struck me that it might come in handy for writing my own letters, speeches, forewords, introductions and various messages for special occasions that I am asked to do.

Anyway, I set to work revising the driving rules on my laptop during the holidays at Balmoral. I started by rearranging the sequence of subjects, and then decided on a comprehensive system of numbering and lettering the articles paragraphs and subparagraphs. This, I believe, is very important, since there is always the necessity to quote a particular rule by its own paragraph. This means that no paragraph should contain more than one identifiable rule.

As I finished a chapter, I would fax it to Jack Pemberton in Canada for his comments and corrections. It was not my intention to introduce any particular changes to the sense of the rules, I just wanted to make them more logical and comprehensible. I thought that changes should remain the responsibility of the Driving Committee and its Chairman.

It was a very time-consuming exercise, but, after a great deal of correspondence by fax with Jack Pemberton, I was quite pleased with the majority of the result. There were the occasional issues on which he and I disagreed fundamentally, but, except for one passage (recognizable to the discerning eye in the current rule book), we usually managed to resolve the problem by compromise. The result of all this is that my draft was eventually accepted, almost in its entirety, by both Jack Pemberton and the Driving Committee.

The only serious disappointment is that the Driving Committee decided to do away with the five-section marathon for championships and went so far as to remove the rules for it from the main body of the rule book. I did at least persuade the Chairman to retain the rules for the five-section marathon in an appendix. I discovered that the FEI had also decided to do away with some of the sections of the cross-country part of the ridden three-day event. This has greatly upset a large section of the three-day-event community in this country. Quite what prompted this odd decision is not clear, but I suspect it is partly owing to the health and safety lobby, which maintains that the competitions are too long and exhausting, and partly to 'professionals', who are anxious to compete as often as possible in order to take advantage of the considerable prize money on offer on the Continent.

As far as driving events are concerned, the time taken in competition on the dressage day is ten minutes, while the cones only take about three. A five-section marathon takes about two hours. If this is reduced to about an hour, I suspect that many people will wonder whether it is worth all the trouble of travelling long distances for such a short time in competition.

It was at about the end of the 1999 season that I began to wonder how much longer I should go on competing. I had never given it much thought before, but I was seventy-eight and considerably older than all the other competitors. Two things decided me to go on for a bit longer. First, Micky Flynn was a genius with the ponies and, as long as he was prepared to stick with them, I knew I would have no problems on that score. The second thing was that these driving competitions gave me a chance to visit some of the most lovely parts of the country. I had come to the conclusion that, while in the early days I had to find somewhere to stay in order to compete, it was now a case of competing in order to stay in glorious country houses and drive through spectacular country. Furthermore, ever since moving from horses to ponies, I had looked at the sport as a means of enjoying myself in congenial company without any great ambition – or expectation – of doing particularly well.

RESULTS FOR 1999

EVENT	Dressage	Marathon	Cones	Pl/No
Brighton	2	7	3	3/5
Windsor	1	E	6	7/8
Dalmeny	1	3	1=	2/5
Sandringham	2	3	1=	2/6
Drumlanrig	1	2	1=	2/4
Barons Court	1	2	4	2/5
Lowther	8	7	8	8/9
Alnwick	4	1	3	2/8

Ponies used: Carrick, Storm, Polly, Peter, Medina.

CHAPTER NINE

FOUR SCORE YEARS

2000–2002

WHENEVER A PROMISING young Fell pony became available from Balmoral, he or she would be taken to Sandringham in January, and introduced to the traumas of being driven in a team of four. We had bought a very nice filly, by the name of Heather, who joined the party in 1999 and showed considerable promise. We turned her out for the rest of that season, and then brought her back to replace Carrick in 2000. Carrick was a faithful soul and always worked his heart out, but he had come to think that he knew it all, and was inclined to take you his way through the obstacles. However, it was not the end of his driving career. He had helped Naomi Ferranti start driving and then went on to get Sophie Wessex started. He is also occasionally ridden by the Queen.

The season began, as usual, with the event at Brighton, but it was different this time. Instead of staying with Micky Nevill, I was staying at Firle Park as a guest of Lord Gage. One of the great attractions of staying with Micky Nevill had been that she had an excellent cook, who not only produced delicious dinners, but also prepared the most sumptuous picnic lunches, which were happily consumed around – or in, depending on the weather – my horsebox. I was therefore a bit anxious about the new arrangements, but I need not have worried. Nicky Gage employed the caterers at Glyndebourne, and their picnics were something to be seen, and eaten.

As it had rained persistently throughout April, the conditions nearly caused the event to be cancelled. The going was soggy, and the marathon course soon became a mud bath. It drizzled all day Friday, but it cleared up for Saturday and, after a dismal start, Sunday improved as the day went on. On the Thursday, I had tried Heather in the wheel with Polly, and put Peter and Storm in the lead. Polly went well enough, but the two old boys behaved atrociously. So I took a deep breath and decided to switch the leaders and wheelers round for the dressage.

Heather was a bit slow to respond at times, but they went really well and I got to within 0.8 points of Emily Bennett, who scored 39.7.

That was the last I saw of Emily. She charged round the marathon obstacles in 97.4, but even that was not good enough to keep up with Georgina Frith, who must have flown to score only 80.4, while I earned 108.2! Anna Grayston, after a bad start in the dressage, got round in 100.6.

I thought it was a bit early to put Heather in the lead for the marathon in her first national event, so I put Polly together with Dina. The course was quite tough, but the ponies were undaunted, and we made all the times, although the leaders shied at supposed horrors at every turn, and Dina drove me mad by persistent titupping in the walk sections. My undoing was bad judgement in selecting routes through the obstacles. That wasted time in obstacle 2 and I overshot in obstacle 5, which wasted more time.

I put the dressage team back together for the cones phase, and I was delighted with the way Heather performed. In spite of having one cone down and 4 time penalties, Georgina Frith swept through to win. Emily Bennett had one down, and, as I did a double clear round (in the fastest time of the whole class), that narrowed the gap between us to 6.6. Anna Grayston was fourth, 12 points further back. It was altogether a very encouraging start to the season.

Ten teams arrived for the Windsor International: Mia Allo and Edwin Flerackers from Belgium, Tobias Bucker from Germany and Aart van de Kamp from the Netherlands, plus the native contingent of Georgina Frith, Beverly Mellstrom, Emily Bennett, Anna Grayston, Philippa Gammell, and me.

The weather was absolutely foul on the Thursday and I got soaked when I took the ponies out for some exercise, as did all the drivers who did their dressage on that day. Fortunately the weather improved dramatically on Friday, and remained brilliant for the rest of the weekend. I put the same team together for the dressage that I had driven at Brighton, and I thought they went really quite well, but, while Joe Moore agreed and put me first, and John Cowdery placed me second, Diana Brownlie was obviously unimpressed, and put me eighth out of ten. It would not have been very significant as there were only 6 points between me in fourth and Georgina Frith in first place, but my only hope of doing well was to get ahead in the dressage to make up for my lack of speed in the marathon obstacles. Mia Allo was in second place and Tobias Bucker was third.

There was a completely new set of marathon obstacles designed by a new course builder, Tony Petitpierre. They were well built, with no nasty traps, but as they were all constructed of posts and rails, there was a certain sameness about them. As George Bowman put it, 'it is a case of hunt-the-letter'. First you had to find a way to distinguish a particular obstacle from the others, and then you had to find the entry and lettered gates, and work out how to get from one to the next in the right order. Finally you had to get the chosen route firmly fixed in your memory. This made putting a plan together quite a challenge. Whatever my long-term memory may be like, it is becoming only too obvious that the short-term version is definitely verging on the unreliable.

The early sections of the marathon took us for a pleasant drive through the Great Park in brilliant sunshine, and it was warm enough to do section E in shirt sleeves. In the obstacles, I just had one brush with a post and overshot the turn into gate F in obstacle 5, otherwise everything, for a pleasant change, went according to plan, but it was still slow compared to the experts, and I finished in seventh place. Mia Allo must have had a serious problem in obstacle 5, as she collected 40.2 penalties and went down to eighth place. Aart van de Kamp came unstuck in obstacle 1 with a score of 36.4, which was enough to drop him to fifth.

The cones course must have been quite driver-friendly, as there were seven double clear rounds, including mine. Philippa Gammell was only 1.8 points ahead of me, and when she hit a cone, I went up a place to sixth overall. Georgina Frith won by some 12 points ahead of Tobias Bucker, in spite of hitting one cone.

It was becoming obvious that Hamble was proving rather too much of a handful for Penny Romsey, and when he carted her in the sixth obstacle at Windsor, I thought it was time to do something about it. On the Monday morning, I swapped him for Storm and drove Hamble myself in the wheel with Peter. He pulled my arms out, but I told her she could drive Storm with Jane in the next Windsor Park Equestrian Club event.

That combination worked quite well for her on the following weekend, except that Jane was at her most idiotic and frustrating in the dressage. At least she managed a quick clear round in the cones phase. Luckily, Jane elected to behave in the marathon, which she always enjoys, and they did a good round with Storm in the wheel. I put Hamble in again for the marathon, and he went perfectly with Peter. The event was somewhat marred when a huge black cloud unloaded its cargo just as I was about to start. I had a waterproof jacket on, but there was no time to put on the trousers. The result was dampening, to put it mildly. The water ran down the jacket onto my moleskin trousers and as all the water on the seat ran down into the depression under my backside, I was given a sharp reminder of what it must have been like to sit in wet nappies.

There must have been general agreement that, however beautiful the grounds at Dalmeny, the place was not really suitable for a driving event, and so, for the next event on the calendar, an alternative venue was required. The chosen place was Hopetoun, the home of the Hope family and the Marquess of Linlithgow, whose grandfather had been Viceroy of India, and my immediate predecessor as

Chancellor of Edinburgh University. The house lies on the south bank of the Forth, but above South Queensferry and the Forth Railway Bridge. The house looks enormous, but it turns out to be quite 'thin'. There is a smallish seventeenth century house with an eighteenth century façade in the middle, and two huge wings attached to the house by colonnades. To the east, it looks towards the railway bridge over a very impressive 'lawnscape', with the main arena on the south side of the drive. The only minor snag about the layout for a driving event is that the stable field is about 400 m from the main arena, and the stable field itself is somewhat uneven. Everything else was ideal, and Adrian and Auriol Linlithgow could not have been more considerate hosts.

There was a fairly modest entry of sixty-five for this event, but only two of them were pony teams. Emily Bennett made the journey, and my Fells and I were the second team. Philippa Gammell was entered but did not turn up.

As Heather and Dina had gone quite well together in the lead for the dressage at the last WPEC event, I put them together again. It was not quite such a success. Dina spooked at everything visible and invisible, and nearly took me out of the arena on one occasion. He also wandered all over the place in the walk. Emily Bennett's test was not brilliant so I found myself only 3.4 points behind her.

There was intermittent heavy rain on the Saturday, and section A of the marathon course was quite badly poached by the time I started as the last to go.

Fig. 9.1 Hopetoun House, a few miles west of the Forth Railway Bridge, looks enormous, but the wing on the right houses the old stables, while the wing on the left includes the ballroom. Only the middle of the centre block is more than two rooms thick. The middle and right-hand end of the centre block are open to the public. The stable field and arena are just beyond the round pond at the top of the photograph. (*Marquess of Linlithgow*)

At least it remained dry while I was on the course. The obstacles were mercifully large and open, but the first one had a lot of bunting decorating it, which flapped noisily in the breeze horrifying Dina, thus delaying me a bit. I was rather slow in the next three obstacles, but I managed the last four faster than Emily, in spite of losing a tyre from one of the back wheels coming out of obstacle 7. However, she still gained another 3 points by the end of the marathon. That gave her one cone and 1 point in hand before the cones phase.

Rather than risk Dina in the lead in the cones phase, I swapped him for Polly and she and Heather went very well together. Unfortunately, I hit 17 after an awkward corner and then hit 18 as well for no reason at all. That gave Emily Bennett a nice margin of 16 points, or three cones and 1 time penalty. She nearly had a disaster at 17, when she somehow got a rein caught in the harness. She hit the cone, but just managed to regain control before the next pair. We were both inside the time allowed, and so she was the winner by 10.7 points.

It is always nice to go back to familiar places, but there is a lot to be said for trying somewhere new, especially when it is set in such glorious countryside, and against the spectacular backdrop of Hopetoun House. It was a thoroughly enjoyable event for the competitors, but, like Dalmeny, it is not easily accessible to spectators. There was much speculation about what might happen in the following year, as Andrew Mylius was expected to want his old dates back again for the event at St Fort. If that were to happen, it looked as if Hopetoun might clash with Farleigh in Hampshire.

Fig. 9.2 There were only two pony teams at the Hopetoun event in 2000. It was a straight duel between Emily Bennett and myself. Although she won all three phases, the scores were quite close and she only won by some 10 points at the end. (*Author's collection*)

The event at Farleigh Wallop in early June had been going for a couple of years before I found it possible to enter. As it is only a short distance from Windsor, if there is anything for me to do at Windsor during the weekend, it is very easy for me to go to and fro. The Farleigh Estate and Farleigh House belong to the Earl of Portsmouth of the Wallop family. I believe his father thought the house was too big or uncomfortable, at any rate he let it to a preparatory school, and then sent his son to the school. Quentin, the present Earl, was fortunate enough to sell a bit of the property to Basingstoke for development, and with the proceeds he was able to get the grey stone and flint house back, and make it into a very comfortable home. I had never met him, but fortunately he turned out to be Micky Nevill's nephew (she was born a Wallop) and she persuaded him to put me up for this new event.

It had rained heavily the week before we arrived, and the stable field had become so soggy that every horsebox had to be towed in by tractors and the resulting quagmire made motorcycling, and even walking, really treacherous.

In the early days, we were allowed to drive round marathon courses in four-wheel-drive vehicles to inspect the obstacles, but with the increase in competitors, all these vehicles tended to make a nasty mess, particularly if the ground was anything but bone dry. Consequently, the organizers decided to ban them. Many people had taken to bicycles, and others had invested in mopeds and similar lightweight motorbikes. I eventually decided that I had better conform and bought myself a very small Honda Easy-Rider. I also bought one for Micky Flynn,

Fig. 9.3 I bought this Honda Easy-Rider when most, if not all, events banned the use of cars to inspect the obstacles. It proved a great success even though I had a couple of spills by skidding in mud or getting stuck in wheel ruts. (*Ian Jones*)

and persuaded Penny Romsey, Sebastian Ferranti and Michael Onslow to get them. I discovered that its maximum speed downhill and downwind is about 48 kph, however you are so near to the ground that even at that speed I felt as if I was nearing the land speed record. In practice, of course, you can never get near maximum speed on the marathon course. My only problem was that I found it a bit difficult to get used to the twist-grip throttle, as it works in the opposite way to the throttle on the collective lever in a helicopter, which was my only previous experience with a twist-grip throttle. My progress in the early days was therefore a bit erratic, but I have improved with practice.

Although I had no intention of using it on a public road, I found I had to license it, and I also had to have a licence to ride it. I discovered that the process of getting a licence is quite complicated, and requires a candidate to do a course. I could see that this might cause problems, so, before going into the regulations in detail, I thought I would have a look at my ordinary driving licence. I got my first licence in this country during the war, and it was simply renewed whenever necessary. I have no idea how it happened, but I was greatly relieved to see that it included motorcycles up to so many ccs, and so that let me off the hook.

I was well aware that this mode of transport would cause comment. I suspect that it was equally divided between those who thought 'Isn't he good for his age', and those who wondered 'What does this old fool think he's doing?' Needless to say, it also attracted some media interest, and I was unwise enough to be photographed giving Penny Romsey a lift while inspecting the obstacles at Lowther. This caused the gossip writers to salivate in a big way. At least they did not notice me giving Georgina Frith a lift at the Windsor event.

Carl Barnard was back among the entries for the Farleigh event, and joined Anna Grayston, Julia Liles, Beverly Mellstrom and Ann Robarts. Georgina Frith drove John Pickford's ponies *hors concours*, having already won the pony tandems class. *Carriage Driving Magazine*, reporting on the pony tandems class, said:

> The Earl of Onslow, cursed his Palomino Welsh ponies around the obstacles, much to the amusement of Stewards and onlookers, before coming to grief in the last gate of obstacle 6. His ponies, eventually caught, reappeared unscathed, as did driver and back-stepper.

As Penny Romsey was unable to drive at this event, I had intended to borrow Hamble to replace Storm, but Micky was not able to enter him in time, and so I was back with the old firm. I tried Polly in the lead with Heather for the dressage, but the result was not brilliant, although I just managed to get 1.5 points ahead of Beverly Mellstrom. Georgina Frith won the dressage by 2.9 points.

Fig. 9.4 In January 1999, I invited Michael Onslow to bring his tandem to Sandringham. He is driving what he described as his yellow 'chip basket' and is well rugged-up against the cold. He names his ponies after Byzantine emperors and empresses. He converted to a team soon after this, and I think he found it rather a different sort of challenge. (*Countess of Onslow*)

Having lost a tyre at Hopetoun, I had to use the carriage I got after the disaster at Drumlanrig. It seemed alright to me, but both Micky and my groom Pip (Paula Pearson) complained that the back end was sliding to and fro. Considering the going, I was not unduly surprised. I took the Portsmouths' younger daughter, Rose (10), with me for Sections A, B, C and D. It was a lovely drive through old oak woods, but the tracks were deep mud and very bumpy. For some reason, which I cannot recall, I put Polly in the lead with Dina and I was a bit shaken when we only just managed the walk sections with a few seconds to spare.

Having unloaded Rose, we started section E full of hope. All went reasonably well through a nicely varied set of obstacles until I got to obstacle 7 when I had a serious memory fade, made a mistake and slipped back 10 points behind Beverly Mellstrom and 12 points behind Anna Grayston.

The arena for the dressage and cones phases was on the old school playing field, so it was unusually flat – for driving competitions – and the going could not have been better. The cones course was ideal, long and open with no trappy bits, but I made a proper hash of it. I hit number 4 hard, and then did the same to 11. I blamed Storm at the time, but it was more probably driver error. It was annoying, but since I could not have expected to catch the two leaders, who both did double clear rounds anyway, and the rest were quite a long way behind, no great harm was done, and I finished third.

The Windsor Park Equestrian Club event in the middle of June gave me an opportunity to do some experimenting. As the Saturday was Derby Day, I had to do my dressage and cones phases at nine in the morning – the first competitor of the day. It was also, incidentally, my seventy-ninth birthday. I discovered two things that were to make quite a difference to the team: Heather had become a brilliant leader, and went equally well with Peter and Dina, and Hamble and Peter went very well together in the wheel. That left Polly, who did not go very well with Hamble in the wheel, and who still threw her head about in the lead. Meanwhile Jane was doing well with Penny Romsey, but I think she found the male presence of Storm behind her rather too exciting. Micky then came up with the solution for both of us; I let Penny have Polly as a wheeler, and I took Storm back into my team.

Sandringham followed at the end of June with only Georgina Frith missing from the regulars. Penny Romsey seemed pleased with the arrangement of Polly in the wheel behind Jane, so Storm stayed with me. The problem now was how to arrange a team for the dressage. I tried Hamble and Storm in the wheel with Heather and Peter in the lead but it was not the answer. For one thing, Hamble was a bit too energetic for Storm, who then let him do all the work, and Hamble was also a little too enthusiastic and insisted on breaking into a canter every time we came to an extension. As a result, I had quite a difficult drive, although two of the judges thought it had been a reasonable performance. The third, and more critical, judge was Caroline Musker, who had been a pony-team driver herself. As it happens, to save the organizing committee the cost of accommodating a judge, I had invited Caroline to stay at Wood Farm for the event. It therefore behove me to be somewhat tactful with my comments! In any case it was not a very serious matter as, although I was lying fifth, I was only 5 points behind Philippa Gammell, who was in the lead.

I put Dina in with Heather in the lead, and Hamble and Peter in the wheel for the marathon. This arrangement turned out to be a great success, although I had problems with Dina jogging in the walks, and he then took to cantering in the fast section. He made up for it by going brilliantly through the obstacles but, even though I was fourth fastest, it was not enough to move me up a place.

John Robertson and John Pickford were not at their best in either the dressage or the marathon, so they were not much of a threat when it came to the cones competition. It turned out that I needed the points gap because I made a dreadful mess of that competition. I succeeded in hitting three cones, and then added 2 time penalties, which left me in fifth place some 20 points behind Beverly Mellstrom. She just had 1 time penalty and retained her fourth place. Anna Grayston had the only double clear round, which put her in third place, one point behind Emily Bennett, who hit two cones but remained in second place. Philippa Gammell hit one cone and kept the lead by 6 points.

Henbury (the home of Sebastian and Naomi Ferranti) was the venue for a new event for me, and it could not have been more fun, except that I did not perform with any great distinction. Sebastian Ferranti had levelled a space big enough for a full-sized polo ground at the far end of the park and it provided ideal dressage and cones arenas. It also provided what must be the biggest collecting ring in Europe. The levelling process had created a bank on one side of the ground, which gave a splendid view for spectators, and room for the secretary's tent, event office and catering facilities close to the stable field. No provision was made to admit the public, which saved a great deal of expense on parking attendants, public lavatories, insurance and safety barriers. It also made it a very jolly 'family' event.

I started quite well by squeezing into second place in the dressage, 8 points behind Emily Bennett, in spite of being marked down by one of the judges. Emily Bennett must have done a particularly good test for a score of only 34.9. Philippa Gammell was not so fortunate and could only manage fifth place out of six entries.

The marathon course was excellent, and the obstacles nicely varied and well built. The ponies went very well and, apart from a couple of minor hiccups, nothing went seriously wrong, and I thought I had done quite well. However, when I saw the scores, I was rather disappointed. Emily Bennett had stormed round in 94, while I was in fifth place with 115. Ann Robarts was eliminated, so at least I was not last.

After my dreadful performances in the cones at Farleigh and Sandringham, I was hoping for something better, particularly as I was less than one cone behind Anna Grayston, and ahead of John Pickford. Sadly it was not to be. John Pickford went in before me, and hit one cone, which gave me a little hope, but when I got into the arena I had to wait for the bell, and I think this must have upset Hamble. At any rate, no sooner did I start than Hamble began to canter and the whole team became unbalanced. I just managed to get round without hitting anything, other than Heather kicking one as a result, I think, of being pushed by Storm, but I was much too slow. My 9.5 time penalties together with 5 penalties for the kicked-down cone dropped me two places to bottom place, apart from Ann Robarts.

The ponies stayed at Henbury until they went on to Barons Court in Northern Ireland, where several improvements had been made. The lawn in front of the house had been ploughed and reseeded, and was like a billiard table. The entries had gone up to sixty, so there was a second dressage arena in the field between the house and the lake.

The house party consisted of the Ferrantis, Penny Romsey, Brian McGrath and me. Naomi was driving Carrick in the novice single-pony class, Sebastian drove his pair in the open pony-pairs class, and Penny Romsey drove her tandem. This group of competitors provided much amusement – and argument – and gave Brian McGrath ample opportunity to offer his advice.

I am sorry to say that the Ferrantis did not distinguish themselves in the dressage, although in Naomi's case, it was partly due to Carrick's lack of enthusiasm. Penny Romsey managed her best score ever with 51, just 2 points behind Anne Gilbert, the leader. I managed a fairly good test which put me in first place, 7 points ahead of Ann Robarts. John Robertson was third, ahead of two Irish competitors, Alwyn Morrison and Millar Paterson.

It had rained on and off all day Friday, and very heavily during Friday night. Then the sun came out on Saturday, and there was a nice cool breeze. In spite of the rain, the going on the marathon course could not have been better. The course was identical to last year, and the obstacles were the same, but the way through them had been altered.

The members of the house party started off at roughly hourly intervals. Naomi Ferranti went carefully and steadily, and moved up from last to ninth out of sixteen entries. Sebastian got round fairly well, and Penny Romsey had a good round, and when Anne Gilbert took a wrong turning in section A and collected 20 time penalties, she went into the lead in her class of three. Andrew Mylius, also driving Fell ponies, had a very good round, but he was still the equivalent of two cones behind her. My ponies went really well, and we opened a lead of 20 points over John Robertson. Ann Robarts was nearly 20 points further back, and then came

Fig. 9.5 Penny Romsey with Jane in the lead and Polly in the shafts driving her much-loved classic two-wheeler in the dressage arena at Barons Court in Northern Ireland in 2000. Jane is working well in this picture, but dressage has never been her favourite occupation. (*Author's collection*)

Alwyn Morrison. Millar Paterson turned over in obstacle 4, after quite a dodgy round and had to retire.

Millar Paterson's crash had very unfortunate consequences. As his ponies ran away towards the stables, the carriage caught the rope marking the spectator boundary, and dragged the loop behind it. Sacha, Duchess of Abercorn, had just got out of her car, and seeing the runaway ponies rushing towards her, she bent down to hold her dog. By sheer bad luck she was standing inside the loop of the rope, and this caught her behind the knees a moment or two after the upturned carriage had passed her. She was thrown over on to the hard road, knocked out and concussed, and was rushed to hospital. Fortunately there were no serious physical injuries, and she was allowed home on the Monday. It took many months, however, for Sacha to get over the effects of the concussion.

Naomi Ferranti had two cones down in the novice single-pony class, and Sebastian Ferranti came second in the cones phase of his open pony-pairs class and moved up a place. Penny Romsey hit two cones and was just not fast enough to maintain her tandem-class lead, and lost to Andrew Mylius by 0.6 points or three seconds. I made yet another hash of the cones, knocking two down, and adding 14 time penalties, but I still managed to win the event by 10 points. The 'hash' was partly the result of Hamble striking into Heather's near hind coronet as we came out of the last marathon obstacle. This put Heather out of the cones phase, and I had to put Storm in the lead in her place, which meant that I had to put Hamble in the wheel. Hamble is brilliant in the marathon, but he has a thing about cones, and tends to lurch through them. In this case he twice succeeded in pushing Peter over to hit a cone on his side.

Unfortunately, Heather was still not quite sound when we got to Lowther, and I had to use the other four ponies for all three phases. Things were further complicated by the fact that I had been invited to open the new pavilion for the Royal Yacht Squadron at Cowes on the Thursday, and it was Queen Elizabeth the Queen Mother's hundredth-birthday lunch on the Friday. Therefore, in order to have a chance to walk the course, I travelled by train to Carlisle on the Wednesday and had a practice run with the new arrangement of Storm and Dina in the lead and Hamble and Peter in the wheel. I walked the obstacles on the Thursday morning before flying by helicopter to Cowes. I then dashed to London for the lunch at Clarence House on the Friday, after which I rushed back to Lowther by helicopter, arriving with thirty minutes to spare before starting my dressage test. By some fluke – and considerate judges – I came second to Philippa Gammell by 5 points, and just ahead of Emily Bennett by 0.3 points.

I had no problems with the first part of the marathon, but things became a little difficult in the obstacles. Storm did his best, but he was obviously mystified by the whole thing, so that I had a number of hesitations, which put me down to sixth place. I then heard that Beverly Mellstrom had, sportingly, owned up to going the wrong way through one of the gates in an obstacle, which had gone unnoticed by the judges. This added 20 penalties to her score and I went up to fifth place.

Micky and I had done a lot of practice with Hamble in the wheel for the cones, but he simply could not contain himself, and once again unbalanced the whole team by cantering and surging through each pair of cones. I did, at least, manage a clear round, but at the expense of 9 time penalties, to retain my fifth place.

There were only four entries for Alnwick and, with Heather fully restored to fitness, I managed to win the dressage by 8 points from John Pickford and 9 points from Emily Bennett. Ann Robarts had a difficult test.

The marathon course through Hulne Park is spectacular, but the first part is a long uphill drag. The ponies went brilliantly in all sections, but I rather let the side down when we got to the obstacles. I came round the end of obstacle 1 rather too fast and overshot gate C, but it only lost me 1 point to John Pickford and 2 points to Emily Bennett. I had real trouble in obstacle 4, when I tried an uphill turn, and the leaders did not quite keep up the momentum. This caused the wheelers to hesitate, and we got a front wheel trapped behind a post. There was nothing for it but to go round again. I had planned an escape route in case of trouble, but in the event I got it wrong, and went much further than necessary, hitting a knock-down in the process.

After that, all went well enough and then, to my great surprise, I found myself held up by Emily Bennett just before obstacle 7. Apparently one of the snap shackles on a trace had broken, and Emily's father/groom had to tie it together with some binder twine. She should have had plenty of time to do this, except that she had slowed down to give her ponies a breather, and lost all the time she had in hand. As a result she arrived late, and collected no less than 18 time penalties in section E. I then saw the scores, and, to my even greater surprise, I found that I was still in the lead, but only by a whisker. I had 173.8 points to John Pickford's 174.1 and Emily Bennett's 175.

Ann Robarts had a dreadful time in the marathon, and an even worse time in the cones. Emily Bennett went in next and hit two cones for a score of 10 points. Then John Pickford went in and had 9.5 time penalties, and I began to think that I might just have been able to win the event. No such luck. I hit the very first pair of cones, but I was still ahead of John Pickford. However, I must have been unnerved as I went on to accumulate 11.5 time penalties and dropped to third by 5 points.

Penny Romsey started badly in the dressage, and was in seventh place out of eight entries. However, she must have gone very well in the marathon, as she moved up to second, and with only a few time penalties in the cones, she retained her second place. Sadly, both Ferrantis ended up last in their classes.

It was a very enjoyable season after rather a shaky start and some irritating pony problems.

Results for 2000

EVENT	Dressage	Marathon	Cones	Pl/No
Brighton	2	4	1=	3/7
Windsor	4	7	1=	6/10
Hopetoun	2	2	2	2/2
Farleigh	2	3	4	3/5
Henbury	2	3	5	5/6
Barons Court	1	1	2	1/5
Lowther	2	5	7	5/7
Alnwick	1	3	3	3/4

Ponies used: Storm, Polly (swapped for Hamble before Sandringham), Peter, Medina, Heather, Hamble.

One of the challenges of driving at Sandringham in January is the weather. It is generally cold and there is often a north or east wind, which comes straight off the North Sea. In Norfolk it is known as a 'lazy wind' because it does not bother to go round you. Over the years I have tried every sort of clothing to cope with the climatic conditions, and for years I used a large padded jacket with a hood. I wore this over a long-sleeved vest, a flannel shirt, a heavy woollen jersey and a padded waistcoat. For the nether regions, I found that a foundation of 'long johns' under a pair of moleskin trousers, under a pair of waterproof over-trousers with gum-boots over Arctic socks, worked quite well. It made walking a bit ungainly, but it preserved life.

The trouble was that the jacket was not waterproof. It then occurred to me that the people who were most interested in keeping out cold, wind and rain were motorcyclists. In due course I managed to acquire a reasonably discreet black Goretex jacket with a zipped-in padded inner jacket. It was both waterproof and windproof and, worn over a fairly lightweight woollen pullover and a heavy Scandinavian jersey, it keeps body temperature at a satisfactory level even in the most arctic conditions. In dry weather, a woollen scarf round the neck keeps the draught out, while a towel scarf keeps the rain out. With the help of the Special Escort Group of the Metropolitan Police, I managed to acquire a pair of padded Goretex over-trousers, which I wear over moleskin trousers and a pair of 'moon boots' from China.

I doubt whether there is any way of keeping hands warm and still be able to handle the reins. After years of trial, I settled on a pair of Daymart gloves under a large pair of heavy pigskin gloves. I then came across some electrically heated under-gloves. You strap a pair of batteries above the wrists and plug them into heating elements that cover the backs of the hands and fingers. They are not 100% effective, but at least you only have to worry about the tips of your fingers getting cold. In case of wet weather, I find that a pair of so-called waterproof gloves over a pair of surgeons' rubber gloves is the best solution I have come across so far. To

Fig. 9.6 Dressed in full winter clobber to withstand the biting Norfolk winds in January. The latest addition to the outfit is a pair of electrically heated gloves designed for motorcyclists. They work brilliantly but, with overgloves, they are a bit bulky for anything except exercising the ponies.

The wooden stables in the background were built when I thought that David Saunders might start a driving school at Sandringham. However, he went off to drive a competition team for Mr and Mrs Kluge. The stables are very popular with both grooms and ponies as they face south and the wood seems to help the ponies dry out after exercise.

From left to right: Micky Flynn, 'Pip' Pearson and Michelle Maynard, who had worked for the irrepressible Richard Margrave. The near leader is Medina (originally bought by Penny Romsey) and Heather is on the offside. The wheelers are Douglas (home bred and starting his second season) on the offside and Peter (bought from John Cowdery) on the nearside. (*Author's collection*)

Fig. 9.7 Another example of winter clobber. (*Author's collection*)

Fig. 9.8 Micky Flynn exercising the pony team in the snow at Sandringham. (*Author's collection*)

top it off, I wear a deerstalker hat to keep the rain from going down my neck. I may well look like Inspector Clouseau in cold pursuit of the Pink Panther in the Arctic, but it is effective.

2001

As a consequence of Georgina Frith winning the previous European Championships for Pony Teams in 1999, the British Horse Driving Trials Association exercised its option to stage the next championships in 2001 and decided that they should take place at Sandringham. When it comes to international events, Sandringham has the great advantage of being near the east-coast ports, which makes it much more convenient for competitors from the Continent. As the host nation has to pay for the travel expenses of foreign teams within the host country, it should also make it less expensive for the BHDTA. However, the FEI rule is interpreted to mean that the Channel crossing is included in the cost to the host nation.

Sadly, owing to a national epidemic of foot and mouth disease, all driving competitions were cancelled in 2001, including the European Championships. This was a bit of a blow as we had spent quite a lot of money getting the main arena levelled, and had been promised generous sponsorship by Bernard Matthews, the Norfolk 'Turkey King'. When the FEI technical delegate came to inspect the facilities before the cancelled 2001 championships, he said that the main arena needed to be levelled. I was all for it, but the questions were, how was it to be done, and at what cost? It then turned out that a driver in the single pony class, Edmund Goodwin, specialized in levelling playing fields, and he generously offered to do it 'at cost'. He brought in a machine that sliced off the turf into rolls. These were then stacked on one side, while the earth was levelled using a laser system. The turf rolls were then replaced and rolled flat. All this was done early in the year, and I refused to believe that the ground would be ready for use by the summer. As it turned out, because of the foot and mouth epidemic, the ground had until 2002 to consolidate, and proved to be a great success.

This cancellation of the 2001 European Championships at Sandringham also put me in a slight dilemma. I had had it vaguely in mind to try to get selected to compete as an individual in the year of my eightieth birthday and fifteen years after taking part in the World Championships for Teams of Horses at Ascot in 1986. I thought this might have been a suitable swan song with which to retire, but when I heard that the FEI had allowed the Championships to be postponed, I persuaded myself to go on for at least another year.

No equestrian activity of any sort was permitted in Windsor Great Park. This was obviously intended to prevent the disease being imported by visiting horses, and I thought it would be politic for me to avoid the Great Park with the ponies, even though they were residents for all practical purposes. However, I continued to drive them in the Home Park, but that has fairly limited potential and most of the driving has to be done on hard roads.

I was discussing these problems with the Deputy Ranger of Windsor Great Park, Philip Everett (my deputy, as I happen to be the Ranger, but employed by the Crown Estate Commissioners as the agent for their Windsor Estate), when he suggested that I might try the tracks in Swinley Forest. This area, including Bagshot Park, is also on the Crown Estate. Most of it is open to the public, but there is no stock in it. It meant boxing the ponies over to Bagshot House, and then driving the short distance into the woods. There is any number of tracks through the woods, and some quite steep hills, but many of them had been badly eroded by a combination of forestry operations and rainfall. My worst problem was finding my way around, and trying to distinguish one track from another in almost continuous forest. As it happened, I had a hand-held GPS set, and this turned out to be most valuable in finding my way back to Bagshot House.

I had resigned myself to the prospect of the whole summer without any driving events, and only being able to drive the ponies at Windsor and Swinley. However, all my regular hosts, at Barons Court, Henbury, Lowther and Alnwick, invited me to stay for the weekends that would have been driving events. This turned out to be almost a bonus as I was able to see other interesting places in the vicinity, and not have to spend hours walking the obstacles. There was some fishing near Barons Court, and in Cumbria on the river Eden, and we were given a conducted tour of the new gardens at Alnwick Castle by Jane, the Duchess of Northumberland, who had initiated the whole project. They were still in the process of being constructed, but there was enough to see to appreciate the sheer scale of the undertaking.

2002

The 'old routine' started again at Sandringham in January 2002 with the same five ponies, Storm, Peter, Hamble, Heather and Dina plus a young home-bred newcomer, Douglas, and I was pleasantly surprised by how well they all went. They seemed to settle quickly into their work, without any dramas or tantrums, and were soon fighting fit – rather too much so, as it turned out. After working quite hard, Douglas had been turned out by the time the first Windsor Park Equestrian Club event came along in mid-April. The others were going really well, and I was beginning to feel quite optimistic. They managed a good score for the dressage, a clear round of the cones with just ½ a time penalty, and a trouble-free round in the marathon.

The fact that the European Championships were to be held this year meant that the members of the national team, and the individual entries, had to be selected and this gave the early part of the season an added zest. A national team consists of three competitors and the team scoring is based on the best two scores from each phase added together. This means that the national team score for the dressage is the total of the two best competitors, say, competitors A and B. The national score for the marathon could then be the sum of the scores of, say, competitors B and C. The national score for the cones could be those of competitors A and C, provided that each competitor had completed all three phases. The beauty of this system is that each of the three team members, apart from having the chance to win an individual medal, can contribute to the overall team score, by doing well in only one of the phases.

Under the FEI rules, in addition to the team members, each foreign nation is allowed a further three individual entries, while the host nation is allowed six individual entries, making a total of nine entries. (These individual entries cannot contribute to the national team score, but they are able to win individual medals.)

Only nine of the eleven competitors at Brighton, therefore, had a chance of being selected for the championships. Georgina Frith, having sold her team, was not in contention, and so the front runners on past form were the 'top girls', Emily Bennett, Philippa Gammell, Anna Grayston, Ursula Hirschberg and Beverly

Fig. 9.9 Micky Flynn's solution to the problem of exercising eight Fell Ponies at Sandringham – drive them all at once. (*Author's collection*)

Mellstrom, and the one male, John Pickford. Barring accidents, three of these would certainly be selected for the team, and the other three as individuals, leaving three places for the rest of us.

The process of selecting members of the national team and individuals to take part in the championships started at Brighton, and this attracted eleven entries. For once, Stanmer started dry, if not sunny, and the rain held off for the whole weekend. As far as I was concerned, things could not have started more inauspiciously. My ponies treated the whole thing like children at their first camping holiday. Micky found them unmanageable on the Thursday and, although they were a bit calmer on the Friday, they were still much too excited to do a proper dressage test. Dina, in particular, was an absolute pain. He would try, and usually succeeded, to trot when he should have been walking, and to canter when he should have been trotting. The result was that I was in a thoroughly bad temper with the dreadful record-low score of 60.8 for sixth place.

They were still much too full of themselves for the marathon on the Saturday and, even after the notorious climb to the top of the Downs in section A, they were still leaning heavily on my arms to the degree that I was developing cramp in my fingers before I got as far as section E. Consequently, getting round the obstacles was quite a challenge, and I was slower than necessary simply because I dare not let them take charge. Oddly enough, although I was only eighth in the marathon, I managed to move up to fifth on the combined score.

The cones course was a brute, and there was not one double clear round. In fact there were only two clear rounds in the cones and only three clear rounds within the time. I nudged one pair and had 9 time penalties, which was enough to drop me back to sixth place again. The competition should have been won by Emily Bennett, but she was eliminated for missing a turning flag. Instead, it was won by Anna Grayston by nearly 30 points from John Pickford with Ursula Hirschberg in third place another 20 points further back. The scores were so close that if I had got round the cones within the time allowed, I would have been fourth and if I had done a double clear round, I would have been third – but then, much the same 'if onlys' applied to all the others.

As Windsor is a CAI (Concours d'Attelage International), all competitors in the international classes are there by invitation, which means that the British drivers are chosen on their position in the points league for the previous year. I have never inquired too closely, but I have a suspicion that my invitation this particular year was due rather more to courtesy than merit. Only five natives were invited: Anna Grayston, Philippa Gammell, Emily Bennett, John Pickford and me. The foreigners were Dirk Sonntag, Cees van Opstal, and Aart van de Kamp. It needed no great judge of form to reckon that the only person I stood a reasonable chance of beating was Opstal, otherwise I was doomed to be last. And this is how it turned out; although I had a moment of glory when I discovered that I had won the dressage (by 0.5 points), perhaps because, for once, Dina behaved impeccably.

The marathon course was excellent, and the obstacles, built by a new course designer, were a great improvement on the old ones. There were no inevitable traps and plenty of options. All was going well until I was about half way round section C, when Heather suddenly fell down in the middle of the Deer Park. Hamble, behind her, fell on top of her and got his hind legs trapped inside her traces. All he could do was to sit there like a dog until Micky pulled the snap shackle and released him. Luckily the ponies were not injured, and there was no damage, so we went on. However, the inevitable delay meant that we were forty seconds late with about 1.5 km to go. The ponies must have realized that we had to make up time, and they fairly flew the last bit so that we finished, pulling up, with half a minute in hand. I later discovered that a small hole had developed over an old drain, bang in the middle of the course, and that three other drivers had fallen into the same hole.

My fate was sealed in the very first obstacle, but for once it was neither due to pony nor driver error. There was a fairly sharp turn into gate A almost immediately after passing the entry flags, and just before I could turn the leaders, they hopped sideways and went into the wrong gap and I had to stop and pull them back. In some mysterious way, the near-leader rein got itself into a tangle, and jammed in the roger ring on Hamble's bridle, which meant that I lost steerage.

Before I knew what was happening, the ponies headed for the exit gate. I thought I had just managed to stop them before they crossed the line, and turn them round, but the rein was still stuck fast. I put Micky down to release it, and all he had to do was to give the 'knot' a tweak and it came free. After that, things went quite well – at least I was a bit faster than Opstal. We flew through the water to what I thought unusual applause, to discover later that there had been several upsets, including George Bowman. It was only after we had finished that it emerged that one of my leaders had put his nose across the electronic timer to stop the clock in obstacle 1, and that we had been eliminated. I did not have much luck in the cones round either – not that it mattered; van de Kamp won by just 2 points from Sonntag with Emily Bennett third, some 25 points further back.

At about this time I was told by Sydney Smith that she had in her keeping a 'golden hippo', which had been given to the Queen by President Tubman during our State Visit to Liberia several years previously. I am not quite sure how it happened, but it seems that the golden hippo had been lent to the British Driving Society to be given as a trophy for something or other. Apparently it was no longer required, and it was given to Sydney Smith for safe keeping. She then contacted Brian McGrath to ask him what she ought to do with it. After lengthy discussions, we eventually decided that it should be given to a competitor at a driving event, who was deemed to have suffered the worst piece of bad luck. The presentation to the winner for 2002 took place at the 2003 event at Brighton and you can imagine my surprise – not to say, shock – when I was declared to be the winner for that incident in the first obstacle at Windsor.

The Monday morning following the Royal Windsor Horse Show witnessed one of the more bizarre equestrian happenings. The pair of ponies that Sebastian Ferranti had bought when he started driving was quite hopeless, so he bought another pair from Georgina Frith, who in turn had got them from Mrs Bolitho. He got them just in time for the 2001 season, but there were no competitions because of the foot and mouth outbreak. I tried to persuade him that competition in the pony-pairs class was very tough, and that he might do better to try his luck in the tandem class. As it happened neither of the new ponies was fit for the start of the 2002 season, and I got the impression that his girl groom was not desperately keen on the tandem idea anyway.

When he came to stay for the Windsor event, I suggested that he might like to bring his ponies and have a little tuition from Micky. As all the obstacles were in the Home Park, I thought he try them on the Monday morning after the event. He took a bit of persuading, but eventually agreed. The snag was, when I went down on the Sunday evening to check the obstacles, I found that all the entry and exit flags, and all the gate letters had already been removed. So I went round with a can of white spray paint, and marked all the left sides of the gates (left gates are marked in white; right gates in red, but I could not find any red paint). I also had to find some sort of markers for the entry and exit gates. I then roped in Penny Romsey and Marina Flynn to act as timekeepers at alternate obstacles, while Micky rode with Sebastian.

I had assumed – wrongly as it turned out – that he would have taken the time to walk the obstacles during the weekend. The result was that Micky had to talk him through each of the obstacles. This was nothing like as easy as it may sound, particularly because, under the stress of the moment, Sebastian was inclined to confuse his left with his right. Having started the stopwatch as he entered an obstacle, Penny tried to be helpful by running ahead from one pair of gates to the next and waving her arms like a demented semaphore to indicate the position of the next gate. Apart from several hesitations, misunderstandings and corrections, he managed obstacles 1, 4, 5, 6 and 8 more or less correctly. He wandered around quite a lot in obstacle 2, until Micky realized that shouting 'left' or 'right' was not producing the right responses. He exited obstacle 3 before he had completed it, and then got himself, Micky and Penny into a real muddle in 7. I was so distracted by this scene of confusion that I almost forgot to stop the clock on his exit. To my great surprise, he managed to finish section E within the time allowed, but by that time a certain level of hysteria had developed at the antics of four people trying to get one driver with a tandem through eight obstacles. However, it did persuade him to try the tandem class that season.

The next event, at Farleigh, came at the end of May, but the heavens delivered a series of monsoon showers all day Thursday, so that, yet again, all the boxes had to be towed into the stable field by tractors. I can only imagine that setting up the portable stabling under those conditions must have been a nightmare. Fortunately, the weather improved on Friday and we had a glorious summer weekend, although negotiating the stable field on foot or on a bike remained hazardous in the extreme.

I thought the ponies did a very good dressage test, and two of the judges put me second, but the third marked me down to fifth. This put me in third place behind Beverly Mellstrom and Emily Bennett, and in front of Anna Grayston, John Pickford, Ann Robarts, Julia Liles, Sarah Jane Cook (recently arrived from the pony-tandems class) and Helen Cruickshank.

The marathon comprised only three sections, but the going was very tough, and in places through deep mud. I just managed the walk section across fields with 5 seconds to spare. The obstacles were all fairly wide with no serious traps except, that is, for 2, which was in the bottom of a pit and, although not particularly tight, it certainly got the adrenalin going. I decided to take things fairly quietly, and to try to get round without any dramas. All went well and I never touched a thing. Poor Beverly Mellstrom was eliminated because one of her grooms took off her hard hat during the walk section. Ann Robarts missed a gate and was also eliminated. Penny Romsey was going brilliantly until she managed to turn over in obstacle 4, as a result of going rather too fast in what was probably the easiest obstacle of the lot, and retired.

The cones course was unpleasantly twisty and, even after walking it endlessly, I only just managed to avoid going wrong. I went clear but collected 15 time penalties. John Pickford did the only double clear round to put him into second place after Emily Bennett. Anna Grayston was third and I was 10 points behind her in fourth.

Sebastian Ferranti started badly by forgetting the dressage test, but he got round the marathon. When driving the cones course, he managed to miss number 8 without the judges noticing, but then he missed 14, which they did notice. The whole event, in spite of the mud in the stable field, was the greatest fun, and I was very pleased with the ponies.

The next outing was a Windsor Park Equestrian Club meeting in June over the Derby weekend. To complicate matters, I had accepted an invitation to start a two-handed round-Britain sailing race on the Sunday morning in Plymouth. I had to start my dressage and cones phases early on Saturday morning so that I could get to Epsom for lunch, and then had to walk the marathon obstacles that evening. I got back from Plymouth at three o'clock on Sunday, and was ready to start the marathon half an hour later. As Micky was accompanying Sophie Wessex, I had Pip as navigator. Luckily, I just managed to get to the start before Michael Onslow. He was on his first outing with a team of ponies, and I thought there might be a chance of my being held up if I went after him. However, I had the misfortune to follow a novice horse-team driver, who held me up at every obstacle but one. Things were not improved by the fact that it had been raining since lunch time, and the whole course and obstacles were badly poached.

Penny Romsey did well to win all sections in her class of three entries. I had persuaded Sophie Wessex to have a go at driving, and this was her first outing with Carrick in the novice-single class. In a class of eleven she did brilliantly to come in fifth in the dressage and cones, and then went up a place after the marathon. She obviously enjoyed it, and I hoped that she was hooked. I had also hoped that Sebastian Ferranti might have tried his ponies in tandem, but he had got into a muddle with his dates and had disappeared to fish on the Helmsdale.

The European Championships at Sandringham took place over the last weekend in June, and attracted twenty-nine entries. There were two from Austria, Josef Kronbichler and Peter Schenk; three from Belgium, Mia Allo, our old friend

Fig. 9.10 *below left* Emily Bennett (née Brookes, who married Peter Bennett, a horse-team driver, in 1997), with her father on the backstep, galloping into the water with her Welsh cross ponies at the European Championships at Sandringham in 2002. Emily had been National Champion in the pony-single, pony-pair and pony-team classes. She was the best-placed British competitor in the 2002 European Championships. (*Alf Baker*)

Fig. 9.11 *below right* John Pickford driving for Britain at the 2002 European Championships. For several years, John Robertson was the only other male driver in the pony-team class until we were joined by John Pickford in 1997 and Michael Onslow in 2002. John Pickford was a successful pony-pairs driver and very quickly mastered the art of driving a team. (*Alf Baker*)

Edwin Flerackers and Bart Verdroncken; two from France, Jerome Cheze and Laure Knell Chartier; five from Germany, Tobias Bucker, Gerhard Gerich, Dirk Gerkins, Edwin Kiefer, Alfred Koppen and Martin Thiemann; six from the Netherlands, Yvonne Houten, Pjotr van der Heyden, Aart van de Kamp, Jan van Dorresteijn, Bert van Lent and Paul van Riet; and one from Switzerland, Anton Hugentobler. Finally, there were nine from Britain, of whom Emily Bennett, Philippa Gammell and Ursula Hirschberg had been selected for the national team, with John Pickford as first reserve. The individual entries were Sarah Jane Cook, Helen Cruickshank, Anna Grayston, Beverly Mellstrom and me.

I was so busy walking the obstacles and getting myself ready for the dressage, that I hardly had time to watch any of the others doing their tests. It was won by Mia Allo with a score of 42.7. Edwin Flerackers and Gerhard Gerich were the only others to score less than 50. Five of the British managed less than 60 and, to my surprise, I had the best score of the locals on 53.6, which put me in seventh place. That, however, was the end of my success.

We were very lucky with the weather, and the going could not have been better, both in the newly levelled main arena and across country. Only six competi-

tors collected any penalties in the first four sections. Even though I say it myself – having chosen it – the marathon course provided a very nice drive.

Because I had no responsibilities to the national team, and there was no likelihood of my being anywhere near the top half in the results, and also because I reckoned that all the others would be going flat out round the course, I decided to take things carefully, and just try to get round without any dramas. I was almost completely successful, but I rather overdid the care. My only difficulty was in obstacle 1, where I got the wrong side of a solitary post in the middle of the very complicated obstacle (Ursula Hirschberg had an even worse time in this obstacle, when she got her leaders either side of that same solitary post). After that, all went swimmingly, but I was much too slow. In fact I only just managed to beat Helen Cruickshank, and a Dutch competitor who gave up in obstacle 7 with a broken carriage. I was some 40 points behind the leader, who must have flown round to score only 80.7.

The cones course was a real pig; in fact only six people managed double clear rounds – none of them British. When it came to my turn, I could see that I was always going to have time penalties, but as I went on, I was beginning to feel that

Fig. 9.12 *above left* Helen Cruickshank in the water at Sandringham during the European Championships in 2002. She and her father, John Robertson, take it in turns to drive and groom and they do not mince their instructions when navigating for each other. (*Alf Baker*)

Fig. 9.13 *above right* Aart van de Kamp from Holland, with his electric Shetlands. Many people underrated these lively little ponies until they won convincingly at Windsor on several occasions. He is here competing in the European Championships at Sandringham in 2002. (*Alf Baker*)

I might go clear. Just then, Peter, or it may have been Storm, took a step sideways as we were going into the very last pair, and down it went. With 16 time penalties, that gave me a total of 21 and a grand total of 195.8 to finish in twenty-second place and sixth out of the nine British entries. One of the Dutch contingent got into all sorts of trouble and amassed no less that 64 penalties in the cones.

According to the report in *Carriage Driving Magazine*:

Iseli's cones course had few of the usual configurations of circles, serpentines and zig-zags. He explained he wanted to get away from them. 'Drivers are used to driving these combinations' he remarked, 'Here I have put cones at tricky angles to one another so that competitors will really have to think and drive that bit more carefully'.

Jan van Dorrsteijn, a Dutch individual driver, was the first to go having had to retire from the Marathon with a damaged carriage; with a double clear he showed that the cones course was eminently drivable. Thereafter, however, few people in the bottom half of the placings were able to emulate this, picking up driving or time penalties, or both. Great Britain's Anna Grayston drove the best round of all the Brits, making the time with only one cone down.

As we got nearer the top, double clears became more frequent, although by no means the norm. In fourth place, German team member Tobias Bucker, stepped up the tension by driving a double clear. Next to go, Allo collected six faults overall which dropped her down to fifth behind individual German driver, Edwin Kiefer.

In second place, Gerkins drove a clear round with just one time fault, giving Gerich, who was only one point ahead, very little room for error. It proved not enough – he made the time, but had one cone down. Gerkins, who was on the German team in 1997 and 1999 when they won the team gold and bronze medals respectively, had never won an individual medal before – now he had the gold. Team mates Gerich and Bucker took the silver and bronze. National placings behind Germany remained the same – Belgium, then Netherlands.

All the other classes went as normal. Penny Romsey did rather well to be second to Michael Onslow in the dressage by less than 1 point. She then won the marathon, which put her in the lead. However, she refused to be told how she had done, and it was only at lunch on Sunday, just before her cones round, that Brian McGrath broke the news to her that she was in the lead and would be going in last. This caused consternation, but the pressure on her was slightly eased by Michael Onslow, who made a complete hash of it. He hit the first pair of cones, which must have unnerved him, and he got lost between cones-obstacles 4 and 5. He then got into a tangle in the box and finished with a huge score. That left Penny Romsey with two cones in hand, but she hit three and dropped to second place. She was quite unperturbed by this as she was so ecstatic about winning the marathon that she could not care less about the final score.

Poor Sebastian Ferranti had a difficult event, to put it mildly. His dressage test was not all that bad, but he had real difficulties with the marathon obstacles. His cones round was even worse. He hit six of the first eight, and then went through 8 the wrong way and was eliminated – not that it made much difference, as he would have been last anyway. I have to say that it did nothing to dampen his enthusiasm for the sport.

After two years of planning and preparation, I was greatly relieved that the weather had been so good and everything had gone so smoothly. Marcus O'Lone, the Land Agent, and Joe Grimwade, the Sandringham Stud Manager and chairman of the organizing committee, had done a brilliant job.

The next outing for the ponies was the WPEC event at the beginning of July. There was nothing very special about it except that it was valuable experience for Sebastian Ferranti. He did a very much better dressage test than usual, and also got round the cones without hitting anything. Micky went with him in the marathon, and he was thrilled to come in second. Having done so abysmally badly at Farleigh and Sandringham, this did much to restore his confidence and morale.

Getting to Barons Court proved rather more complicated than usual. There was a Jubilee Garden Party at Sandringham on the Thursday afternoon, and I could only leave at half past seven that evening. I then had to drive to RAF Marham to fly to Aldergrove, and then continue by helicopter to Barons Court. By the time I arrived it was nearly ten. At least it all went according to plan. Micky, on the other hand, had a chapter of problems. He left Windsor on the Monday morning and spent the night at Henbury before driving on to Stranraer to catch the ferry to Belfast. Unfortunately, one of the tyres on the trailer blew out on the way and, by the time he could get a new one fitted, he had missed the ferry. He then discovered that the next ferry would not accept the horsebox. He eventually arrived at Barons Court at one in the morning – in pouring rain. Luckily it cleared up by Friday midday, and we had glorious weather for the rest of the weekend.

I thought that the pressure might be off when I saw that the only other competitor was Julia Liles. I was seriously mistaken. Julia's dressage was not brilliant – fortunately for me – because she went on to beat me in the marathon by 0.6 points and again in the cones.

My ponies went really well in the sticky conditions in the dressage arena in front of the house, and I established a crucial lead of 10 points. They also went brilliantly on the spectacular marathon course, and fairly whizzed through the obstacles – or so I thought. The record shows that I beat Julia Liles through obstacles 1, 2 and 3, but then she beat me through the rest to score 108.6 to my 109.4. That gave me just two cones in hand for the last phase on Sunday. She went in first and had two cones down plus 8 time penalties. I thought I was reasonably safe, but then I proceeded to hit two and add 13.5 time penalties, so my lead was whittled away to 4.3.

Sebastian Ferranti, driving his ponies as a pair, started brilliantly by beating his two pony-pairs competitors in the dressage, but he slid to second place in the marathon. This was partly due to one of his rivals turning over in an obstacle. Sadly, everything went horribly wrong in the cones, when he drove determinedly straight from 3 to 9 and was eliminated.

In the tandem class, Penny Romsey was up against Anne Gilbert, who was certainly the favourite to win. By the time they came to the cones, Anne Gilbert was 17 points ahead, or three cones plus some time in hand. It should have been ample, particularly as Penny Romsey hit one cone and had a few time penalties. It looked like a foregone conclusion until, about halfway round, Anne Gilbert's leader got a leg over a trace and she had to put her groom down, which cost her 5 penalties. Her leader then started to play up and she accumulated sufficient time penalties to let Penny Romsey through to win her very first red rosette.

It was another most enjoyable weekend for all the competitors, but Brian McGrath, who loved to bask in the Irish atmosphere, had the misfortune to slip one leg between the bars as he crossed a cattle grid, and damaged the knee of an already injured leg quite badly. Getting his leg out again was much more painful. As luck would have it, the wife of one of the guests in the house had been a nurse, and he was given much tender loving care by all the other ladies, but it took a long time to mend completely.

Owing to sponsorship and other problems, we were all very sad to hear that it had been decided that this would have to be the last event in the splendid Barons Court setting.

I am a great supporter of the Commonwealth Games, but my enthusiasm wore a bit thin when I discovered that I had to rush from lunch with the athletes in Manchester on Friday to get to Henbury in time to do my dressage test that afternoon. The day was rather muggy, and the ponies were not at their most enthusiastic. Storm spent the first part shaking his head, which was unusual for him, and then I noticed that he had a cleg behind his ear. He eventually managed to dislodge it, but we could still do no better than fourth place out of eight.

I then just had time to go round the obstacles with Micky before attending a party in the catering tent, where I was to be given an album of photographs to mark my thirty years of driving or my eightieth birthday, I am not quite sure which. It had been put together by Naomi Ferranti, whose death from cancer the previous November was a shattering blow for Sebastian and all her friends. John Richards handed over the album in the presence of several old rivals from the early days, among who were Albert Menaged, Jack Collinson and George Bowman, and there was much reminiscing. It was a very jolly occasion, and after a delicious dinner with Sebastian Ferranti, I went out again to walk the obstacles until it got dark.

As the obstacles were all so different from each other, I found them reasonably easy to remember, and I planned ways of avoiding any really awkward bits. However, the last obstacle posed a dilemma. I noticed that it might be possible to get through gates A and B in one by turning sharply round a tree, but the gates were so arranged on either side of the tree that if you turned too tightly it might be possible to fail to get the whole carriage through both gates. I appreciated the risk, but I thought that I would be very unlikely to be able to turn tightly enough to fail to cross the line and, in any case, I thought it was very unlikely for a course builder to include such a trap deliberately. In the end I decided to risk it.

Everything went beautifully on the day and I was quite chuffed to see that I had equalled or beaten Philippa Gammell in every obstacle, and even managed to beat Emily Bennett through the water – but then, so had Ursula Hirschberg, Beverly Mellstrom and Sarah Jane Cook. It was soon after finishing that I discovered that I had been eliminated in obstacle 8, and that the same fate had befallen Ursula Hirschberg, as well as Sebastian Ferranti in his class.

The *Carriage Horse* put it this way in its report of the event:

Obstacle 8 was the downfall of a number of competitors and 11 were eliminated. Those eliminated had not realised they had to go wide of the tree before they turned to ensure that their rear axle had cleared the line of gate A.

…It was unfortunate that not all competitors were aware of the potential problem in obstacle 8. Most of those eliminated accepted their fate with grace or humour; …as did one competitor – he sent a note to the stewards to say 'Good job we no longer put people in the Tower'!

Michael Onslow was driving his team for only the second or third time in a national event, and clocked up the enormous score of 307.2. As eliminated scores are based on the highest score in the class, it meant that I acquired 433.9 and Ursula Hirschberg 499.3!

On the Sunday, Ursula Hirschberg was the first to go in the cones phase, and did an impeccable double clear round. I then followed and, much to my delight, I did the same. It turned out that we were the only two in the whole class to manage double clear rounds. Perhaps it shows what a difference it makes to have nothing to worry about! Michael Onslow went in next and his ponies jumped out of the box to vociferous abuse from their driver. The box was put together again, and he made another attempt to even louder abuse, and they jumped out again. He then retired. This meant that Ursula Hirschberg and I both moved up a place and I ended up sixth. Brian McGrath did some calculations and found that even if I had not been eliminated, I would only have made fifth place anyway.

Sebastian Ferranti did a fairly good dressage test on his home ground to achieve fourth place, and got round the marathon without too much trouble, until he was eliminated in obstacle 8. Unfortunately things went wrong for him, yet again, in the cones and he hit seven, although it hardly mattered as his elimination in the marathon put him last anyway.

Nine of the regulars plus Michael Onslow assembled at Lowther at the beginning of August. Anywhere else in the country, you would have expected early August to be fine and dry – not the Lake District. It rained every night on the Thursday, Friday and Saturday, and the stable field was a real mess. The only redeeming feature was that it did not rain during the day. The main arena is normally free-draining, but this time it was really soggy, and the going was heavy. It obviously affected all the dressage tests, as John Pickford won with a score of 48.5 and the rest of us were in the 50s, 60s and 70s. I was third with 54.9 points, just 1.3 points behind Beverly Mellstrom.

Emily Bennett did one of her usual lightning rounds of the marathon for 92.6, the only one to crack the century. The first sections of the course were very sticky, but my ponies coped with them very well, and completed the fast section C without a problem. I then had a very scrappy round of the obstacles. I started badly by going wrong in the very first – and easiest – obstacle. I had no trouble in obstacle 2, but then I went wrong again in 3. I got through 4 quite well, but I then got a leader either side of a post in 5. I was pleasantly surprised to find that I was third fastest through the water, but then I blew it again in the last obstacle and had to put in a loop. After all that, I was rather expecting to be well down the order, and so I was slightly amazed to find that, although only fifth in the marathon, I had gone up a place to third in the combined scores. However, I was only 0.2 points ahead of Sarah Jane Cook and 0.8 ahead of Philippa Gammell. Both Beverly Mellstrom and Michael Onslow were eliminated.

When it came to the cones, my one chance of keeping my third place was by doing a double clear round, but only Emily Bennett did that to score a convincing win. Philippa Gammell's 3 time penalties gave me a very slight breathing space, and Sarah Jane Cook knocked one cone down, but was within the time, which meant that I had a few time penalties in hand from Philippa and a single cone from Sarah Jane. All went well until I hit the eighteenth pair for 5 penalties, but it was the additional 0.5 time penalties that dropped me to fifth place. Philippa Gammell went up to third place and Sarah Jane Cook was placed fourth by just

Fig. 9.14 Splashing through the Lowther River at the 2002 event. As it came near the end of the marathon it must have been quite a refreshing experience for the ponies. (*Author's collection*)

0.3 points. Michael Onslow had no problems with the cones this time, although he clocked up a score of 38.5.

Sebastian Ferranti got round the marathon rather slowly, and then hit seven cones. However, two of his pony-pairs class in succession missed out the same pair of cones, and he moved up two places to sixth out of twelve.

Only three other pony-teams entries, Ann Robarts, Michael Onslow and Philippa Gammell, turned up at Alnwick, but there were no less than thirteen in the pony-tandems class. The weather during the week had been ghastly, and everything was terribly wet. However, it cleared up and we had lovely weather throughout the weekend.

I managed to win the dressage by just 1 point from Philippa Gammell and 7 points from Ann Robarts. Michael Onslow did a much improved test for 64. Penny Romsey achieved seventh place, but not by much.

Saturday provided glorious weather for the marathon through the challenging countryside of Hulne Park. There were four obstacles in front of the castle and the other four on the other side of the river. I thought I was doing quite well through the rather long and complicated obstacles, but I was not fast enough to keep up with Philippa Gammell, who gained 10 points. At least I got through them all without making a mistake. Michael Onslow got round, but his driving was a bit erratic. Penny Romsey and her tandem went really well and she moved up to third place in her class.

The cones course looked fairly straightforward at first glance, but it turned out to be quite twisty with a perfectly horrid circle just after the start. Michael Onslow hit four while Ann Robarts hit five and had some time penalties. I went in next and managed a double clear round. I just had to hope that Philippa Gammell would hit a couple, to let me end the season on a high note. She very nearly obliged me by hitting one, but retained her place by just 3 points. Penny Romsey surprised everyone by doing a double clear round to retain her third place, until John Garlick hit a couple of cones to let her through to second place. Penny was so sorry for him that, after the prize-giving, she put her second prize in his horsebox!

Sebastian Ferranti was unable to compete, and his ponies were driven into third place by his groom. It just shows that there was nothing seriously wrong with his ponies, when his groom took the trouble to work them properly.

The day ended with a dinner in the castle restaurant for all the party. Sadly, Penny Romsey's groom and her temporary horsebox driver were under the impression that they had not been invited to the dinner, and they flounced off in a huff. The rest of us had a wonderful dinner amid gales of laughter, as we looked back on the ups and downs of the season. As far as results were concerned, this was not one of my best and, I have to admit, it was nothing to do with the ponies. They were about the best combination I had ever driven.

Results for 2002

EVENT	Dressage	Marathon	Cones	Pl/No
Brighton	6	8	7	6/11
Windsor	1	E	6	9/9
Farleigh	3	4	2	4/9
Sandringham	7	27	23	23/29
(European Championships)				
Barons Court	1	2	2	1/2
Henbury	4	E	1=	6/8
Lowther	3	5	4	5/9
Alnwick	1	2	1	2/4

Ponies used: Storm, Peter, Medina, Hamble, Heather.

CHAPTER TEN

HOW MUCH LONGER?

2003

A s I was about to reach the advanced age of eighty-two, I had a feeling that it was about time to give up taking part in these driving competitions. I am sure I would have done so but for Micky Flynn, whose management of the ponies is nothing short of miraculous. He is supported by two of the best girl grooms in the business. Pip Pearson (with her collie, Fran) has been with me for six years; she is strong, keen, very experienced in looking after horses and ponies in several equestrian sports, and a hunting enthusiast. Michelle Maynard, slim and with hair that has a way of changing colour every now and then, gained a lot of experience when she worked for Richard Margrave. He must have been an interesting employer, as I remember that he had an impish sense of humour, and an exuberant attitude to driving a team of horses. Both Pip and Michelle have a shrewd understanding of the Fells, and the ponies respond to their love and care.

I have to admit that I had another motive to keep going. The old green horse-box and trailer had become increasingly unreliable on long journeys and, if I wanted to go on competing, I knew they would have to be replaced. This would have been an excellent excuse to give up, but I thought, perhaps unreasonably, that I would be damned if I was to be forced to give up just because the horsebox and trailer had run out of puff. I argued that if I bought a second-hand box in reasonable condition, it would still have a sale value when I had finished with it. Furthermore, the old box was not fitted with proper accommodation and I really owed it to Micky and Marina Flynn to provide something a bit more comfortable for them to live in at events. Micky found such a box in Northern Ireland, and it came into use for the 2002 season.

Getting a new trailer for the carriages and portable stabling was another matter. Danny Harvey, the mechanical engineer at Sandringham, had acquired quite

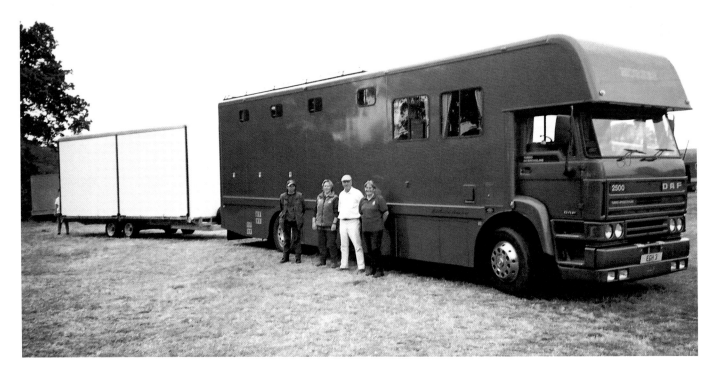

Fig. 10.1 The new 'road train'. The box has proper accommodation for the Flynns and the new carriage trailer, built by Danny Harvey at Sandringham, makes it much easier to erect the portable stabling and more comfortable for the ponies. (*Author's collection*)

a lot of experience in maintaining and improving the old trailer (bought from Sydney Smith in 1991), and in designing or building new trailers for Penny Romsey and Sebastian Ferranti. These were only intended for two ponies, but they provided the opportunity to incorporate various new ideas and features, which made it much easier to set up the portable stabling. In 2002 I asked him whether he would be prepared to build a new trailer capable of taking two carriages and six stables. He willingly agreed, but it turned out to be a bigger enterprise than either of us anticipated, particularly as the building work had to be fitted in to his first responsibility for the mechanical equipment on the Sandringham Estate. In the end it was only completed in August 2003, just in time for the Lowther and Alnwick events. It included a number of novel features, and turned out to be a huge success. It used to take nearly an hour to set up the old stabling, but the new version went up in minutes and with much less physical effort.

After years of experience with Fell ponies, I have come to appreciate their very special characteristics. They are quick-witted and intelligent, and while some have their anxieties and dislikes, on the whole they are remarkably calm and laid-back. They have immense stamina, and are willing to work their hearts out. Above all, they are forgiving and always willing to get you out of difficulties. The fact that I happened to have an exceptionally good team of ponies at the end of the 2002 season was yet another inducement for me to carry on.

Peter and Storm were getting on a bit, but Peter still had a few years in him, and should see me out. Storm is a great character, and was sound in January, but at that time I was not to know that he was going to have a fitness problem. The others were younger and, provided they remained sound, they had plenty of life in them. The two old boys, together with Heather, Hamble, Medina and Douglas – the latest home-bred addition – assembled at the stables at Appleton in early January and quickly settled down to the business of getting fit.

Douglas had started well in the previous year, and we were fairly confident that he would fit into the team in 2003, at least for the dressage and cones phases. He is a big strong pony but, as luck would have it, he has a wonderful temperament, and turned out to be pretty reliable both in the wheel and in the lead. His great talent is that he shares the work with the other wheeler, whichever side he is on, and goes evenly with the other leader. Nothing seems to spook him and he is remarkably relaxed in the stables. By the time the ponies returned to Windsor, we were confident that he could be included in the team for the next Windsor Park Equestrian Club event. I now had six good ponies and the only problem was to decide which one to leave out when the season started in earnest. The choice lay between Hamble and Storm, but we did not have to make a final decision before going to Brighton at the end of April. In the event, the choice was made for us when Storm developed a problem with one of his hind legs and he had to be turned out.

I am not quite sure for what reason, but Micky Flynn had taken to referring to the two leaders, Heather and Dina, as the 'fairies'. They do tend to live in a world of their own, but they do, at least, get on with each other and they do not pull. They are brilliant for both the obstacles and the cones, provided always that there is nothing scary like flapping flags, or anything resembling an umbrella either in the obstacles or too close to the cones. However, it is rather too evident, at least to the judges, that they are not madly enthusiastic about dressage. In order to keep what little interest they have, I limit dressage practice to very short sessions. They do nothing wrong in the movements, but they tend to get a bit bored, and fail to show that zip and sparkle, which would get me much better marks from the judges.

When I gave up playing polo, I offered to do some umpiring, but I soon discovered that it was one of the best ways of losing friends. For this reason, I was in two minds about accepting an invitation, several years ago, to judge dressage at the early-season WPEC events, even though I had written a small book called *Driving and Judging Dressage*. As a regular competitor, I was not in a position to be able to judge at national events, but I hoped that I would not come to too much

Fig. 10.2, 10.3, 10.4, 10.5
(*pages 270 and 271*) The new home-built portable stabling in use. The sides of the trailer hinge upwards in two sections on each side, assisted by small hydraulic rams. The old system needed nearly an hour to erect: these stables can be erected in twenty minutes. On the first such trailer I had, the 'doors' to the individual stables were rigid. The snag was that, on uneven ground, they were very difficult to fit. These heavy-duty cloth doors are hung on chains top and bottom and attached by small 'snap-shackles', which makes them much easier to manage. Zip fasteners help to close up the stables at night or in bad weather. The two carriages and the two sets of harness occupy the middle of the trailer. (*Author's collection*)

harm if I accepted the invitation to judge at a club event. Incidentally, according to the FEI, I am too old to be an international judge but, fortunately, not too old to be a competitor!

On the vexed subject of driven dressage, the British Horse Driving Trials Association arranges an annual judges' clinic, usually in March, very generously hosted by Sydney Smith at her splendid Unicorn Trust establishment at Stow-in the-Wold. I tried to attend these clinics as regularly as possible because I found it a very valuable experience, and there was always much to discuss. My only consistent criticism has been that, more often than not, experienced ridden dressage judges, and sometimes riders, are invited to attend and to lecture to the meeting.

It has always been my contention that there is a very significant difference between ridden and driven dressage. In fact, I very much regret that, when the *FEI Rules for Driving Events* were being written, we did not use some other expression for what became known as the 'dressage phase'. In retrospect, 'compulsory figures' (as in figure-skating competitions) might have been more appropriate. This was recognised by the FEI in 2003 when Jack Pemberton, the Chairman of the FEI Driving Committee, told me that he had proposed that it should be referred to as 'driven dressage' in the revised rules for 2005, in order to emphasize that it is different from the ridden version.

This whole issue rather came to a head at the 2003 clinic when it was suggested that judging dressage on the continent was done a little differently, and that if British drivers were to compete with any hope of success, they would have to be judged according to continental standards (I refrained from pointing out that I had done the best dressage test of the host nation teams to come seventh at the European Championships the previous year, and that it had been judged by an international jury). The suggestion was that there would be greater emphasis on the conformation and paces of the horse/s than on the accuracy and style of the driver. This is all very well, but it has serious implications for those who are thinking about a choice of breed for a single, pair, tandem or team, if only certain breeds are considered to have the right conformation.

In the light of this discussion, I was interested to see the results of our drivers at the World Pony Driving Championships later in the year. The combined dressage score for the six drivers in the British team put it in second place after Germany. The best score in the four-in-hand class was the German Dirk Gerkins' 48.1. Emily Bennett was sixth with 58.4 and John Pickford was given 63.5, which put him in ninth place out of twenty. I would guess that these scores were only about 8 points more than the average in national competitions.

Apart from the very obvious difference that in ridden dressage, the rider sits on the horse, whereas a driver sits on a carriage behind a horse or horses, there are two other fundamental differences. In the first place all ridden dressage involves one person riding one horse. There may be many different standards of tests, but the problem for the individual rider is always the same. By contrast, in driven dressage, there are four separate classes: singles, pairs, tandems and teams (of horses and ponies), and so in each class the problem for the drivers, and the judges, is different.

Secondly, it is very much easier for a rider to steer a horse to follow the track of the test accurately. The critical element of the ridden test, and what is being judged, is the performance of the horse in each of the different paces, i.e. the difference between and within the paces, plus the different movements, as required in the particular test.

In driven dressage, the most difficult problem is to get the horse/s and carriage to follow the required movements accurately; to start a movement at the right point, and to end it at the right point; to follow the required track accurately, and to make the transitions smoothly and precisely. Only three kinds of trot, a walk, a halt and a rein-back, and some circles are required. With more than one horse there are the added problems of getting the horses to work evenly together. All this has to be done using the reins and voice alone. It is obvious that the required paces need to be done willingly and actively (in other words, with impulsion), but I do not believe that the paces themselves should be the sole criterion in marking. What matters just as much is the general attitude of the horse/s. The judges need to see that they are alert and interested, willing and anxious to please, and, above all, easy and pleasant to drive.

The problem is bad enough for drivers of singles, but it gets progressively more difficult through pairs, teams and tandems. That is certainly my experience as a driver and as a judge. Cutting corners, egg-shaped circles, stopping yards short of the mark, and failing to show a change of pace, are common faults. All these factors, at least in my opinion, should be marked down long before worrying about 'bending', 'roundness', 'suppleness', 'expression' or 'cadence'. Those qualities should only be taken into account if the movements are correctly and accurately driven in the first place.

There is one further difference between ridden and driven dressage. In the original rules, there used to be an additional competition for what was known as 'presentation'. This entailed each competitor being judged separately by each judge, who carefully inspected the whole turnout; the condition and cleanliness of horses, carriage and harness, and the dress of the driver and grooms. Presentation, as a separate phase, has long since been abandoned, but there is still a box, on the sheets provided for dressage judges, marked 'Presentation' and it carries a maximum of ten points. Unlike ridden dressage, appropriate, sparkling and properly fitting harness is essential. Badly fitting harness has a major influence on the way the horse/s go, and an appropriate and gleaming carriage improves the picture of the whole turnout.

A report on the 2003 clinic was later published in *Carriage Horse* and it drove me to write the following letter to Tom Pettifer, the Chairman of the British Horse Driving Trials Association:

I have just been reading the April edition of *Carriage Horse* with the article about the National Judges Clinic at the Unicorn Trust. I am a bit worried to see that the discussion about the definition of the 'collected trot' is reported as if there had been general agreement with the views of Diana Brownlie, Jane Goldsmith and Andrew Counsell. I seem to remember that there was quite a lot of uncertainty about what they were getting at. I think it is worth bearing in mind that the definition of the collected trot in the FEI Rules starts by stating quite precisely that '*The pace is slower than the working trot*' and goes on '…*the steps are shorter and lighter and more mobile*'. Is the BHDTA really going to suggest that the FEI should change the definition of the collected trot just because there is a change of fashion in judging?

I, for one, remain highly dubious about the suggestion that '*Collection should not be just slowing the horse down but more as a way of* **containing the energy and creating more engagement***.*' and '*However accuracy should still be regarded as 'icing on the cake' when handing out the high marks*'. I draw your attention to the marks for General Impression under FEI Article 942.5 'Driver'. You will see that it ends with the sentence '*The mark should reflect the consistent level of accuracy.*' That is a basic requirement; it is not icing on the cake.

I am particularly concerned about the suggestion that '*In future slow trots lacking energy and impulsion will be penalised*'. Up till now, it was a common experience to read in the comments column of the Judges' sheet that there had been 'little variation in pace' or 'little extension shown'. I am confused about how it will be possible to judge a collected trot if there is to be little or no difference in pace between it and a working trot.

What worries me is this 'puritan' intellectual approach to the Dressage phase of a combined driving event. It is equivalent to suggesting that 3-day event riders should be able to perform 'Haute Ecole' standard of Dressage. In both the riding and driving event, Dressage is just one - and not the most important one as far as scores are concerned – of the three Phases.

Considering that the only means of controlling a 'multiple' is by the reins and the voice (the idea of using a whip during a one-handed circle at a collected trot – other than to touch a wheeler – is absurd), quite how any driver is to get a team to '*create more energy and engagement*' while doing a one-handed circle is a mystery to me. Even in ridden Dressage, the horse moves forward more slowly when it is doing a collected trot, but it can be made to show more energy and engagement by the use of the spurs and reins.

Furthermore, I am not at all confident that the average driving Dressage judge would know how to interpret the article 'Dressage Judging'. For example, you cannot possibly alter the rhythm without altering the pace.

I have no quibble with the general ideals, but I think the experts have got their priorities upside down. The basic requirement of a driver will always be to show a change of pace between the three degrees of trot, and to perform the figures as accurately as possible. The presence, or absence, of these features should be clearly visible to the Judges. After that, the **quality** of the collection, working and extension in the trots becomes a matter of the judge's personal opinion. This means that '*creating more energy and engagement*' is what should be seen as the 'icing on the cake'.

I was judging novice single ponies the other day, and I can only say that it came as a pleasant surprise to see a pony showing distinct changes of pace and a driver managing to do the figures accurately. If Judges are really going to try to implement the gist of what is written in *Carriage Horse*, I fear that it will only serve to confuse and discourage novice drivers, as well as experienced drivers attempting to bring on novice horses.

By the end of the driving season, I had a feeling that I was losing that argument. I also had some correspondence with Jack Pemberton, the Canadian Chairman of the FEI Driving Committee, about the revision of the driving rules due in 2005. This prompted him to send me a copy of the sixth draft of my original re-write of the rules for my comments. I think he was rather taken aback when I sent him about a hundred suggestions for improvements. Most of them were minor points about wording. I was disappointed to see in this latest draft that the criteria for judging dressage had all been rewritten. His covering letter also mentioned that the major national federations were anxious to reduce the marathon to three sections (A, D and E) for international events and championships. I suspect that this will lead to a demand for 'one-day events' before long. I was also unhappy about the suggestion that the penalty for knocking over a cone should be reduced from the present 5 to 3, and to reduce the time penalty from 0.5 to 0.2 penalties per second. The reason given was that it was unfair for someone who had done well in the dressage and marathon to lose a place because they hit a cone. I pointed out that, if someone had a combined score of, say, 150 before the cones, a penalty of 5 points was a very small proportion of that score. In any case, someone who was good enough to lead a class before the cones, should be able to do a clear round. If they failed to do so, it seemed only reasonable that the competitor in second place by less than 5 points should be the winner.

Meanwhile the 2003 season began with a Windsor Park Equestrian Club event in early April. For once the weather was perfect and the going dry. I put Douglas on the nearside in the wheel with Peter for the dressage and cones. This was his first competition and, he really did quite well, even though I got a dreadful mark of 64 from Caroline Musker. It later turned out that the stand-in scorer had omitted to multiply the score by 0.8, a calculation that would have produced a rather more respectable score of 51.2. The only other four-in-hands present were the horse teams of Adrian Puddy, who scored 46, and Dick Lane with 59. In the cones phase, I was quite happy with one cone down and 6.5 time penalties. Adrian Puddy had two down but only 1 time penalty, so he beat me by 0.5 points. Dick Lane had an unusually expensive round.

Sunday dawned cloudy with a nasty northerly wind, and by the afternoon everyone was frozen. It is on days like this that my sympathy and gratitude goes out to all the voluntary officials. I put Douglas in with Hamble in the wheel, but this time on the nearside, as Hamble has always worked on the offside. They went brilliantly, and were still going like steam engines at the end, although they were a bit strong for comfort.

I had started Sophie Wessex with Carrick in 2002, and she had shown evidence of keenness and considerable talent; I was, therefore, hoping that she might progress this year, and possibly get herself qualified for national events. Bagshot is no distance from Windsor, and I was expecting her to pop over occasionally before the season started for some practice and coaching from Micky Flynn. Nothing happened, and I began to wonder whether she had gone off the idea. Then the happy thought entered my head that she might be expecting a baby. It was only a matter of days before we got a message to say that a public announcement was to be made to the effect that I had guessed right.

If I had any optimism about the coming season it was rudely shattered at the next WPEC event. I started at half past nine on a cold morning by judging the open single-ponies class dressage and was pleasantly impressed, but, when I thought we had finished, and I had delivered my writer back to the secretary's caravan, I was informed that there was another competitor waiting to be judged. Fortunately, it turned out they had been left off the list.

Things are pretty informal on the Cannon Ground at Windsor, and I am quite used to being told 'You can go in whenever you like'. This time the call came rather sooner than I would have liked, as I had not done any warming-up. As I did not want to keep the judge waiting, I went straight into the arena, with dreadful results. This time I had put Douglas in the wheel with Storm and, apart from a crooked rein-back, they managed quite well. The 'fairies', on the other hand, were hopeless. This produced such gems on the judge's sheet as 'Oh dear…! Are they short of sleep?', 'Oh dear…! They must have got out of the wrong side of the bed' and 'Things are improving…or so I thought'. However, he must have been in a very generous mood to give me 49.2. It was the only test, other than the very last one at Alnwick, when I scored less than 50 in that season. I will pass over the cones score and, just to add to this dismal performance in the preparation for Brighton, I was unable to do the marathon because of other engagements.

For a change, everything was dry and the going hard at Stanmer Park in Brighton. The layout for the event had also changed. The main arena had been moved up to what had been a cricket pitch between the house and the church. It was a great improvement, but it was sad to see the house in such a derelict state. The event was also made a good deal more entertaining by the presence of both Penny Romsey and Sebastian Ferranti in the pony-tandems class. Both had new grooms. Penny Romsey had secured the services of Jenny, a cheerful, intelligent person in what might be described as approaching sensible middle age. She had lots of experience with riding, but this was her first encounter with driving. Sebastian Ferranti had found Karen, a splendidly enthusiastic northern girl for whom driving was also a new experience. We were all bivouacked together and it turned out to be a very happy party, which boded well for the rest of the season. The drivers, together with Brian McGrath, our unofficial Chef d'Equipe, were again comfortably housed by Lord Gage at Firle Park.

Earlier in the year, Sebastian Ferranti had turned over while driving his pair at Henbury and damaged his carriage. Fortunately, he happened to have a single carriage, so he decided to put the ponies together as a tandem. I thought it was quite a courageous decision, but I am sure it was a good idea for him to get out of the very competitive pairs class. Micky Flynn spent a lot of time working on both the driver and his ponies. Sebastian was, therefore, now in the same class as Penny Romsey, and all her best motherly instincts were aroused to help the newcomer to her class. I am not altogether sure that this was received with unreserved joy by Sebastian, who did not have quite the same dedication to preparing for the marathon and walking the obstacles in the early hours of the morning.

It was just before we set off for Brighton that Storm developed a problem with a hind leg, and so he had to be left out. This meant that Douglas would have to face his first national event. I had decided long ago that Hamble and dressage were incompatible, which meant that Douglas was paired with Peter. I was very pleased with their performance, and I thought they deserved better than 50.9, but, at least, I was second to Emily Bennett by just 3 points. Sadly, the marathon was a chapter of disasters. We were some nine seconds late on the second walk thanks to Douglas breaking into the occasional trot. Bearing in mind that this was a new experience for him, I intended to be rather cautious, but I started badly by losing my way in the first obstacle. I was careful and slow in the next four, but I got stuck and went wrong in obstacle 6 and again in 7 and ended up last, apart from Michael Onslow, who had only just started driving a team. Micky Flynn put it down to Douglas's inexperience, but I was beginning to think that Hamble was at the root of the problem. He has a heart the size of a bucket and is as strong as an ox, but he gets anxious in tight obstacles and pulls; these factors, plus a good deal of driver error, were the real problems.

On combined scores, there were only 3 points between Julia Liles, Beverly Mellstrom and me. The others, Emily Bennett, Anna Grayston and John Pickford, were all at least 30 points ahead. I partially redeemed myself in the cones phase. Michael Onslow went in first, and collected nearly 40 penalties. I went in next and, by some miracle, managed a clear round, but with 11 penalties for time I had an overall total of 187.7. I was then amazed to watch Beverly Mellstrom knock down two cones and add 6 penalties for an overall total of 192, so I moved up a place. Julia Liles went in next and hit three cones and added 8.5 penalties for time, which gave her a combined score of 198.4, so I went up another place to end up in fourth place.

There were eight entries for Windsor: Mia Allo from Belgium, Aart van de Kamp with his Shetlands and Harrie Burghoorn from the Netherlands, and Emily Bennett, Anna Grayston, John Pickford, Philippa Gammell and I were the British entries. I was rather in two minds about accepting the invitation to compete at this event. I do not think I had qualified according to the points league for the previous year, and I also had a new, relatively inexperienced pony in the team, but I allowed myself to be persuaded to have another go.

I had been worried about having Hamble in the wheel, and I was thinking of trying Douglas with Peter for the marathon when, to my relief, Micky Flynn suggested it himself.

The ponies went well in the dressage, and I managed to get into fourth place. However, the next day I was slowest through the marathon obstacles with 125 points compared to Aart van de Kamp's 86. In obstacle 4 I hit the outside post going into gate A, and was just saved from being pitched out by Micky Flynn grabbing my jersey. The only reason I was not last was that Emily Bennett missed a gate in obstacle 8, in spite of going back with the intention of correcting her mistake. John Pickford was not having a lucky weekend either; he went wrong in the dressage, and then had to retire after injuring a pony in obstacle 7. He put an inexperienced pony in for the cones and failed to get round a very tight double box obstacle after two attempts.

I managed a clear round of the cones, but had to add 12 time penalties and ended up in sixth place, 5 points behind Harrie Burghoorn and 15 behind Philippa Gammell. However, the main thing was that Douglas had turned out to be a real star.

The next event involved a migration to Hopetoun at the end of May. Penny Romsey was unable to make it, but Sebastian Ferranti brought his ponies, and we were very comfortably housed by Adrian and Auriol Linlithgow in the big house. The local driving club had been allowed to create a new arena to the west of the house, and conveniently close to the stable field. The only trouble was that the ground had not had time to consolidate, and, after heavy rain, the going was definitely sticky. However, the ponies coped very well with the conditions, including doing the only good rein-back in the class. A score of 53.9 put me a close second to Emily Bennett on 53.1, but nothing like far enough ahead of Philippa Gammell and John Pickford.

The heavens opened on Saturday morning, but the sun came out just as I started section E. I thought I was really motoring through the obstacles, but the others went much faster. However, I did manage to beat both Philippa Gammell and John Pickford through obstacle 4, the water obstacle. I was very unlucky in 5, when Douglas hesitated on a sharp turn to his side and I hit the post on the nearside a glancing blow. This whipped the back of the carriage round, and Pip was catapulted off the back step, much to her mortification as it earned me 10 penalties for having a groom down in an obstacle. But for that, I would have been only 10 points behind Philippa Gammell. Yet again, I was saved from being last by Emily Bennett, when she missed a gate in obstacle 2. Some wag suggested that if she went on doing that sort of thing she would earn a place in the Honours List.

The ponies went brilliantly in the cones on a very stodgy course to get round inside the time, although some sixteen seconds slower than Emily Bennett. Unfortunately, I hit the first pair of the slalom, to be the only one of the class to hit anything. This mistake was entirely my fault as I had forgotten the need to go a little wide to make the turn, and it was too late to get everything straight by the time I got to the start of the slalom. John Pickford could afford his 2 time penalties to win by some 10 points from Philippa Gammell. The other three drivers were selected as the team drivers to represent Britain in the Pony Driving World Championships in Austria in August 2003.

Sebastian Ferranti managed quite a good dressage test with his tandem, but he was very slow through the obstacles, missed a gate in 3, and was eliminated. He got round the cones with only one down, but his ponies were struggling in the soggy conditions, and he accumulated some 30 time penalties. In spite of this he thoroughly enjoyed himself, as did everyone else throughout the weekend.

Fig. 10.6 *right* Anna Grayston, another of the very successful 'flying fillies'. She had a very nasty accident at Alnwick in 1999 when her ponies spooked at something in the collecting ring before the cones section. They spun round, throwing her off the box and took off for the stable field. All was well in the end, and she was back on the circuit the following season. Here, Anna and her team are at Windsor in 2003. (*Alf Baker*)

Fig. 10.7 *below* Every now and then everything goes right. After some ten years competing, Penny Romsey eventually reached the heights by winning at Lowther in August 2003. (*Lady Romsey*)

I have not written an account of every Windsor Park Equestrian Club event, but the one in early June should be mentioned. I was unable to get to Windsor until after lunch on the Saturday, as that morning I had been taking the salute at the Colonel's Review, the last rehearsal before the Queen's Birthday Parade on Horse Guards. When I eventually got to the Cannon Ground, I discovered that Penny Romsey had had an interesting experience in the dressage arena. Apparently she had forgotten to do the second extension and the walk, but the Judge (Lex Ruddiman, who had started driving a team of horses towards the end of my time in that class) failed to notice the mistake, so she just went on. There then followed a panic-stricken discussion in whispers between Penny Romsey and her groom, Jenny, about what to do next. They managed, somehow, to incorporate all the missing parts and ended up with 36, the best score in her class and her best score ever.

The next day, I was making my way to the start of section E at the end of the walk section, when I came across Sebastian Ferranti going the wrong way in search of the compulsory halt. I then realized that I was not too certain myself, and I could see no signs. I made a guess, which luckily proved to be right, and he was only one minute late starting E.

I had no problems with the first obstacle, but things went wrong in the water crossing at what is known as China Island. We had to go through the water and round a tree for gate A, then back across the water for B and over the bridge, this time, for C, which was at right angles to A. The ponies whizzed into the water at great speed and shot through A, but then went too far and took me through C as well. Micky Flynn shouted, but I blandly said that it did not matter as we had been through it already, which was, of course, sheer nonsense. Having gone through C before B I had made an error of course and collected 20 penalties, but I was not eliminated because I went back to do B and then came back, as planned, to do C. All this was enlivened by a young artist, Alexander Talbot-Rice, who wanted to take some photographs of the ponies going through the water for a picture he was intending to paint. I saw him on the far side as we went in, and then, while I was negotiating A, and unintentionally going through C, he nipped across the water and took some more photographs from the other side. As we came galloping up out of the water, he suddenly stepped forward towards the track from behind a bush, and gave the ponies such a surprise that we nearly went up a steep bank on the other side of the track.

The next event was at Farleigh Wallop at the end of Ascot Week. I decided to enter, even though I knew it was going to make for a very complicated weekend. Fortunately, it is only about an hour from Windsor because the only way I could walk the obstacles was to drive over to Farleigh from Windsor on the Thursday morning, and back to Windsor for lunch before going racing, and then drive over again after tea in the Royal Box at Ascot, and back again to Windsor for dinner. I then drove back to Farleigh again after tea at Ascot on Friday to do my dressage, and stay the night before doing the marathon on the Saturday, but I had to get back to Windsor again that evening for my grandson William's twenty-first birthday party. The next morning I had to go back to Farleigh again for the cones. There are two ways of getting to Farleigh from Windsor, and I got to know both of them quite well.

Luckily, it was only a three-section marathon, as the weather was scorching, but it was over quite a demanding course. It took us to the top of the hills with dramatic views over Basingstoke to the north and into Hampshire to the south and east, and through some lovely old oak woodland. The obstacles looked manageable, the weather was set fair and the going was firm. My dressage was not very good, largely due to Heather, who appeared to be half asleep most of the time. This put me 6 points behind Beverly Mellstrom and 9 ahead of Julia Liles with Michael Onslow some way back. I put Hamble with Peter for the marathon and lived to regret it. Hamble became anxious and pulled my arms out, which made steering difficult. What made it worse was that I had fallen onto my left shoulder from my small motorcycle while 'walking' the obstacles on the Thursday. I was riding through some longish grass between obstacles, and failed to notice a deep rut. The front wheel went in and turned down the rut while I went straight on. Because of this fall and Hamble's eagerness, by the end of the marathon my shoulder was aching quite badly and, later, the whole shoulder and arm came out in a spectacular blue and yellow bruise.

Both Beverly Mellstrom and Julia Liles got ahead of me in the obstacles. However, Julia Liles had a disastrous round in the cones, with three down and 21 time penalties, and as I managed to get round with only one down and a few time penalties, it was enough to let me through into second place some 18 penalties behind Beverly Mellstrom.

The tandem drivers did not have a very successful event. Penny Romsey was fourth out of six entries in the dressage and Sebastian Ferranti was last. Penny then started the obstacles by going wrong in the first and getting lost in the second. At least she won the cones phase, which was a slight compensation. Sebastian got round the obstacles rather slowly and then had trouble in the cones, but at least he finished without getting eliminated.

Sandringham followed at the end of June and the two tandem drivers, our Chef d'Equipe and John Stevens came to stay at Wood Farm. Although in his nineties, John Stevens had driven himself from the West Country. He was one of the early band of enthusiastic supporters, organizers and officials at driving events. He had been a regular official at previous events, and had kindly agreed to chair the Appeals Committee.

This was another complicated weekend for me, because President Putin of Russia was only due to depart after his State Visit on the Friday morning. Fortunately, I was able to leave London for Sandringham after a reception on the Wednesday evening, so that I could spend most of Thursday driving the ponies and walking the obstacles. I then returned to London by helicopter for the dinner given by the President, and then back to Sandringham by the same means after his departure on Friday morning.

I had spent quite a lot of time in January trying to find a new route for section A, and eventually managed to get an abandoned track along the Babingley River sufficiently restored to form part of the course. It was still a bit soggy on the day, but it seemed to be popular with the competitors. The first walk was through a plantation of blackcurrants, and section C started through part of an apple orchard. Section E was the usual series of loops that ran between the obstacles beside the main arena. The obstacles were the same as the ones built for the European Championships but, of course, the routes through them were quite different.

I thought I had done quite a good dressage test, and many others agreed, but none of the judges thought so. That meant that I had to start the marathon with a handicap of some 10 points more than the first four competitors. This time I put Douglas in with Peter, and it made all the difference; it was a pleasure to drive the obstacles, but I was nothing like fast enough. The only mishap was in the carousel area of obstacle 5, when the flapping flags, ribbons and cut-out circus horses caused panic in the leaders, and I had to do quite a lot of improvising, which must have added another 10 penalties at least. Beverly Mellstrom had even worse problems in that obstacle, and collected 45.8 penalties. Philippa Gammell confessed to going wrong in obstacle 2, and should, therefore, have been given 20 penalties after correcting her mistake. The judges were reluctant to believe her until she produced a video to prove her confession, and was thus dropped to fifth position, just 0.6 points ahead of me before the cones, while I was only 5 points ahead of Helen Cruickshank.

It was quite an awkward cones course, and there were very few double clear rounds in the previous classes. A difficult decision had to be made about whether to circle to the left after 3, or to make a slightly longer – and safer – circle by turning right and going round 4 to get a better entry to it. As I had little to lose, I thought I would go for the shorter route, but I was somewhat unnerved before I even got there by hitting the second pair of cones. I had no real excuse for this mistake, although it had caught out quite a lot of people in the other classes. I had no difficulty in getting from 3 to 4 the short way, but I just nudged a ball off at 12 and finished with 10 penalties plus 4 time penalties, a total of 14. Philippa Gammell went in next and also had two cones down but she went the long way round to 4 and finished with 10 plus 5 penalties, which put me ahead of her by 0.4 overall. Beverly Mellstrom collected 20.5 penalties, and so she dropped below me as well and, much to my surprise, I moved up another place to finish fourth.

Penny Romsey had mixed fortunes. Her dressage test was not one of her best, but she was still in second place; she then drove brilliantly to win the marathon, but sadly made a mess of the cones and dropped to third. Sebastian Ferranti did a much improved dressage test, but he was rather slow in the obstacles again, and then collected quite a high score in the cones phase; this does not sound very good, but it was only his first season with a tandem.

For once the weather was glorious throughout this Sandringham event, other than some heavy rain during the Friday night, which did at least settle the dust. The Country Fair proved to be very popular again with the total attendance only slightly down on the previous – record – year. The weekend was brought to a pleasant close with an evening barbecue for our whole party in a hut we normally use for shooting lunches.

There was the usual long gap after Sandringham before we all reassembled at Henbury at the end of July. After weeks of hot dry weather, I arrived at Henbury in time for dinner on Thursday, to be told that heavy rain was forecast for Friday, which proved to be true; it absolutely sluiced down all day. I was lucky enough to do my dressage about midday, before the arena got really badly poached, but I do not think I have ever had to do a dressage test in such a non-stop deluge before. The sound of the rain on the video is deafening. Mine was the last of the five pony teams to do the test, by which time any trace of the sawdust mark at X had long since disappeared, and so I was slightly put out to read on one of the judges' sheets that I had halted too soon. I thought the ponies went reasonably well considering the conditions, although the 'fairies' were not at their best. I ended up 8 points behind Philippa Gammell and 3 behind John Pickford. I later discovered that John Pickford's team had been spooked by something just after his final salute, and bolted out of the arena heading straight for the president of the jury. The team wrapped itself round his car, and moved it bodily several metres, and both the car and the carriage were damaged. You would be forgiven for thinking that this might have incurred some penalties, but the test ends with the final salute, and after that the sheet just says 'Leave the arena at a trot' without specifying by which route.

This accident presented John Pickford with an awkward problem. The FEI had decided to organize the first World Pony Driving Championships in Austria in August. There had been separate World Championships for single, pairs and teams of horses for some time, and the pony people were agitating for the same system. However, the FEI felt it would be impractical to organize separate championships for each of the pony classes. The idea, therefore, was for each nation to enter two team members and one reserve in each of the four-in-hand, pairs and singles classes. Quite why tandems were left out is not clear. John Pickford and Emily Bennett, with Philippa Gammell as reserve, had been selected for the teams class, and as they would have to leave the following week, there was not much time for John Pickford to get his best carriage repaired.

Meanwhile, owing to the heavy rain on the previous day, it was decided to leave out sections C and D of the marathon, but I am not sure that it was really necessary. I was very happy with the way the ponies went through the obstacles. Every time Peter and Douglas go together, they get better, and give me the confidence to try to go a bit faster. Most of the obstacles were quite manageable although 5 was on quite a steep slope and caused many problems, and 6, which started with a sloping wooden bridge, was also quite tricky and proved very difficult for the horse teams. Penny Romsey was convinced that Jane would refuse to get onto the bridge, but a stentorian bellow of 'Jaaaaane' as she approached it, did the trick. Unfortunately for Philippa Gammell, she had a serious problem in obstacle 4, which must have unnerved her, as I beat her through the last four obstacles. That meant that, on combined scores, I got some 50 ahead of Philippa Gammell and John Robertson and 13 points behind John Pickford.

On the Sunday morning, I heard that John Pickford had eventually decided to withdraw because of his damaged carriage. He might have been able to borrow one, but he felt he had to set off as soon as possible to get his best carriage repaired in time to travel to Austria. That left me in first place with a very comfortable lead, which was just as well because the cones course was a real brute. It might have been even worse as the designer had included a clump of flags quite close to the course. Luckily, one of the judges had noticed several horses and ponies shying at the flags during the dressage tests, and asked for them to be moved. As I was in the process of walking the cones course, I saw a party advancing on the flags. When I discovered that they were about to move them, I hastily offered to help, and I got them moved rather further away than I think they had intended. One of the party asked me where I wanted to put them, and I suggested that the best place for them was in the middle of Macclesfield.

The rules allow no more than four multiple obstacles in the cones course and this particular course included two slaloms and two 'open' boxes. There were, therefore, twenty-six pairs of cones in the twenty cones obstacles. Michael Onslow drove the course first and collected 48 penalties. Philippa Gammell went in next and did a clear round but she overshot 19 and collected 9.5 time penalties. John Robertson hit one and added 21 time penalties to his score, which let Philippa

Gammell move up into second place by 6 points. I went round as fast as I dared and got 5.5 time penalties, but I also hit three cones, starting with the fifth, which gave me a massive total of 20.5, although still with 40 points in hand. Andrew Cowdery, the commentator, announced that it was 'his first win of the season'. He should have said that it was my first win for years.

Penny Romsey did a brilliant dressage test with her tandem (53 to my 56) and then flew through the obstacles. Sadly, things fell apart in the cones and Penny hit six to drop from second to fourth. She was greatly comforted when George Bowman hit no less that seven cones, for which, I told him later at Lowther, she said that she could have happily kissed him, whereupon he set off in search of her and, somewhat to her astonishment, gave her a smacking kiss before explaining the reason.

Sebastian Ferranti got round without any dramas, but rather slowly. His groom, Karen, did a wonderful job in guiding him through the obstacles. Both the words and the gestures in obstacle 6 were recorded on the video. Andrew Cowdery was stationed near 6 and, after listening to Karen giving rather audible instructions, he announced over the public address system that any further commentary from him would be superfluous. I showed the video to all the grooms that evening, although I was a bit anxious about Karen's reaction. I need not have worried, as she burst into helpless giggles at the sight and sound of her antics.

After the marathon on Saturday, Philippa Gammell invited me to tea and drop scones in her horsebox. Having tried them on previous occasions, I accepted with pleasure and anticipation because she is without doubt one of the master drop-scone makers. With the addition of a bit of butter and some golden syrup, they are food fit for the gods.

There were now two weeks before the next event at Lowther in August. Rather than take the ponies all the way back to Windsor, Micky Flynn, the two tandem drivers and the grooms, all agreed that the whole party should go to Sandringham on the Monday. Penny Romsey just stayed for a day's driving on the Tuesday, as she had things to do at home, returning on the following Tuesday before the whole caravan set off for Lowther. Sebastian Ferranti stayed with me at Wood Farm, and did some serious training with Micky Flynn. I made an excursion to the Royal Albert Hall in London to attend a special evening at the Proms, and then a round trip to Cowes and back via the Bicester and Finmere Horse Show, which was celebrating its twenty-fifth anniversary.

The weather was perfect: sunny, but not too hot and we took the opportunity to turn the ponies out as much as possible. A few days in a field does wonders for Fell ponies. They come back to work calm and refreshed. I just pottered round the lanes on most of the outings, but as I had some cones there, and after our rather dismal performances, we all needed to do a bit of serious practice. I was also able to give Danny Harvey (Sandringham's mechanical engineer) a hand in putting the finishing touches to the new trailer. It was ready just in time to go to Lowther. The 'trailer stables' went up so fast that the grooms stood around wondering what they had forgotten to do.

Inexplicably, the entries for Lowther were significantly down, even though the whole event had been revamped – including the weather. In contrast to the previous year, the sky was blue, the sun blazed down and the temperature soared, except for a short shower on Sunday morning. There was a new and very helpful stable manager, and most of the driving classes were allowed to do their dressage in the main arena. I was rather sorry to see that the marathon course had been considerably shortened, but there was a completely new and imaginative set of obstacles built by George Prince. The first five were in a row below the castle, and easily viewed by the spectators. The other three were down by the river crossing, which attracted the usual crowd of spectators, who enjoy watching competitors going through the water.

The great thing about these new obstacles was that they were all very different in character, and, therefore, easier to learn. The first one looked like an Indian camp with wigwams; the second was called the Petrified Forest; the third was based on a pinball table with round straw bales wrapped in different colours; the fourth consisted of what looked very like standing stones and was a bit confusing; the fifth was called Klondike and was based on a gold diggers' camp; the sixth was the usual crossing of the Lowther River; the seventh was in the sandpit, renamed The Bomb Hole, and was quite a challenge; and the eighth was the only conventional post-and-rails-type obstacle. Klondike, the fifth obstacle, started with a steep drop and then you were expected to turn sharp right at the bottom, although there was an escape route if you had to go straight on. There was then another sharp right turn on an uphill slope, which is always a problem as the leaders usually go into draught uphill.

Owing to the absence of the competitors at the World Championships, there were only three pony-teams entrants for this event: Anna Grayston, Michael Onslow and me. Anna Grayston led the field throughout. She was 3 points ahead of me in the dressage – 49.1 to my 52.3 – with Michael Onslow much closer than usual on 66. He distinguished himself by being the fastest of the class through the water. Both the tandems did quite well, and Sebastian Ferranti was not last in the class.

I was delighted with my ponies in the marathon, but I made a serious mistake in obstacle 1 when I misunderstood an instruction from Micky Flynn and got into a time-costly muddle. Otherwise all went well, if rather slowly compared to Anna

Grayston who fairly shot round, and got 30 points ahead of me, although I gave away at least 5 of those points in the first obstacle. I watched the singles and tandems through the first five, and they all seemed to manage the steep slope in obstacle 5 without a problem, except for Sebastian Ferranti, who got firmly stuck on the uphill right turn and had to retire with a damaged carriage. When it came to my turn, the wheelers failed to hold the carriage back on the slope, and we shot out of the escape route at the bottom. Otherwise, I only had a moment's anxiety in The Bomb Hole, when a lot of quick changes of rein were needed while going up and down the sides of the hole. I also went slightly wrong in the last obstacle, but managed to correct myself, more by good luck than good judgement.

Penny Romsey fairly flew round the obstacles, just 2 points slower than Anna Grayston, but she would have been faster had she not overshot in obstacle 2 and had to do a circle; despite this, she ended up leading her class by some 40 points. She got round the cones with only a couple down and a few time penalties, and duly won her class. I noticed, too late, that the course builder had failed to widen the gap between the cones from 160 cm for the previous, pony pairs, class, to 170 cm for the pony-tandems class. As she drove out of the arena, the steward, who had been doing the job for years, congratulated her warmly adding 'I never thought I would see the day when you won this class'!

My ponies set off round the cones in great style, and were going really well until I must have had a lapse of concentration and nudged the last pair of the slalom cones, but we were inside the time allowed. Anna Grayston also hit one of the slalom cones, and finished in exactly the same time, but with an overall score some 40 points better.

Sebastian Ferranti had rather an unhappy experience after retiring in the fifth obstacle with a broken carriage. When he started to lead his ponies back to the stables, he naturally set off down through the park to cross the road, and then down round the arena and up the hill to the stables. When he reached the road, an official tried to prevent him from going on down to the arena on the grounds that this area was out of bounds according to an 'instruction' given to drivers. It later transpired, however, that this 'instruction' only related to exercise areas before the event. The official informed him that the route back to the stables was on the public road down the steep hill past the church, up to Askham village and back along the route for competitors returning from the end of section E. He thought this was an unreasonable detour, and that his first concern was for the welfare of his ponies, so he continued on his way. The next thing he knew, he was summoned by the ground jury and, without being given a chance to give his account of the incident, was told by the president that, as a punishment for ignoring the 'official', he had been 'eliminated' – even though he had already retired. In addition he had been 'disqualified', which meant that he could not compete in the cones. Everyone tried to get him to lodge an appeal, but he decided not to do so. The general view was that the ground jury had no right under the rules to punish him in this way.

The only other cloud over the event was that George Bowman was unable to compete in his thirtieth 'home' event, as a result of two of his horses getting injured in their portable stabling during the Thursday night. Other than these unfortunate incidents, it was a very happy and enjoyable weekend.

In previous years, there had been a problem of finding somewhere for the ponies and grooms to stay between the stables at Lowther closing and the stable field opening at Alnwick. This year the same chap was stable manager at both events and he arranged matters so that he closed the Lowther stables on the Tuesday morning and then drove over and opened the Alnwick stables that afternoon. Meanwhile, I had to go to Edinburgh for a dinner on the Monday and a reception at midday on the Tuesday before joining the others at Thirlestane Castle, where we were given very comfortable shelter by Rossie and Bunny Maitland-Carew.

On the Thursday we transferred to Friar's Well in Hulne Park to stay with Elizabeth Northumberland, and then spent the afternoon walking the obstacles. They appeared to be driveable without any really tricky bits, but I thought they were rather long and hideously complicated. As most of them were built of plain posts and rails, I found it hard to distinguish between them. My heart sank when I saw the last obstacle, which resembled the dreaded carousel at Sandringham rather too closely, and I foresaw trouble.

The ponies were in good form for the dressage and I scored under 50 for the first time that season. Even so, I was just over 3 points behind Beverly Mellstrom, while Michael Onslow was in the 60s. I was expecting great things of the ponies in the marathon, but then I got into a muddle, yet again, in the very first obstacle. It so happened that Beverly Mellstrom made almost exactly the same mistake. This obstacle must have had an evil spirit in it, because Penny Romsey got into all sorts of trouble and earned 20 penalties for going wrong in it. After that, Beverly Mellstrom and I ran neck and neck, including both having difficulties in the last obstacle, but she just managed to get ahead by 7 points, or 10 on the combined score.

The cones course was really tough, again with two slaloms. I did not appreciate that there was a delay in starting the cones, and I got the ponies down much too early. The result was that they were thoroughly bored and fed up by the time it came to my turn in the late afternoon. I did not think there was much chance of my catching Beverly Mellstrom, but if I could do a clear round, it would put some pressure on her. I had no such luck. I started badly by hitting the very first pair of cones, which does nothing for morale. It then went from bad to worse and

I could not get a spark of enthusiasm from the ponies. I ended up with three cones down and 9 time penalties. Even Michael Onslow got round faster, although he hit ten cones in the process. Beverly Mellstrom sailed round inside the time and with only one cone down. It was a disappointing end to what had been a very enjoyable, and fairly successful, season.

While we were at Alnwick, news was trickling through about the World Championships. The British team was second in the dressage, third in the marathon and fifth in the cones, and made fourth place overall behind Germany (1st), The Netherlands (2nd) and Austria (3rd). Individual placings in the singles class were: Julie Camm, second in the dressage, and Sara Howe, second in the cones. In the pairs class, Jo Rennison dropped a bit in the dressage, but she came sixth in the marathon and ninth in the cones. Ursula Hirschberg was eliminated due to an unfortunate accident, and sadly lost one of her ponies. In the teams class, Emily Bennett was sixth in the dressage, fourth in the marathon, but must have had an off day in the cones as she was eleventh with a score of 23.5. Things cannot have gone well for John Pickford, as he was ninth in the dressage, eleventh in the marathon and eighteenth in the cones.

On our last evening at Alnwick, our whole party, consisting of some twelve people, gathered in the Alnwick Castle public restaurant, with champagne kindly provided by the Duke, for the usual end-of-season dinner before the ponies were turned out, and everyone prepared for their autumn activities. The only absentee was David Key, my driver and video operator, who had to return to London that afternoon.

Will I be competing again in 2004? I can only say that nothing has changed since I wrote the first paragraph of this Chapter.

RESULTS FOR 2003

EVENT	Dressage	Marathon	Cones	Pl/No
Brighton	2	6	2	4/8
Windsor	4	6	7	6/8
Hopetoun	2	3	4	3/4
Farleigh	2	3	1	2/4
Sandringham	5	6	3=	4/8
Henbury	3	2	2	1/5
Lowther	2	2	1=	2/3
Alnwick	2	2	2	2/3

Ponies used: Medina, Heather, Peter, Douglas, Hamble.

Years (ponies)	20
Total competitions	116
First place	15
Second place	30
Third place	27
Fourth place	15

Fell ponies used from 1982 to 2003 (hb = home-bred):

	Dates
Bramble	82–90
Roy	82–89
Martin	82–87
Carawich	82
Rosie	82–83 and 89
Laddie	83–85
Dawn	84–93
Ebony	84–93
Tom (hb)	87–96
Gina (hb)	88–89
Cilla	89–91
Lady	90–93
Carrick (hb)	92–99
Sacha (hb)	93–95
Myrtle (hb)	93–97
Storm	94–02
Jane	95–98
Polly	97–00
Peter	98–03
Medina	98–03
Hamble	00–03
Heather	00–03
Douglas (hb)	03
Twenty-three ponies	

Grooms employed with the ponies:

	Dates
David Muir Sen., Head Groom	81–86
Duncan Watt (Stalker)	81–82
David Muir Jun.	82–86 (Head Groom 87–93)
Paul Muir	82–88
Alison Leslie	83
Michael Muir	84–91
David West	87
Robert Chambers	87
Dean Clarkson	88
Joanna Reep	89–91
Elizabeth Milan	92–93
Elizabeth Halcombe	92–93
Micky Flynn, Head Groom	94–present
Marina Flynn (part time)	94–present
Barbara Duncan	94–96
Rachel Stokes (one event)	94
Roger Oliver (June-August)	94
Sarah Stinton	95–96
Elizabeth Elwick	96–98
Carole Scott	97
Paula Pearson	98–present
Rebecca Topping	99–01
Laura Owen	02
Michelle Maynard	03–present

Postscript

I SET OUT TO WRITE up my records of driving events when I realized that in 2002 it was thirty years since I had taken part in my first driving competition. However, it was not my thirtieth year of competition since there were no competitions in 2001, thanks to the outbreak of foot and mouth disease. That is why I have included the record for the 2003 season. It also occurred to me that such a book would be a record of the inception and development of what was, effectively, a new sport.

Taking up a sport as a beginner is always rather daunting. No-one likes to be a complete novice, in spite of the fact that experienced performers are only too delighted to welcome beginners, and to give them as much help as possible. If a copy of this book should ever fall into the hands of a would-be beginner, I hope the accounts of the many disasters that I suffered will give them the encouragement to persevere; things do get better with practice, patience and experience.

I have explained why I took up competition carriage driving with a team of horses but you may well wonder why I have continued to compete for quite so many years. The simple answer is that I have enjoyed every moment of it, or, more accurately, *almost* every moment of it. It gets me into the fresh air, and it keeps me reasonably fit. I suppose I could just drive about the country, but the challenge of the competition is a great inducement to get out and practise, even when the weather conditions might be a bit discouraging.

Driving a team through the countryside is great fun in itself because you experience it in a very special and different way: you go faster than someone on foot; you sit higher and, therefore, get a better view; you are in the open and so you can say 'good morning' to people as you pass; it is less physically demanding, since you sit there while your team does all the work; and, above all, you get to drive through some of the most spectacular landscapes in this country. As I have already mentioned, when I started driving, I had to find people who would be kind enough to put me up so that I could take part in the competitions but now I drive so that I can stay with these kind people, and drive through the glorious countryside.

When I was driving a team of horses, my Head Groom at the time, David Saunders, found a sleigh in the carriage house at Windsor, and suggested taking it to Sandringham in case it snowed in January. By one of those extraordinary coincidences, we had a serious blizzard, and I was able to drive the team to this sleigh for a week. It was a memorable experience. The whole countryside was white and the sleigh slid across the snow in an eerie silence. The horses accepted this novel situation without concern, even though the snow tended to 'ball' under their hooves. The traditional cure for this problem was to apply grease to the undersides of the hooves, but it was only effective for a short time.

One of the great attractions of the competition is the driving community itself, and its curious peripatetic existence during the competition season. It is rather like a mobile weekend party. A glance round the stable field on arrival at an event will quickly reveal who is there, as you recognize horseboxes and trailers. You bump into old friends at odd moments through the day, both from your own, and the other driving classes. With a common interest in driving, there is always something to talk about. Nerves are a bit stretched in the collecting ring before the dressage, and meeting friends as you walk an obstacle, or on the cones course, is a mixed blessing. If you stop for a gossip it ruins your concentration, and the chances are that you will have to go back to the beginning and start all over again. There is also quite a lot of cross-entertainment when the work of the day is done, and there is a moment to relax.

I am also attracted to the sport because the competition is a matter of individual performance, rather than a contest between teams, or a one-to-one confrontation like tennis. You may not be going fast enough through the obstacles, but you are not aware of it at the time. You are just relieved to get round without a mistake or a mishap. By the time you get to see the scoreboard, the adrenalin has ceased to flow.

As a driver, you obviously have to be able to drive a single, a pair, a tandem or a team with a fair degree of control and accuracy. After that, you need, first, to be able to remember the dressage test – at least more often than not. It sounds fairly simple, but if you happen to have any difficulty with your horse/s during the test, it is quite easy to lose track of where you have got to, or you can simply have a mental blackout and just go wrong.

Next, you have to decide which routes to take through the obstacles in the marathon course, and then get them firmly fixed in your mind. I suspect that the most physically demanding aspect of the competition is the exhausting business of walking the obstacles. There is also the mental strain involved in finding a reasonable compromise between the fastest and the easiest way through them. The number of times you walk them is dictated by age and memory-fade, versus endurance. It also helps to be able to read the letters on the gates at not less than about fifty paces. It is of no use if your navigator instructs you to go through gate B next if you cannot see it. It is also a great help to be able to tell your right from your left because it is useless for the navigator, who usually stands behind the driver, to point and say 'that way' when the driver cannot see where the navigator is pointing. The main thing is that, provided you do not unduly hold up the competitors behind you, it does not really matter how much time you spend finding your way through the obstacles. If the competitor behind you catches up, and starts breathing down your neck, no-one will object if you let them go through.

Finally, in the cones course you have to remember the sequence of the pairs of cones. Driving the course only takes about three minutes but, depending on the state of your memory – and your fitness – you may need to walk the course three or four times to get it fixed in your mind. If you can manage all this, there is no reason why you should not take part, whatever your age, provided you do not mind coming in last.

The fact is that the competition provides the incentive to go out and drive, and the challenge is to master the art of driving an accurate dressage test, to judge the pace accurately, so that you arrive at the end of each of the marathon sections at the right time, and then to get the team through the marathon obstacles as quickly as possible. The final test is to drive the team through the cones course with only about 10 cm to spare on each side between the wheels and the cones. For that sort of thing, you need a well-trained team of fit, willing and temperamentally calm and unflappable horses or ponies. In my experience of driving teams of horses and ponies, you are extremely fortunate if you can ever get three such animals in a team of four at the same time.

The whole thing is obviously very much a team effort. As a driver, you need to understand the characters, talents and limitations of the animals in your team, and they need to have confidence in you, as their driver, and get used to the way you send your signals through the reins, and by your words of command. Constant shouting makes little impression on the animals, and certainly does not impress the judges or the spectators. The horses or ponies have to get on with each other without bickering. The leaders must work together and come out of draught when going round corners or downhill. The wheelers also have to share the work between them, and the inside wheeler has to learn to go into the corner and not follow the leaders immediately when they turn. It is also the wheelers' job to hold the carriage back when going downhill.

But that is only part of the whole team. The way the grooms do their work in the stables and on exercise is a vital factor in the whole organization. Affection and care in the stables, a varied exercise routine, and a diet appropriate to the needs of each animal are essential, but so is strict discipline and schooling during ridden exercise. This is when the ponies are taught the paces required for the dressage, and the fast trot and walk for those particular sections of the marathon. This is also when bad habits are corrected, and instant responses to commands are encouraged. Come the marathon, one of the grooms has to become the navigator and give the driver clear and distinct instructions about where to go through the obstacles.

I only started driving in competitions when I had reached the advanced age of fifty, and after twenty years of highly competitive polo, and the last thing I expected to do was to get involved in World and European championships. I drove the horses from the Royal Mews because they were available and, later, I took to driving Fell ponies because they too just happened to be available. I have enjoyed every minute of my competitions with the Fells, but they are nothing like as flashy, as eye-catching, or as agile as the majority of Welsh ponies. I was always keen to do reasonably well in competitions, but I do not think I have ever been seriously competitive; certainly not since giving up driving a team of horses – the Formula 1 of the world of competitive driving.

I am getting old, my reactions are getting slower, and my memory is unreliable, but I have not lost the sheer pleasure of driving a team through the British countryside. There may be problems and disasters in the competitions, but they happen to everyone, and there is always the hope that things will go better the next time. I have been fortunate to have had a longer innings than most, and I have no intention of giving up while I have a team of willing ponies and dedicated grooms, while I can still cope with the challenges and, above all, while I still have Micky Flynn to manage the ponies, to get them to the events, and to guide me through the obstacles.

What happens next is anyone's guess, but this book ends here.

Index